Martyn Whittock is Head of Humanities and History at Kingdown School, Warminster. A lecturer in local history, he has written numerous textbooks for the educational market. He has been a consultant for the BBC, English Heritage and the National Trust and has written for *Medieval History Magazine* and archaeological journals.

D0288262

Highlights from the series

A BRIEF HISTORY OF

THE THIRD REICH

MARTYN WHITTOCK

ROBINSON   RUNNING PRESS
PHILADELPHIA · LONDON

Constable & Robinson Ltd
3 The Lanchesters
162 Fulham Palace Road
London W6 9ER
www.constablerobinson.com

First published in the UK by Robinson,
an imprint of Constable & Robinson, 2011

Copyright © Martyn Whittock, 2011

The right of Martyn Whittock to be identified as the
author of this work has been asserted by him in accordance
with the Copyright, Designs & Patents Act 1988.

All rights reserved. This book is sold subject to the condition
that it shall not, by way of trade or otherwise, be lent, re-sold,
hired out or otherwise circulated in any form of binding or cover
other than that in which it is published and without a similar condition
including this condition being imposed on the subsequent purchaser.

A copy of the British Library Cataloguing in Publication
Data is available from the British Library

UK ISBN 978–1–84901–299–7

1 3 5 7 9 10 8 6 4 2

First published in the United States in 2011 by Running Press Book Publishers

All rights reserved under the Pan-American and International Copyright Conventions

*This book may not be reproduced in whole or in part, in any form or by any means, electronic
or mechanical, including photocopying, recording, or by any information storage and retrieval
system now known or hereafter invented, without written permission from the publisher.*

9 8 7 6 5 4 3 2 1
Digit on the right indicates the number of this printing

US Library of Congress Control Number: 2010928999
US ISBN 978–0–76244–121–1

Running Press Book Publishers
2300 Chestnut Street
Philadelphia, PA 19103–4371

Visit us on the web!
www.runningpress.com

Printed and bound in the UK

MIX
Paper from
responsible sources
FSC® C018072

To fellow historians Tom Morgan and Kirstin Harrison;
with thanks for their support and friendship.

CONTENTS

ACKNOWLEDGEMENTS

As always, my wife Christine and our daughters, Hannah and Esther, supported me with their encouragement and interest as I researched and wrote, and we discussed many of the issues central to this book. I am very grateful.

I am grateful for assistance and advice from the following people whilst I was carrying out research into this book: Professor Richard Overy, Professor in History, Exeter University; Professor Richard J. Evans, Regius Professor of History, Cambridge University; Dr Kay Schiller, Senior Lecturer in the Department of History, Durham University; Wiltshire County Library Service and my friends at Bradford on Avon library. I am particularly grateful to my agent, Robert Dudley, and to Leo Hollis, my editor at Constable & Robinson, for all of their encouragement and support.

It goes without saying that all errors are my own.

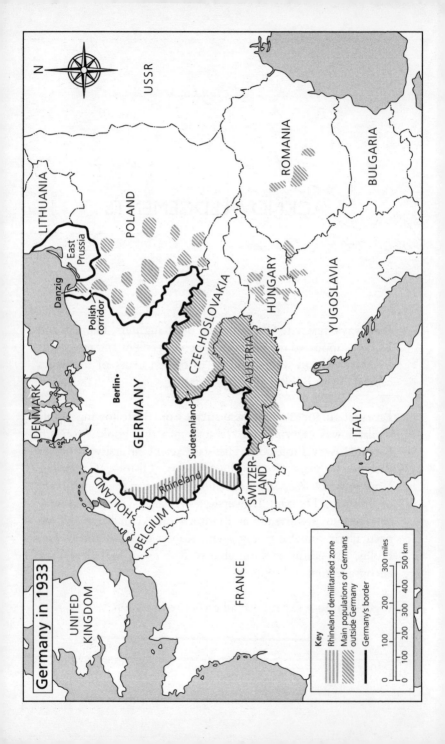

Germany in 1933

N

USSR

LITHUANIA

East Prussia

Danzig

Polish corridor

POLAND

ROMANIA

BULGARIA

HUNGARY

CZECHOSLOVAKIA

YUGOSLAVIA

Berlin•

GERMANY

AUSTRIA

DENMARK

Sudetenland

SWITZER-
LAND

ITALY

HOLLAND

Rhineland

BELGIUM

UNITED
KINGDOM

FRANCE

Key

Rhineland demilitarised zone

Main populations of Germans outside Germany

Germany's border

0   100   200   300 miles

0   100   200   300   400   500 km

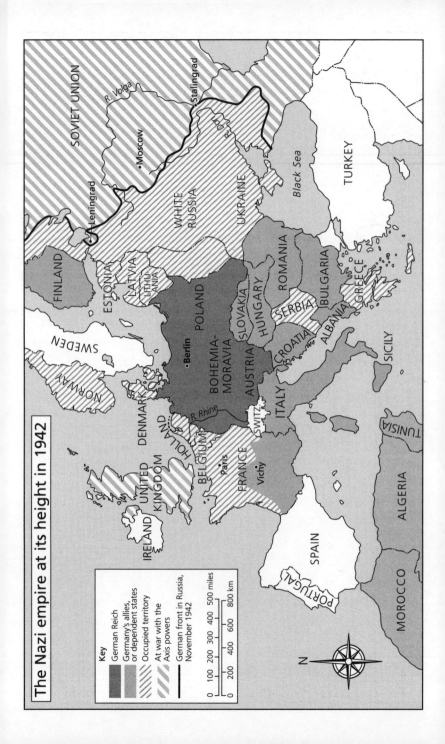

The Nazi empire at its height in 1942

Key
- German Reich
- Germany's allies, or dependent states
- Occupied territory
- At war with the Axis powers
- German front in Russia, November 1942

0 100 200 300 400 500 miles
0 200 400 600 800 km

SOVIET UNION

R. Volga

Stalingrad

•Moscow

R. Don

Leningrad

FINLAND

SWEDEN

NORWAY

ESTONIA

LATVIA

LITH-
UANIA

WHITE
RUSSIA

UKRAINE

Black Sea

TURKEY

POLAND

BOHEMIA-
MORAVIA

•Berlin

SLOVAKIA

HUNGARY

ROMANIA

BULGARIA

SERBIA

CROATIA

ALBANIA

GREECE

AUSTRIA

DENMARK

UNITED
KINGDOM

IRELAND

HOLLAND

BELGIUM

SWITZ.

ITALY

SICILY

R. Rhine

Paris

Vichy

FRANCE

SPAIN

PORTUGAL

MOROCCO

ALGERIA

TUNISIA

N

INTRODUCTION

The Third Reich remains one of the most striking episodes of world history in the twentieth century. The genocide against the Jews, the launching of the Second World War, the multiple abuses of power, the cruelty and suffering that were imposed on millions were all central features of Hitler's Nazi regime. Yet the Nazis were also highly successful in manipulating images and information: they mobilized and engaged vast numbers of people; they caught the imagination of the young and appeared remarkably modern to contemporary observers. This reminds us how complex the Third Reich was and how difficult to easily categorize. Was it aiming to create a throwback to a mythical past or was it looking forward to a brutally modernist and technologically advanced state? Was Hitler a strong and controlling dictator who achieved his clear goals, while dividing and ruling, or were his indolent personality and chaotic style of government the symptoms of a weak dictator who was unable to control the complex and contradictory forces that he unleashed? Was the Third Reich directed from above, or strongly influenced from below? Was it ruled by terror, or largely supported by a compliant German population? Was Hitler a popular dictator? Was the genocide against the Jews a peculiarly German phenomenon, or a particularly German version of terrible wider trends?

The aim of this book is to explore these – and other – key questions and to give an overview of the complex evidence. Historians' interpretations will be examined in order to suggest conclusions that take account of the different views that they represent. The evidence from the time itself is varied and complex: official statistics, state-sponsored art, secret police reports, public speeches and propaganda combine with diaries, letters and memoirs, humour and personal reminiscences to provide a multi-faceted view of life in the Third Reich. We will hear the thoughts of SS officers, German peasants, extermination-camp victims and survivors, opposition politicians, Nazi loyalists and resistance plotters, businessmen, ordinary men, women and children. Some will reveal the thoughts of 'insiders'; others will reveal the outlook and experiences of those who were very much 'outsiders' in the ruthlessly categorized Third Reich.

Finally, it may be helpful to explain something of the approach of this book. History must put us firmly in touch with the lives of – and issues facing – people in the past. It is right that the examination of the evidence makes the personal experiences of those in the past more accessible, as well as outlining the wider processes and developments that acted on individuals. In order to assist in this balance, each chapter will frequently refer to individuals' lives, thoughts and experiences in order to illustrate the wider issues in personal terms. In this way, we see the people within the history and appreciate how the historic events impacted on them. For in the vast numbers, appalling sufferings and huge distances covered in any history of the Third Reich, we must never lose sight of the individuals whose lives were caught up in these titanic events. For history is fundamentally about his-story and her-story . . .

I

THE NAZI RISE TO POWER, 1918–23: FROM THE END OF THE FIRST WORLD WAR TO THE MUNICH PUTSCH

Anton Drexler was born in Germany in 1884 and first worked as a machine-fitter, before becoming a locksmith in Berlin in 1902. Despite his extreme nationalism he was judged physically unsuitable for military service and so, to his great disappointment, did not fight in the First World War. In 1919 – bitter at the defeat of Germany and alarmed at the social and political turmoil of post-war Bavaria – he co-founded the German Workers' Party (the DAP) in Munich. Drexler was typical of a vulnerable section of the German population, the lower middle class. Possessing sufficient skills and independence to raise them above the mass of workers, such people were desperate to avoid any downwardly mobile pressures that might force them into the ranks of the working class. Made insecure by the economic and political upheaval in post-war Germany, such people were quick to blame Jews, socialists and communists for Germany's plight.

The DAP was only one of many tiny *völkisch* (ethnic/racist) parties in Bavaria. Their common feature was their racist belief in the purity of German blood and German culture. Beyond that, their beliefs were a strange mixture of extreme nationalism, anti-Semitism and right-wing militarism, blended with a radical and semi-socialist resentment of capitalism, large department stores and unearned profits. As such, they were difficult to place on any political spectrum as they represented the anxieties, fears and resentments of those who felt themselves squeezed from above and below. Below them were the unionized workers with their internationalist allegiances to class rather than race; above them were the more comfortably off and the rich, whose nationalism was basically conservative.

In 1919, one of the DAP's meetings was attended by an obscure army corporal of Austrian origin – Adolf Hitler. Drexler gave Hitler a pamphlet entitled 'My Political Awakening' and, according to Hitler's later thoughts expressed in his own political biography, *Mein Kampf (My Struggle)*, Drexler's pamphlet reflected many of Hitler's own emerging beliefs. As a result, Hitler decided to join Drexler's tiny party and, by 1920, his rhetorical skills were both drawing in the crowds and overshadowing Drexler. That same year, he persuaded Drexler to change the party's name to the National Socialist German Workers' Party (the NSDAP, or Nazis). In 1921, Drexler's leadership was challenged by Hitler and, after a brief resistance, Drexler resigned. Without the skills or organization to resist Hitler, Drexler left the NSDAP in 1923 and was a largely forgotten figure by the time he died in Munich in February 1942. By that time the party that Hitler had hijacked had been in power for almost ten years and had unleashed a world war of unbelievable savagery. German troops occupied Europe from the Atlantic to southern Russia and the mass killing of Jews in Eastern Europe had been taking place since the previous summer. That would have been impossible to imagine in the years immediately following Germany's defeat in 1918, but the roots of what Hitler would come to call the Third Reich went back deep into that troubled and turbulent period and into the whirlpool of contradictory beliefs which lay at the heart of Drexler's little political party.[1]

National defeat and the establishment of the Weimar Republic

As Germany faced defeat in November 1918 it was disintegrating. Sailors mutinied in the ports of Wilhelmshaven, Kiel and Hamburg; workers and ex-soldiers set up revolutionary *soviets* (revolutionary councils, named after those recently established in communist Russia) in Berlin and other cities. The German Emperor – Kaiser Wilhelm II – fled to Holland and a new democratic government replaced him. This was a moderate socialist government, led by the leader of the German Social Democratic Party (the SPD), Friedrich Ebert. On 11 February 1919, Ebert was elected as the first President of the new German republic. He remained President until his death in February 1925. Under his presidency, Germany was to survive the upheavals of 1919 and eventually achieved sufficient stability to make it appear that Germany really did have a democratic future.[2]

But first, Ebert's new government faced massive unrest. Armed workers and soldiers – inspired by the recent 1917 revolution in Russia – attempted communist uprisings in various parts of Germany. These were bloodily put down by the army and groups of nationalist and right-wing ex-soldiers known as the *Freikorps* (Free Corps). By 1919, there were nearly 200 of these Freikorps groups in Germany. While they were used by the new government to crush revolts by communists, they had no love for democracy either. In January 1919, a group of communists attempted to seize power in Berlin. These were the Spartakists, who shortly before this revolt had set up the German Communist Party (the KPD). The 'Spartakist revolt' was bloodily crushed by the Freikorps, who were prepared to help Ebert's government because they hated communism even more than they hated the Social Democrats.

As a result, the government of Ebert survived, but this led to a bitter split between the moderate socialists of the Social Democratic Party (SPD) and the Communist Party (KPD). This meant that left-wing political parties in Germany hated each other as much as they hated their nationalist opponents. In Munich, the capital of Bavaria (which was one of the German states), the Bavarian government was overthrown and an independent communist soviet republic was briefly set up under Kurt Eisner. But this too was eventually crushed by the army and Freikorps and its leaders killed.[3]

While Germany was in the middle of this unrest, a new constitution was created for the nation. This constitution was settled in the city of Weimar because the capital, Berlin, was in chaos due to the Spartakist revolt. As a consequence, the German government from 1919 until Hitler came to power in January 1933 is called the 'Weimar Republic'.

In 1919, the new Weimar government agreed to the Treaty of Versailles which formally ended the First World War. The victorious Allies (most notably Britain, France and the USA) imposed a very harsh set of demands on Germany in order to weaken it so that it would never again threaten the peace of Europe.[4] The aim was also to extend the principle of self-determination by which people were able to be part of countries made up of their own ethnic group. In this way, Poland was formed from land that had once been ruled by Germany, Austria-Hungary and Russia. But millions of Austrians (now a small country, without its great empire) were not free to join their fellow Germans in an *Anschluss* (union) of the two countries. Consequently, democracy and the new Weimar Republic seemed associated with defeat and humiliation and this would assist those more extreme groups who hoped to undermine it in the 1920s. To them the politicians who had led Germany out of the war in 1918 were the 'November Criminals' and the 'criminals' had compounded their guilt by signing the humiliating Treaty of Versailles.

Many Germans were unwilling to believe that the mighty German army had been defeated in the First World War. They preferred to believe it had been betrayed by socialist politicians, communist revolutionaries and Jews (despite the small size of the German Jewish population and its high level of integration into German society). The unrest after the end of the war also made it easier for these people to believe that Germany was in danger of a communist revolution. As a result there remained a great deal of support in the 1920s for the army and for nationalism, despite the disaster of defeat in 1918 that these two forces had, in reality, brought on Germany. On top of this, the harsh treatment by the Treaty of Versailles made it easier to direct anger at enemies abroad than admit that Germany's military ambitions had brought many of these problems on itself.[5]

The increasing problems of the Weimar Republic

The new Weimar Republic faced a number of escalating problems. Firstly, the Social Democratic government's fear of communist revolution caused it to over-estimate the threat and to rely on conservative and military forces in Germany. This encouraged groups who, in reality, hated the Social Democrats and had no love for democracy either.

Secondly, the working class, who might otherwise have provided a foundation of support for the Weimar Republic, was deeply divided. In 1917, wildcat strikes had affected many urban areas. Then the Spartakist revolt had ended in bloody defeat. In May 1919, the Munich soviet republic had finally been crushed by the army and Freikorps. In 1920, radical workers (the 'Red Ruhr Army') had seized power in the industrial area of Rhineland-Westphalia. The uprising was again ruthlessly crushed by army and Freikorps units on behalf of the central government. Ironically, many of these soldiers had earlier in the year supported a Freikorps uprising (the 'Kapp Putsch') against that very government.[6] In each of these failed uprisings it was radical workers (many of whom were communists) who had fallen in a battle that was as much against the Social Democrat-led government as against the forces of capitalism. With better-off and more qualified workers (and their trade unions) backing the government, this left the German working class bitterly split. This inability to unite against the forces of the right would be a major weakness of this social group right up to Hitler coming to power in January 1933.

Thirdly, the very structure of the Weimar constitution created problems for the government. The voting system of proportional representation tended to encourage the growth of many small parties. This made it hard to form a strong government to deal with problems. The elected president had the power to make laws without the agreement of the *Reichstag* (parliament) in times of national emergency (Article 48). This weakened the power of the Reichstag and, therefore, weakened the new democracy.

Fourthly, many middle-class Germans distrusted the new democratic system. Most civil servants and judges continued in post into the Weimar Republic, although many were not sympathetic to Weimar, or democracy, and were biased towards right-wing nationalist groups. Similarly, the army remained very influential and had little loyalty towards Weimar, or democracy. General Seekt, Chief of the Army Command (1920–6) kept the army under control and reduced the power of the Freikorps but was determined to keep the army independent of the government. And many in the army believed they had the right to decide what was best for the nation. All of these factors made it hard to establish a modern and democratic government.

Furthermore, there were just too many paramilitary groups in Weimar Germany. The Nazis had their brown-shirted fighting units of the SA, the Communist Party had its 'Red Front Fighters' League', the Social Democratic Party had its 'Reich Banner, Black-Red-Gold' organization, the conservative nationalists had the ex-soldiers of the 'Steel Helmets'. And these were in addition to the death squads operated by the Freikorps. This general level of paramilitary violence undermined political stability. Indeed, some German states would even come to ban glass ashtrays at political meetings and the carrying of walking sticks in public as both were all too frequently used as offensive weapons![7]

As if its political problems were not severe enough the Weimar government faced severe economic problems too. The pressure to pay reparations (compensation) to the victorious Allies was high and the government printed money to pay its debts, causing inflationary pressures within the German economy. Also, paying for new social reforms was expensive and the government struggled to afford it. This was made worse in 1923, when the French occupied the German Ruhr coalfields. The French hoped to force payment of reparations, as Germany was falling behind on these. This was another blow to the German economy. All these problems led to hyperinflation in 1923. Money rapidly lost its value. By November 1923 it cost 200,000,000,000 marks to buy just one US dollar. To put this into perspective, an egg cost 100 million marks! Two women out shopping with a basket crammed with bank notes put down the basket to look in a shop window. When they turned back they found that the money was still there but that the basket had been stolen. After all, a basket was worth something! Members of the middle class, and others with savings and fixed pensions, saw these become worthless overnight and workers' wages collapsed in value. However, many larger German firms actually benefitted from this as it kept their labour costs down and these firms resisted attempts to stabilize the currency.[8]

The early years of the Nazi Party
For the parties on the extreme right of German politics the crisis of 1923 was fortuitous and for none more so than for the NSDAP – the Nazi Party. The roots of the Nazi Party reached back, as we have seen, to January 1919 when Anton Drexler and a sports journalist named Karl Harrer started a small political group in Munich, which they called the German Workers'

Party (the DAP). Its formative period coincided with Hitler's return to Munich.

Having fought in the German army during the First World War, despite his Austrian citizenship, Hitler returned to Munich (his adopted city since 1913) in 1919, where he was recruited into the political department of the army. His job was to spy on the meetings of political parties in the city. Visiting a meeting of the DAP in September 1919, Hitler liked many of its ideas and realized it was a party in which he could have real influence. Later, Nazi legends claimed he was the seventh member, but in reality he joined as member number 555.

In February 1920, Hitler and Drexler put together the '25 Point Programme' – the aims of the party. At this time the party also changed its name from the German Workers' Party (DAP) to the National Socialist German Workers' Party (the NSDAP), or the 'Nazis'. The fact the word 'socialist' still had a place in the title shows the party was attempting to appeal to German workers and draw them away from the attractions of communism. These '25 Points' were never altered and remained the official aims of the party, even though Hitler soon came to ignore them.

In 1921, Hitler became the party's *Führer* (leader).[9] The growing cult of the leader can be seen in the terminology used in the Nazi-owned press.[10] In December 1922, an article in the Nazi newspaper the *Völkischer Beobachter* (*Racial Observer*) made the claim for the first time that he was '*the* Führer, for whom Germany was waiting'.[11] Under his influence the party took on the Nazi salute, the brown-shirted uniform, the swastika flag and the presence of armed squads to defend its meetings and break up the meetings of opponents. These would eventually become the brown-shirted *Sturmabteilung* (Storm Division), or SA, led by Ernst Röhm.

The new Nazi Party programme proclaimed beliefs including: the unity of all German speakers, tearing up the Treaty of Versailles and discrimination against Jews. Amongst these typical demands of the right wing, there were also left-wing calls for nationalization of major industries and profit sharing. And the concerns of the lower middle class appeared in the pleas to shut department stores to protect small shopkeepers and grant land to peasants. But Hitler was always reluctant to be tied down by a political manifesto. For him the seizure of unfettered power was crucial. Otto Strasser, one-time friend of Hitler, recalls an early argument they once had:

"'Power!'" screamed Adolf. "'We must have power!'" "Before we gain it," I replied firmly, "let us decide what we propose to do with it. Our programme is too vague; we must construct something solid and enduring." Hitler thumped the table and barked, "Power first! Afterwards we can act as circumstances dictate!"[12]

As part of this ruthless pursuit of power, Hitler deliberately provoked his political enemies and the Bavarian authorities. This both intimidated opponents and drew attention to the Nazi Party through acts of beer-hall violence.[13] But the most ambitious provocation was yet to come . . .

The Munich Putsch, 1923

In November 1923, Hitler and a group of nationalists tried to seize power in Munich, the capital of Bavaria, in southern Germany. This was the infamous 'Munich Putsch'. The Nazis hoped that a march on Berlin, following a seizure of power in Munich, might win popular support because so many Germans were angry at the French occupation of the German Ruhr coalfields in January 1923 and the economic crisis that followed, leading to hyperinflation. During 1923, the Nazi Party membership rose from 20,000 to 55,000 and seemed to suggest the tide of public opinion might be starting to flow their way. It appeared that the Weimar Republic was doomed. In addition, a new government, opposed to the Weimar Republic, had come to power in Bavaria and it was possible that its members would be sympathetic to Nazi ideas. On the evening of 8 November, Hitler and his supporters seized control of a beer hall in which the leader of the Bavarian government, Gustav von Kahr, was speaking to a large meeting. Hitler declared that a 'National Revolution' had started. Persuading von Kahr to agree to support him, the next morning Hitler led a march into central Munich. But von Kahr, now convinced that Hitler would fail, decided to resist the revolt[14] and loyal troops and police fired on the marchers. Fourteen of Hitler's supporters and four policemen were killed as the two sides exchanged fire. The man next to Hitler was killed, but Hitler escaped with only a dislocated shoulder.

Hitler went into hiding at a supporter's house south of Munich, but on 11 November he was arrested by the police and charged with High Treason. Placed in cell number 7 at Landsberg Prison he awaited trial. It looked as if he was finished. The Nazi Party was banned and its leaders were arrested, or went into hiding. The Bavarian völkisch movement (the collection of racist political organizations allied to the Nazis) broke apart into its squabbling little groups again.

However, Hitler (who could have faced the death penalty for both treason and the deaths of the four policemen killed during the Putsch) was only sentenced to five years in prison and a fine of 200 gold marks, with the prospect of early release. The court rejected the idea of deporting him to his native Austria, despite the fact that he was not formally a German citizen. This raised the question: why the leniency? The reason was a mixture of sympathy for Hitler's anti-Weimar beliefs and the fact that the Bavarian government had been keen to cover up its own treasonable actions against the Berlin government. Leniency towards those accused of leading the Putsch helped to encourage the burying of embarrassing facts.[15] In Landsberg Prison, where he only served nine months of his sentence, Hitler enjoyed a large and comfortable cell, had free access to visitors (over 500 visited him), and could receive flowers, letters and presents. He was allowed to dictate his life story (*Mein Kampf*) to the two Nazis imprisoned there with him (his chauffeur Emil Maurice and Rudolf Hess, who would one day be deputy leader of the Nazi Party).

In *Mein Kampf*, Hitler's earlier attacks on Jewish capitalists became overshadowed by his new focus on what he called 'Jewish Bolshevism'. In his mind, the Jews dominated the world through their control of the two forces of Bolshevism (Russian communism) and world capitalism. The fact that these two groups were completely opposed to each other posed no difficulty to Hitler. As far as he was concerned, the Jews were behind both and both were the enemies of German nationalism. This astonishing conspiracy theory was widely accepted by many anti-Semitic groups and it gave coherence to the otherwise mutually irreconcilable twin hatreds of the lower middle class: communism and capitalism. The fact that some leading capitalists were Jewish and that Karl Marx had been Jewish, as were a number of leading communists in the USSR, seemed sufficient evidence to back up belief in this fantastic conspiracy. The weightier fact that most capitalists and communists were not Jewish was ignored. As was the fact that communism and capitalism were systems that were utterly opposed to each other. In the world of anti-Semitic conspiracy theorists such awkward realities had no place and these theorists lived in a strange mental landscape, which suited their personal needs and phobias but bore no resemblance to the landscape of the real world. As a consequence, for Hitler, what lay ahead was a struggle to the death between Germany and these two linked systems.[16] When, later in 1941, Germany invaded the USSR, it was the climax of this crusade against 'Jewish Bolshevism'. Hitler's ideas and plans were developed further in the *Zweites Buch* (*Second Book*). This unedited manuscript of Hitler's thoughts on foreign policy was written in 1928 and was never published in his lifetime. Undiscovered until 1945, this book was not published until 1961 (in German) and lacked an authoritative English version until 2003. (For a more detailed exploration of Hitler's foreign policy plans, see Chapter 15.)

However, the fact that Hitler committed his general goals to paper should not lead us to assume that he had some clear and detailed plan of how to achieve his aims. It is clear that, although Hitler was willing to be flexible on short-term goals and methods, the long-term aims laid out in these books remained fixed in his mind and actions until his suicide in Berlin in 1945. Similarly, the fact that Nazi ideas were often confused and that the Nazis were willing to promise contradictory things to different groups of people should not make us think they did not have strongly held beliefs. At the core of all the confusion were things that Hitler and his followers were determined to do, even if the methods and details were unclear in the mid-1920s.

2

THE NAZI RISE TO POWER, 1924–33: FROM THE MUNICH PUTSCH TO HITLER'S APPOINTMENT AS REICH CHANCELLOR

Few people are more associated with the 'might-have-beens' of German history between the two world wars than Gustav Stresemann. Born in Berlin, it was in 1906 at the age of 28 that he became a deputy in the Reichstag (parliament) and he was elected the leader of the National Liberal Party in 1917. By this time he had moved to the right wing of this party and had come to support the Kaiser's expansionist policies and the unrestricted sinking of merchant ships by German U-boats.

In 1919, he gathered most of the right wing of the old National Liberal Party into the German People's Party (the DVP), with himself as chairman. At first, Stresemann opposed the Weimar Republic but, by the middle of the 1920s, he had become a reluctant supporter; not because he believed in it but because he thought it was necessary for the good of Germany. As a result, he was prepared to work with the parties of the moderate left (such as the Social Democrats) and the Catholic Centre Party to promote stability.

As a liberal politician and statesman he served as Chancellor and Foreign Minister and oversaw the introduction of a new currency, which assisted Germany's recovery from the hyper-inflation of 1923, and he was responsible for the negotiations leading to the Dawes Plan of 1924, which reduced Germany's reparations payments. His most notable achievement was reconciliation between Germany and France, for which he and the French Foreign Minister, Aristide Briand, received the Nobel Peace Prize in 1926. The period of apparent stability that Weimar Germany experienced from 1924 to 1929 means that his name has since been closely associated with this so-called 'Golden Age of Weimar'. He seemed to embody what *might* have happened to Germany as an alternative scenario to the Third Reich: Democratic government, humane policies, increasing prosperity and the settling of international issues by diplomacy with Germany as an international player once more.

On the other hand, he was complex. He refused to deal firmly with those responsible for the Munich Putsch and he supported anti-Polish policies and engineered a trade war between Germany and Poland. Furthermore, while he accepted Germany's western borders (in the Locarno Treaty, 1925), there was no such commitment to accept the eastern borders. Along with most German politicians – from the reasonable to the fanatic – he felt that there was unfinished business there with Poland. As such, his career reminds us that even the most attractive of Germany's Weimar politicians had not accepted the Versailles settlement and would undermine it – at least in the east – if possible. Even at the time there was uncertainty over whether his policies represented a temporary ruse until Germany had recovered its strength, or a genuine desire for accommodation with other European nations.[1] Little wonder then that the desire to revise the Versailles settlement – but by much more brutal means – was strongly represented amongst the hardline politicians of the right wing. And, ironically, as Weimar Germany seemed to be gaining in legitimacy under Stresemann, international scrutiny of its behaviour was reduced, unintentionally making it more likely that these right-wing groups would challenge Weimar's constitution.[2]

Nevertheless, the career of Stresemann reminds us that alternative scenarios exist in history. But the question remains: could even he have weathered the storm that would strike Germany – and the world – at the end of the 1920s? The question must remain unanswered because he died of a stroke on 3 October 1929 at the age of fifty-one. On 24 October, Wall Street crashed.

The Nazis after the Munich Putsch

Following the failure of the Munich Putsch, the Nazis faced major problems. In the national elections in 1924, the German nationalist groups were crushed. In all of the electoral constituencies except one, the Nazis gained less than ten per cent of the vote. The Nazi Party was in disarray without Hitler's central leadership.[3] Things looked very bleak. Even when Hitler was released from prison in December 1924, he was still subject to controls because he was only released on parole. In most parts of Germany, he was banned from public speaking until 1927. In Prussia (the largest by far of the different regional states of Weimar Germany), the ban on public speaking lasted until 1928. As well as this, Hitler faced dissent from leading Nazis in the north of Germany and in the Rhineland. In these areas, Gregor Strasser and Joseph Goebbels favoured a form of Nazism with a greater emphasis on socialism.[4] If Hitler was to reassert his authority these would have to be tamed.

Hitler began by rebuilding the Nazi Party. He re-founded it in 1925 and called on all its old members to rejoin and completely accept his leadership. Old Nazis who refused to accept Hitler's total authority were pushed out of the party. The SA leader Ernst Röhm refused to accept Hitler's decision that the SA should be brought fully under the control of the Nazi leadership and, as a result, he was forced out of a position of authority in the SA, left the party and went to Bolivia to train the Bolivian army. In February 1926, Hitler called the northern party leaders to a meeting in the town of Bamberg.

Over two hours, Hitler attacked the northern Nazis' ideas for seizing the private property of the German princes (who had lost power in 1918 but still owned huge areas of land) and instead he argued that nothing should distract the Nazis from their central belief in conquering *Lebensraum* (living space) in Eastern Europe. Goebbels was unimpressed, but kept silent. However, Strasser gave way and this made it difficult for his allies to continue to resist Hitler. Afterwards, this meeting would be known in the party as the 'Führer congress' because it resulted in the triumph of Hitler and his concept of both the party and his leadership style.

In April 1926, Hitler invited Goebbels to Munich. Here he lectured him on his 'errors' but promised to forget about them if Goebbels accepted his leadership. Goebbels was finally completely convinced. He wrote in his diary: 'I bow to the greater one, the political genius.' And a few days later, he wrote: 'Adolf Hitler, I love you because you are both great and simple at the same time. What one calls a genius.'[5] From this moment – until he shot himself in Hitler's bunker in April 1945 – Goebbels would remain totally loyal to Hitler and completely under his control. In return, Hitler made him the *Gauleiter* (regional party boss) in 'Red Berlin', with the job of battling the communists there. Soon Goebbels' adulation knew no bounds, describing Hitler as 'like a meteor before our astonished eyes'.[6] At the 1926 party rally, the representatives accepted Hitler's total domination of the organization. Only Hitler would decide who held the most important jobs. In addition, the 'Heil, Hitler' salute was made compulsory in the party.

Between 1927 and 1928, Hitler followed on from his success in disciplining the party by reorganizing it. He gave the job of doing this to Strasser. The Nazi Party was restructured into 35 regional areas, or *Gau*. Each one of these regional areas was the same as a Reichstag constituency. This was important because it meant these regional organizations had as their main function getting Nazis elected to the Reichstag. Hitler was now committed to gaining power through the ballot box.

The final piece in the creation of the new structure of the Nazi Party came in January 1929, when Heinrich Himmler was appointed head of Hitler's bodyguard, the *Schutzstaffel* (protection formation), or SS.[7] Originally formed out of units of the SA, the SS had appeared in public for the first time in July 1926, when 116 of the SS paraded, along with 3,600 SA, at the party rally at Weimar and the SS was then presented with the 'Blood Flag', the banner that had led the march in the Munich Putsch of 1923. When Himmler took control, the SS numbered 290 men. Within a year this had risen to a thousand and within two years to nearly three thousand. In 1930, Himmler persuaded Hitler to make the SS fully independent of the SA. The SS, with its black uniform and military organization, regarded itself as an elite formation. SS members tended to be better educated and with an older age-profile than the SA. As one leading historian reminds us, 'The SS included bullies too, but they were superior, academically educated examples of the type.'[8]

It soon became an internal Nazi Party police force, collecting information on SA leaders as well as on external enemies of the party. Later, in 1934, it was the SS who would be used by Hitler to destroy the SA leadership. By the 1940s, the SS had grown to many thousands. It had, by then, developed its own security organisation (the SD), its own security police (the SIPO SD), gained control over the *Gestapo* (secret police) and Himmler had created a terror and police organization that ran concentration and extermination camps and even had regiments fighting alongside the army (the *Waffen* SS). Nazi Germany, after 1933, developed into an 'SS state'. But, in the late 1920s, all this lay ahead. In the meantime, the Nazis had to face the uncomfortable truth that extremism struggles in times of stability, and the second half of the 1920s brought much-needed recovery for Weimar Germany.

Recovery and 'the golden years of Weimar', 1924–9

To solve the problem of worthless German money, a new currency was introduced in December 1923. This was called the *Rentenmark* and was organized by Hjalmar Schacht (a famous German finance expert appointed by Stresemann). These actions helped draw the economic crisis to a close. In addition, Germany was increasingly accepted as a member of the international community again. In 1924, the Dawes Plan led to the USA loaning Germany 800 million gold marks to help economic recovery and allowed a longer period of time for Germany to make its reparation payments. The amount paid each year was also fixed according to how much Germany could afford. Tension with France was reduced as Germany's western border was guaranteed by the Locarno Pact of 1925, while Germany was still free to contest the eastern frontiers where it was most anxious to revise the map-making of Versailles. In 1926, Germany was invited to join the League of Nations. In that same year, the Treaty of Berlin continued Germany's friendly relations with the communist USSR, which dated from the Rapallo Treaty of 1922. This put further pressure on the Poles who were sandwiched between Germany and the USSR. Germany seemed of consequence once more. In 1929, the Young Plan reduced and rescheduled German reparation repayments, although these would continue to be repaid until 1988.

As a result, unrest in Germany decreased, and it seemed possible that some of the effects of the First World War on Germany might be solved through negotiation. From 1924 to 1929, Germany seemed to be experiencing both an amazing economic recovery and a surprising degree of political stability. By 1928, production in heavy industry was back to the levels it had reached before the outbreak of war in 1914. Foreign investors were keen to invest in Germany again and exports also rose. Other aspects of Weimar society were also positive: workers' spending power was higher than in 1914; health care was better and covered more people than before the First World War; crime levels fell; living standards were rising.[9]

This made life difficult for extremist groups (such as the Nazis and the communists), who thrived on unrest, and whose support had increased during the troubled years of the early

1920s. By 1928, the Nazi share of the vote had fallen to 2.6 per cent and they gained only 12 out of the 491 seats in the Reichstag; similarly, the communists could not achieve higher than 10.6 per cent of the vote in this year. At the same time, those parties who supported the Weimar Republic increased their share of the vote. In 1928, the Social Democrats gained 29.8 per cent. When its leader, Hermann Müller, formed a coalition that year he led a group that was supported by over 60 per cent of the Reichstag. Even the conservative nationalists of the German National People's Party (the DNVP) decided that, if they were to have any influence over the government, they would have to give up their total opposition to the Weimar system. As a result, they joined Weimar coalition governments in 1925 and in 1927. So it seemed in the mid-1920s that economic stability was being accompanied by political stability and that Weimar democracy was firmly established.

There were, though, clouds on the horizon. In 1925, the First World War hero Field Marshal Paul von Hindenburg was elected President. He would remain President until 1934 and his influence on Weimar democracy was mixed. On one hand, he was loyal to the Weimar constitution and kept within its rules; he made no attempt to restore the German monarchy; he made the Weimar Republic a little more acceptable to some right-wing Germans and his military reputation increased the loyalty of the army to the office of president. On the other hand, his advisers were men who opposed the idea of the Weimar Republic. He was unwilling to appoint Social Democrat members to the government and, when he could, appointed conservative nationalists instead; as Germany faced unrest after 1929, he would increasingly use his power as President to bypass the Reichstag and so weakened the Weimar democracy.

And there were yet other clouds on the Weimar horizon. The German liberal parties lacked unity and while this could be managed in good times it did not bode well if Germany were to enter another period of unrest; the economy was heavily dependent on US loans; German farmers found it hard to compete in a world where trade still had not fully recovered from the First World War; unemployment never fell below 1.3 million. And even before the crisis of 1929, support for middle-of-the-road parties was declining as many middle-class voters felt that Stresemann's foreign policy successes had little positive impact on their local economy and wellbeing. The Weimar Republic was therefore much more vulnerable than it appeared. In fact, it was built on the equivalent of a financial faultline. A tremor in the world economy would threaten the stability of the whole Weimar economy (and with it, Weimar democracy). And the Wall Street Crash in October 1929 was not a financial tremor – it was a financial earthquake.

The economic and political impact of the Wall Street Crash
On 24 October, the largest stock market in the world, on Wall Street in New York, crashed. By 1932, six million Germans were out of work. This meant that about one third of all German workers were unemployed and becoming desperate. Between 1929 and 1932, there was a 24 per cent increase in arrests for theft in Berlin.

The membership of the communists rose from 117,000 in 1929 to 360,000 in 1932. To many middle-class people the threat of a communist revolution seemed very real, despite the fact that support for the communists never reached the level that made such an event likely. These people looked to the right-wing groups, such as the Nazis, to protect their interests. This helps explain the growth of extreme politics at this time of national crisis. The support for the moderate middle ground melted away as desperate people looked for desperate answers to their problems.

The Wall Street Crash brought down one of the most stable governments Weimar Germany had enjoyed – the so-called 'Grand Coalition'. In March 1930 it collapsed. This was one of those events that time shows to have been a significant milestone on the road to the end of Weimar democracy, although it would not have appeared so at the time. Its significance lies in the fact that it was the last Weimar government to command a majority of seats in the Reichstag. From this point onwards power shifted increasingly from the Reichstag to the President. Many of the leading advisers around President Hindenburg thought it would be a positive move to give up relying on changing groups of parties in the Reichstag and, instead, to establish a more authoritarian kind of government in which chancellors they approved of used the president's power to rule by decree, under Article 48 of the constitution. The leaders of the German army were particularly keen on this style of government, as it seemed to offer them more influence and promised the kind of stable society that they wanted for Germany.

The new government, which replaced the Grand Coalition, was led by President Hindenburg's choice as Chancellor, Heinrich Brüning. He was leader of the Catholic Centre Party, which had given the most consistent support to the Weimar Republic. But his party was changing and moving to the right. The signs for democracy were not good.

The drift towards dictatorship

Brüning planned to change the Weimar constitution by uniting his role of Reich Chancellor with that of Prussian Minister-President. The Prussian Minister-President headed up the largest of the *länder* (states) of Germany. By uniting the two roles, Brüning would greatly increase his power and reduce the influence of the Social Democrats, who dominated Prussia. It was the first of Brüning's attempts to reduce democratic controls and increase the power of the government. Despite the failure of this attempt – because Hindenburg would not allow it – its importance lies in that it indicates where Brüning's sympathies lay, and it was a suggestion that the Nazis would later take up. In March 1931, Brüning reduced the power of newspapers to criticize his government.

In the summer of 1931, the economic situation worsened and the German banking system seemed on the brink of collapse as more and more foreign investment flowed out of Germany. The Reichsmark soon could not be exchanged for any foreign currency. In December 1931, Brüning issued his fourth emergency decree; this one would reduce wages to the level of 1927. Not surprisingly, opposition to his policies was growing. This was seen in the Reichstag election of September 1930, which turned out to be a breakthrough for the Nazis.

The results of this election were a fatal blow to Weimar. For the Centre Party there was some good news, as the number of Centre Party seats rose from sixty-two to sixty-eight. The Social Democrats did less well and lost ten seats, taking their total down to 143. However, Brüning's allies amongst the moderate nationalists did disastrously, while more extreme groups did well. The Communist Party share of seats rose from fifty-four to seventy-seven. But the shock was the success of the Nazi Party, whose number of seats catapulted from 12 to 107. In 1928, only 0.8 million people had voted Nazi but by 1930 this had increased to 6.4 million (or 18.3 per cent of the votes cast).

Conflicts between uniformed Nazi Reichstag deputies and Communist Party ones made the Reichstag virtually unmanageable. Between 1920 and March 1931, the Reichstag met for business on average one hundred days a year; in the year from April 1931 to July 1932, it met for only twenty-four days; between then and the end of January 1933, it met for only three days. Parliamentary government had virtually ceased well before the Nazis eventually came to power in January 1933.

As anxiety gripped large numbers outside the closed circle of political influence, actual political power in Germany became increasingly concentrated in the small group of men around President Hindenburg. These included General von Schleicher (responsible for relations between the army and the government and a natural intriguer) and Oskar Hindenburg (the President's son). General von Schleicher began to plot to remove Brüning, with his reliance on the support offered him by the Social Democrats, and instead to try to harness the popular support and power held by the Nazis.

While this was happening, Hindenburg had come to the end of his seven years as President. Hitler eventually decided to stand and arrangements were hurriedly carried out to make him a German citizen in February 1932. Hitler flew from city to city in his 'Hitler over Germany' campaign and eventually gained 37 per cent of the vote compared to the communist Thalmann's 10 per cent and Hindenburg's 53 per cent. The old Field Marshall had won but the election had shown that Hitler was now a national figure.

On 30 May 1932, Brüning handed in his resignation as Chancellor and was replaced by Franz von Papen. The appointment of von Papen marked the end of parliamentary democracy in Germany. Most members of von Papen's new cabinet had no connections with political parties and no support in the Reichstag. It became known as 'the cabinet of barons'. Von Papen seems to have thought he was creating a new system that was above party politics – unfortunately it was also disconnected from popular support.

The results of the July 1932 election brought another massive boost of power to the Nazis. Their vote more than doubled, from 6.4 million to 13.8 million. This was a jump from 18.3 per cent of the vote, gained in September 1930, to a huge 37.4 per cent. They gained 230 seats in the Reichstag and this was nearly one hundred seats more than their nearest rivals the Social Democrats, with their 133 seats. The communists also increased their vote, but with 89 seats were no rival to the Nazis. The Centre Party gained its highest ever number of seats at 75, but it too was incapable of challenging the Nazis. The nationalists lost heavily and the old liberal parties collapsed.

Von Papen returned as Chancellor but without a majority in the Reichstag. His intention seems to have been to dissolve the Reichstag as soon as it met and to use the presidential power of decree to declare that there would be no more elections and, instead, to create a virtual dictatorship with Hindenburg at its head and von Papen running the government. How this would have survived the reaction amongst those excluded from power was never explored because von Papen was outmanoeuvred in the Reichstag. The Nazi who was now chairing the Reichstag meetings – Hermann Göring – ignored von Papen's attempt to dissolve the Reichstag and, instead, allowed a communist vote of no-confidence in the government to go ahead. The result was such a crushing humiliation for von Papen that he had to abandon his plan to end elections. It was clear from the vote that he had next to no support in the country. Instead, von Papen, in desperation, called another Reichstag election. There were possibilities that the Nazis might weaken: they were running short of money and the economy was starting to recover. In fact, the results of the November 1932 Reichstag election were mixed. On one hand, the Nazi vote did decline and the turnout of voters was much lower than in July 1932. As a result, the Nazi share of the vote fell from 13.8 million to 11.7 million and so the number of Nazi Reichstag deputies fell from 230 to 196. On the other hand, the communist share of the vote rose to 17 per cent, frightening many of the wealthy and conservative leaders of Germany who advised Hindenburg. This was good for the Nazis as it made these conservatives more likely to work with them.

The new Reichstag was even more unmanageable than the previous one, with 100 communist deputies facing 196 Nazi ones. Von Papen was in deep trouble. He had little support in the country and was now losing the support of the army. Without the support of the army, he could not possibly go ahead with a plan he was considering to ban both the Nazis and the communists and to rule by presidential decree. Furthermore, von Papen had also fallen out with a former ally who had assisted him to come to power. General Kurt von Schleicher had become Minister of Defence earlier in the year and resented von Papen for trying to put together an authoritarian answer to Germany's crisis without cooperating with him.

Unable to prevent the increasing street violence or proceed with his plans for an authoritarian government, von Papen resigned in December 1932. General von Schleicher replaced him as Chancellor. However, he, like von Papen, faced a major problem. Along with Hindenburg and his closest advisers, he wanted to create a form of rule whereby the President would appoint the Chancellor to run the government without any reference to the Reichstag. However, to do this risked starting a civil war, unless a majority in the Reichstag could be persuaded to vote for the change. But why should the Reichstag vote for its own end?

In December, hoping that the Nazi leadership could be divided, von Schleicher offered the job of Vice-Chancellor to a leading Nazi, Gregor Strasser. Strasser was concerned at the fact that the party organization, which he had built in the 1920s, was on the verge of collapsing due to lack of funds. Strasser refused to join the government without Hitler's agreement, but Hitler was furious as he was holding out for the top job of Chancellor for himself. As a result of this disagreement, Strasser resigned from the party. The failure of his strategy to split the Nazis meant that von Schleicher had to rely on presidential decrees to rule because he lacked sufficient support in the Reichstag. However, by January 1933, he was fast losing the confidence of both the President, who resented the fact that his friend von Papen had been forced to resign by von Schleicher,[10] and the army, who feared civil war if a Chancellor could not be found who could command a majority in the Reichstag.

Faced with these problems, von Schleicher requested that Hindenburg give him wide-ranging emergency powers to rule Germany. Von Schleicher's strategy was to have the Reichstag dissolved but not to hold elections until the autumn of 1933, in the meantime ruling by declaring a state of emergency. Hindenburg refused. Instead, he responded to a request by von Papen, who persuaded him to appoint Hitler as Chancellor with himself as Vice-Chancellor. On 15 January 1933, the Nazis increased their share of the vote (compared with November 1932) in the parliamentary elections in the tiny German state of Lippe-Detmold, as a result of a massive campaign by the Nazis, which they could never have managed in national elections.

This made it seem that Hitler would not accept anything less and was in a stronger position than he really was. This solution, von Papen thought, would allow him to control Hitler but give the government the support of the Nazis and other right-wing groups in the Reichstag. Since the majority of the new cabinet would not be Nazis, von Papen and the nationalist Alfred Hugenberg (leader of the German National People's Party, the DNVP) believed they could manipulate Hitler. The German army supported the idea too, as it seemed to offer stable government. On 30 January 1933, Hitler was appointed Chancellor of Germany. A combination of factors – the economic crisis, the lack of deep-seated democratic traditions within German society, the wheeler-dealing of ambitious political figures who cared more about power than democracy – had brought down the Weimar Republic.[11]

That night, thousands of SA, SS and 'Steel Helmets' (the First World War veterans' association) marched through Berlin in a vast torchlit parade. Thousands watched them and Hindenburg took the salute. To many in the crowds it was like the unity that had swept the nation in August 1914 at the start of the First World War. It was as if the years of defeat and humiliation had never happened, as if the longed for national revival was at last taking place.

3

WHO VOTED NAZI? AND WHY?

Ernst Hanfstaengl, nicknamed 'Putzi', was born in Munich, the son of a rich German art publisher named Edgar Hanfstaengl, and an American mother. Putzi spent most of his early years in Germany and later moved to the United States. While there he attended Harvard University. A gifted pianist, Putzi composed several songs for Harvard's football team and was a member of the famous Harvard 'Hasty Puddings Theatrical Club'. Putzi graduated from Harvard in 1909.

Moving to New York, he took over the management of the American branch of his father's fine-arts publishing business. He knew Franklin and Theodore Roosevelt, the newspaper baron William Randolph Hearst and actor Charlie Chaplin. In 1920, Putzi married Helene Elise Adelheid Niemeyer from Long Island. Their only son, Egon Ludwig, would eventually serve in the US Army Air Corps. Sadly, their daughter Herta died at the age of five. In 1922, Putzi returned to Munich, Germany.

Putzi was fairly intelligent, sophisticated and well connected. He had benefited from US democracy and the open culture of a free society. So why did he become one of the members of Hitler's close circle in the 1920s? Not only that but he took part in the failed Munich Putsch and it was to Putzi's house that Hitler fled after the collapse of the Putsch. Legend has it that it was Putzi's wife, Helene, who persuaded Hitler not to commit suicide at that point. The Hanfstaengls' support for Hitler reveals how he was seen to represent many of the values that such a wealthy German family held dear: the rise of a new and powerful Germany, the overthrow of the despised Weimar Republic and the thrill of access to power. After all, it was Putzi who had played on the piano whilst Hitler gave vent to his political frustration in the 1920s and these experiences clearly made the former believe he had some significant influence on the latter. But Hitler was not dependent on Putzi, nor on the wide range of disparate people who gave him their allegiance. This was a reality that only time would reveal.

After Hitler came to power, Putzi fell foul of Joseph Goebbels in the in-fighting that characterized the 'jungle' of competing interests at the heart of Nazi government. As a result, by the end of 1933, he was removed from Hitler's staff and three years later he was divorced from Helene. After questioning the courage of German troops fighting in the Spanish Civil War, he became the victim of an elaborate hoax in which he was placed on a German aircraft bound for Spain, only to discover during this flight that he was to be dropped into enemy territory on a dangerous secret mission. His terror mounted as the flight drew closer to the destination. In fact, the plane had merely been circling Germany all the time. The whole charade had been masterminded by Goebbels but Putzi did not see the joke. In 1937, he fled Germany and eventually arranged for his son to join him in exile. Imprisoned by the British on the outbreak of the Second World War, Putzi (from 1942) worked for the US government, giving it insights into the organization of Hitler's inner circle. Returning to Germany after the war, he died in 1975.

Who was expecting what from the newly installed Nazi government in 1933? And would all these groups of supporters be satisfied by their experience of the Third Reich? Clearly, the Nazi support base was wide and varied.[1] In fact, some historians have claimed that the Nazi Party was the first modern 'protest party', in that it had no single clear base, or ideology, but attracted the support of a wide number of different groups because they were angry with the current system and situation. But how far is this true? And were there sufficient common features that might be said to characterize a Nazi voter?

The Nazis and religious believers

In the Reichstag election of July 1932, the Nazi share of the vote was twice as high in Protestant areas as in Catholic ones. The Catholic Centre Party regularly gained 11–12 per cent of the vote and did not really lose a great deal of support to the Nazis. This is not to say that no Catholics voted Nazi. In special circumstances this could occur, such as in Silesia, where there was strong nationalist resentment against neighbouring Poland, which had gained parts of Silesia after the First World War. Here, many Catholics did vote Nazi but this was the exception to the rule that the average Nazi voter was likely to be a Protestant. This characteristic was assisted by a strong tradition amongst German Protestants of patriotism and loyalty to the state. This had its roots in the Kaiser's Germany and some historians have argued that it had even deeper roots in the sixteenth- and seventeenth-century German Reformation, which created Protestant churches that stressed the importance of matters of religion being decided in line with the wishes of those in control of government. On the other hand, German Catholics, even the highly patriotic ones as most were, looked outside Germany to the supreme leader of the Roman Catholic Church – the pope in Rome. This tended to compete with the German-centred demands of extreme nationalists. As a result, for many reasons, Nazis had greater appeal in Protestant areas.

The Nazis and first-time voters

The Nazis had considerable success attracting young, first-time voters.[2] These were people who had not developed a traditional voting pattern, whose formative years had been under Weimar and whose job prospects were deeply affected by the 1929 Wall Street Crash. In January 1931, over 42 per cent of Nazi Party members were under 30 years old and 70 per cent were under 40 years old. This made the Nazis a very 'young' party. This contrasts with similar figures for the Social Democrats, who had only 18 per cent of their members under 30 and only 44.6 per cent under 40 years old. Furthermore, the way to the top in the Social Democratic Party was to work one's way upward through a hierarchy of committees. It was a process that, frankly, was boring to most young people raised on a 1920s diet of Hollywood films, consumerism and dancehalls.[3]

As early as 1922, the Nazis had set up a youth wing catering for those aged 14–18 years. At first called the Youth League of the NSDAP, it changed its name in 1926 to the catchier title of the 'Hitler Youth'. Its main aim was to act as a recruiting ground for the SA. At first though, the Hitler Youth had only limited success. In January 1932, it still only had a thousand members in a city as large as Berlin. Alongside the Hitler Youth there was the National Socialist School Pupils' League, founded in 1929, and the League of German Maidens, formed in 1930. These organizations had limited success compared with the National Socialist German Students' League working in universities: founded in 1926, this gained an energetic leader in the young Baldur von Schirach in 1928. By July 1931, under his leadership, it had taken over control of the national organization representing German university students. As a result of this success, von Schirach was appointed leader of the Hitler Youth in October 1931. Under his leadership, Nazi youth organizations would grow in importance after Hitler's appointment as Chancellor in January 1933 and during the 1930s considerable pressure would be put on young people to join one of the Nazi youth groups, since all other youth groups were soon banned in the Third Reich.

The importance of the youth activity before this date though lies in its effect of mobilizing support for the Nazi Party among young people, even if they did not actually join a Nazi youth organization. The energy of the Nazi Party and its promise to revitalize and restore Germany had great appeal to many German young people. And the Nazis were more active, more eye-catching than the traditional and very conservative groups who, until this time, had sought to organize and attract right-wing young Germans.

The Nazis and the rural population

As early as 1923, the Nazi newspaper the *Völkischer Beobachter* (*Racial Observer*) praised the German peasantry as examples of what the Nazis considered to be good traditional Germans squeezed by the communists seeking to take their land and wealthy capitalists demanding high interests on loans. This was part of a complex Nazi approach to those who worked on the land. It involved ideas ranging from reducing the debts of farmers to fantasies of German industrial workers returning to work on the land – a completely unlikely situation. In 1921, the Nazi writer Hermann Esser wrote that: 'The fellow country-men toiling in the factories, workshops and offices must be brought into contact again with the soil.' Even as late as the 1940s this racist fantasy continued as Nazi plans for the occu-pation of the USSR included settlements of heavily armed SS farming communities exploiting the land with the assistance of Slav agricultural workers reduced to slavery. It was a fantasy that mixed images of simple medieval peasants with the mili-tary ambitions of twentieth-century German nationalists.

Despite this, the Nazi attempt to win the support of German farmers was slow in developing. For much of the middle years of the 1920s, it was overshadowed by propa-ganda campaigns aimed at the middle classes and workers. This was not helped, from the Nazi point of view, by the fact that the rural communities of the original Nazi heartland in Bavaria were Catholic and not easily won over to allegiance to the Nazi Party, which, as we shall see, harboured an antag-onism towards the Catholic Church.

It was after 1927 that the Nazis began to put their energies into capturing rural votes, and the target group then was Protestant farmers in northern Germany. The Nazis hoped that here it would be more successful than in its recent attempts to break into industrial areas and win them from the Social Democrats and the Communist Party. The Nazis were encouraged in this hope by peasant unrest in many rural areas of northern Germany. Here, poorer farmers were in deep trouble. They were hit harder by agricultural downturns than wealthier landowners who were able to buy farm machinery on hire purchase and modernize their farms relatively cheaply. Poorer peasant farmers, on the other hand, had tended to save their money and it had become worthless as a result of the inflation of 1923. After the end of the inflation, the government had attempted to encourage a revival of agriculture with low interest rates on loans made to farmers. As a result, peasant farmers borrowed heavily, assuming that further inflation would reduce the value of their borrowing. This was not the case and they soon found themselves heavily in debt and unable to repay these large loans. By the late 1920s, many peasant farmers found they were forced out of their farms because they had failed to repay debts. Even wealthier farmers were angry as they resented paying the higher taxes needed to support the Weimar Republic's welfare state. Then the crisis in world trade in the late 1920s and early 1930s caused further severe problems for German farmers. Unable to sell their produce and further affected by the drop in demand at home (due to the rise in unemployment), many were unable to pay back loans and mortgages on their farms. As a result, there was widespread unhappiness across farming communities.

As farmers faced these problems they began to demand high tariffs on foreign farming goods imported into Germany, in the hope that this would protect their produce from competition from cheap overseas imports. Since the Nazis were in favour of 'autarky' (or self-sufficiency) and the banning of foreign food imports, the farmers' desperation and the Nazis' ideas began to converge.

In order to win farming votes in northern Germany, the Nazis played down any socialist-type features of their programme for fear that these would frighten off farmers. For example, where Point 17 of the Party Programme demanded 'expropriation of land for communal purposes without compensation', Hitler was quick to assure farmers that this only referred to taking land from Jewish companies who had bought it in the hope of selling it on at a high profit. This was not what this point of the Party Programme had really meant but the Nazis realized it needed reinterpreting.

Nazi successes in rural areas in the Reichstag election of May 1928 convinced them that rural votes could be won easily and cheaply. As a result, the Nazis promised farmers that they would have a special position within the promised Third Reich. The state would protect farming interests and provide a 'corporation' in which farmers of all types could work together and in which their voices would be heard. To prove their rural credentials, the Nazis were careful to pair any upper-class speakers in country areas with a farmer.[4] Furthermore, the Nazis promised that any farm labourers, who were often Social Democrat voters, would be brought under control and forced to give up their demands for higher wages. Across Schleswig-Holstein large numbers of middling and small landowners rushed to join the Nazis and many younger men joined the SA and were dispatched to fight for the Nazi message in nearby cities. Throughout 1928 and 1929, the support for the Nazis increased in rural areas.

While support for the Nazis increased amongst smaller farmers it was slower to grow amongst farm labourers. This changed in the early 1930s when the Nazi trade union – the NSBO – established groups (cells) amongst farm workers. The striking success of the Nazis in Schleswig-Holstein in the July 1932 Reichstag elections revealed how successful these strategies were. It was the only state in which the Nazis gained over 50 per cent of the votes cast.

The Nazis and women

Under Weimar, many German women experienced a greater degree of personal freedom than before 1918. So what appeal would Nazism have for them, with its emphasis on a return to traditional female roles and its opposition to a female presence in the workplace? The Nazi programme, published in 1920, stated that it disapproved of women working. Hitler claimed that the emancipation of women was a slogan invented by Jewish intellectuals. He argued that for the German woman her 'world is her husband, her family, her children, and her home'.[5]

The view that women should remain at home was reinforced when a third of male workers became unemployed during the depression after 1929. Nazis argued that men were being replaced by female workers who, on average, only received 66 per cent of men's wages. Therefore, the Nazis concluded, a reduction in the number of women workers would help bring down male unemployment.

During the election campaign in 1932, Hitler promised that, if he gained power, he would take 800,000 women out of employment within four years. This was accompanied by an emphasis on the value of starting families in order to boost the German birth rate. When the Nazis came to power, they followed through in this intention to promote women rearing families at the expense of those who did not have children. In August 1933, a law was passed that enabled married couples to obtain loans to set up homes and start families. To pay for this, single men and childless couples were taxed more heavily. Incidentally, the decline in unemployment after the Nazis gained power meant that it was not necessary to force women out of manual work. However, action was taken to reduce the number of women working in the professions.

With all this emphasis on traditional female roles it might be thought that the Nazis would have only limited appeal to German women. But this was not the case. In fact, in the early 1930s, German women were more likely to vote for the Nazis than for the parties of the left.[6] The Communist Party, for example, seems to have had very little appeal to women. Most of its voters were men. Why was this? Clearly, religious, class and local issues motivated women as much as they motivated men, but German women were more likely to turn to right-wing groups and, as the Nazi Party grew in size, it became the most obvious of these groups. This right-wing tendency may be explained by the fact that many German women still held traditional roles within their families. In this case, the beliefs of the Nazis would have been more appealing than might be assumed. Furthermore, the Nazi emphasis on racial purity afforded women a vital role in the making of a new German community. In addition to this, the fact that many German women already played a key role in the raising of children and in the maintenance of homes may have made them particularly open to the message that only the Nazis could restore economic prosperity and social order. This promised protection for homes and families from the disruption caused by unemployment. And the left-wing parties' male-orientated structures often overshadowed their more unisex theories.[7]

There is also some evidence to suggest that the Nazis played upon female fears of crime and disorder that would occur if communists took power. The idea of marauding communist thugs out to destroy German society might today sound like a bizarre fantasy but, set against the violence and atrocities of the Russian Revolution, the Russian Civil War and Stalin's collectivization campaigns in the 1920s and early 1930s, the fear of violence that might accompany social disintegration seems to have had a particularly large impact on German women, even more than on German men.

And what about social class?

Even in the early 1930s, people realized that the Nazis had been highly successful in recruiting support amongst lower-middle class Protestants. Many middle-class Germans were bitter at losing their savings during the hyperinflation of 1923 and were gripped by a fear of being forced down into the working class. Along with this, having more to lose than their poorer neighbours, they feared social unrest, and those with small businesses feared the spread of left-wing influence in their workshops. Instead, they hoped for a new-found national unity to replace class conflict. On top of this, many civil servants resented Weimar job cuts in the early 1930s.[8] It was a cocktail of emotions that propelled many towards the Nazi Party. This cocktail was stirred by witnessing escalating street violence, which seemed to threaten the stability prized by middle-class German citizens. As Albert Speer was later to remark, it was the sight of disciplined marching SA units that persuaded his mother that only the Nazis could restore order in Germany. This, of course, was true in large measure, since *they* were causing a great deal of the disorder.

Amongst wealthier businesspeople, the attraction of the Nazis lay principally in their promises to control workers and end trade-union activities. The Nazis promised the end of the Social Democrats and the Communist Party. Furthermore, Nazi plans for military expansion promised increased profits for industry, and the pursuit of *Lebensraum* (living space) in Eastern Europe offered opportunities to gain cheap resources and increase profits even further. As a result, it was leading industrialists who, in November 1932, put pressure on Hindenburg to pull the Nazis into a broad-based nationalist authoritarian regime.[9] Nevertheless, it was only after Hitler became Chancellor in January 1933 that big donations flowed in from this quarter. Prior to this event, many German capitalists were content to watch and see whether or not the Nazis had a political future. For most of the period 1930–3, it was ordinary Nazi Party members who dug deep into their meagre pockets to fund the party's election expenses.[10]

However, the appeal to industrialists should not obscure the fact that the Nazis were also successful in pulling in working-class support. This was obscured at the time by the fact that middle-class people tended to 'go Nazi' as part of large recognizable communities and groups, whereas workers tended to join individually. In contrast, the non-Nazi trade unions (for example, those run by the Social Democrats) continued in existence until destroyed by the Nazis in May 1933 and this gave the impression that most workers had not gone over to the Nazis. This was despite the fact that high unemployment levels had already reduced the numbers in non-Nazi trade unions and made these groups even less representative of the working class than they appeared. The historian Conan Fischer has suggested why it was the middle-class nature of Nazism that most people were aware of, despite large numbers of workers voting Nazi:

> The pattern of the Nazi advance probably provides the most convincing explanation, for whilst entire middle-class organisations had been penetrated by, or even switched to the National Socialists, the workers usually joined as individuals or sometimes as members of communities which lacked any pronounced class profile or awareness.[11]

Furthermore, the Social Democrats in particular were unwilling to admit to the fact that large numbers of workers would support the Nazis. This phenomenon was less of a problem for centre and right-wing groups to admit to when they lost middle-class support – but they were still powerless to actually stop the loss of their supporters to the Nazis. Interestingly, the Communist Party *did* recognize that it was losing workers to the Nazis. In 1932, one communist report noted: 'SA members have no bank account and no salary; most have no job.' They were 'without work or hope' and, as such, were drawn into the SA by promises of work and bread. But most of these frank concerns were restricted to internal party documents and reports and so few people outside the Communist Party leadership were aware of the conclusions.

But the question remains: why did some workers vote Nazi? The answer involves a range of factors. There was a tradition of anti-capitalism from the early years of the Nazi Party and this lingered in a number of areas even after Hitler reined it in. In addition, Hitler's language of resentment towards the wealthy struck a chord amongst the unemployed and the desperate, who were also impressed by his lowly social origins.[12] This was enhanced by the socialist-type slogans and symbols that the Nazis sometimes used in working-class areas. And in such areas it was noted that the SA contained many unemployed workers, who had found purpose in their new-found Nazi membership.

Nazi trade-union activists promoted strike activity in early 1930 to destabilize Weimar. That gave the Nazi Party an illusory appearance of radicalism, which had significant appeal as the numbers of the jobless mounted after 1930. As one worker remarked to a US historian in 1934, Hitler offered more concrete objectives than the revolutionary theories of the communists: 'Instead of prophecies and far-off visions, in National Socialism he gave us a good working scheme of things we could get busy on right away.'[13] And finally, the German working class was not a united group. Only about 30 per cent worked in large union-ized industries and had a strong tie to the Communist Party or the Social Democrats. About 60 per cent of workers were not even members of a trade union and were far from predictable in their voting patterns. The parties of the left certainly could not take their support for granted. Some were Protestants, others Catholics – and this too affected voting traditions.[14]

Even so, it seems to have been the *fear* of unemployment that motivated Nazi voters. The actual unemployed themselves were twice as likely to vote for the Communist Party as for the Nazis. In the middle of 1932, only 13 per cent of the unem-ployed supported the Nazis, compared with 37.3 per cent of the nation as a whole. This reminds us that the role of unem-ployment was complicated.

Research in the 1970s emphasized the Nazis' ability to unite middle-class groups but more recent work, in the 1990s and early twenty-first century, has shown that they were in fact highly successful in forging links across class boundaries. This was combined with the Nazis' skill at talking the different 'languages' of particular groups at the same time, but in different places, whilst also uniting these groups with the common language of race and national identity. That some of these groups would be disappointed by the Nazis' inability to deliver to everyone is hardly a surprise, but all this lay beyond 1933. In the run up to gaining power, it was the ability of the Nazis to appeal to widely different groups and offer the promise of national unity that caused a surge in their popularity. In this appeal – even if contradictory and unlikely to work in practice – no other political party could compete with them. And the mere hope that such a national community could be created was enough to persuade vast numbers of Germans to vote Nazi in the context of national instability and unrest in the early 1930s. In order to appeal to less racist members of the electorate, the Nazis were even prepared to play down their anti-Semitism, as William Sheridan Allen found in his detailed study of support for the Nazis in the small town of Northeim.[15]

This attempt to create 'a German party for all Germans' was greatly assisted by the wide range of Nazi Party special-interest groups set up before 1933. These ranged from youth groups to factory cells, groups for civil servants and groups for wounded veterans of the First World War, groups for women and groups for farmers; the list is long. Even though many of these groups had only small memberships, they were important in creating the image of a party that could appeal to virtually all Germans. In the short term, this meant that the Nazi message was adapted and targeted at many different sections of German society and, in this way, had a political influence on groups that, before this, had considered themselves non-political. In the longer term, the existence of such a wide range of different groups gave the party a structure that could rapidly expand to absorb new members and, after Hitler came to power, would contribute to the Nazi aim of a society in which all the institutions were dominated by the beliefs of the Nazi Party under its Führer.

The role of the Führer

The personal appeal of Hitler was also a major part in swinging support behind the Nazis. This is not to downplay the role of wider social trends and the part played by Strasser's party machine. It is simply to make the point that the role of Hitler as Führer was crucial in both holding together such a complex and mutually contradictory group as the Nazis and in providing a focal point for national unity at a time of crisis and apparent disintegration. To a nation in which democracy was a relatively new experience, tainted with defeat and national humiliation, and in which the authoritarian regime of the Kaiser was very much within living memory, the idea of a person claiming to embody national unity had great appeal. Hitler's conscious presentation of himself as the hope of Germany and the Nazis' relentless propaganda, which centred on his role and authority, had a great impact on many disillusioned Germans.

His whole style of speaking and presenting his message in a highly staged and theatrical style now seems contrived and deeply unappealing, but at the time many Germans recorded how it deeply moved them and created an almost religious atmosphere of worship and hope. For such people, Nazism had become a kind of secular religion, in which Hitler was presented as a German messiah. And this was not just a phenomenon seen among the young and inexperienced. Many older Germans also wrote of the impact on their minds of Nazi discipline, unity and apparent hope of national revival in the middle of a time of turmoil, despair and uncertainty. In all of this, Hitler himself played a key role – though not of course the only one.

Making sense of the evidence: was there such a thing as a typical Nazi voter?

So, what did the 'typical Nazi voter' look like? People were more likely to vote Nazi if they were Protestants from rural areas and small towns; this was especially so if they were middle class, female and young. Workers, Catholics, those from the big cities and the unemployed did also sometimes support the Nazis, but, overall, were not a major source of their votes. Research in Saxony has shown that the Nazis tended to win working-class support only in areas where the Social Democrats and Communist Party had not established a traditional influence. Overall, the Nazis, despite being under-represented among some groups in society, won support from across the community. They attracted some support from every group, from both men and women and from the old as well as the young. They were, indeed, the first real 'protest party'. As one Hamburg schoolteacher confided in her diary in 1932, it was Hitler who 'rescues the Prussian prince, the scholar, the clergyman, the farmer, the worker, the unemployed, who rescues them from the parties back into the nation'.[16]

The historian Richard Evans summed up this ability to attract widespread support in the aftermath of the Wall Street Crash: 'The Nazi Party had established itself with startling suddenness in September 1930 as a catch-all party of social protest, appealing to a greater or lesser degree to virtually every social group in the land.'[17] The unpredictable nature of such a disparate combination of voters helps explain Hitler's actions after he came to power: to try to ensure that his dictatorship was not dependent on such a shifting and complex support base. Once he was free from relying on the unpredictable nature of democracy, his dictatorship was secure. However, how he would satisfy the contradictory expectations of so many different groups remained the greatest challenge facing the Nazis after they came to power. They had promised something to almost everyone. Somebody was going to be disappointed.

4

BRINGING GERMANY INTO LINE

Marburg was just one of many German cities that found all areas of life affected by the Nazis' coming to power in 1933. And this showed itself in the oddest corners of city social life. For example, the leaders of the gymnastics and sports club decided to imitate the new style of government ruling Germany. Its chairman, a high-school teacher named Dr Wilhelm Stier, was re-elected with the support of local Nazis. But now he was styled the führer of the club and in May dismantled its democratic constitution; instead of elected organizers, he appointed those who would henceforth run the club. The same trend occurred in the local swimming club. Only here, its new führer declared that further changes were unnecessary as its leadership and activities had 'always been strictly nationalistic'. Another local sports club, in May, selected new leaders to the sound of the Nazi salutes of 'Sieg Heil'. It should be noted that – despite this enthusiastic display of loyalty – all these loyal Nazis had only joined the party since January.[1] Such displays of mirroring the new government were happening across Germany.

Hitler came to power in January 1933, legally and constitutionally. This is a very important point: it affected how most Germans regarded the regime. Despite the fact that it would soon become one of the most violent and criminal govern-ments in world history, it had been brought to power legally.

This meant that for most Germans – even for its opponents – it was the legitimate government. This would make it harder to oppose and eventually to attempt to overthrow it, even when the extent of its criminality and violence was clear. It also partly helps explain why so few Germans ever really opposed the regime between 1933 and 1945. It was not only down to its fearsome violence, it was also partly because of the German tradition of obedience to the state and the fact that Hitler had come to power legally.

However, in January 1933, all this lay ahead. Indeed, there were those at this point who believed that the Nazis were on the brink of being 'tamed'. They assumed that bringing Hitler into government would force him to modify his more extreme demands as he faced the realities of running a nation in coop-eration with other political groups. They also wanted to harness the energy and dynamism of the Nazis to crush communism and create a more stable and united Germany. To those such as von Papen, who had engineered this piece of political tight-rope-walking, it seemed achievable.[2] They assumed that, instead of falling into a chasm of violence and division, Germany would develop into a stronger and less volatile society.[3]

That this would follow right-wing, authoritarian and milita-ristic policies – in contrast to the democratic and multi-party democracy of the Weimar Republic – was acceptable to many of the elites within Germany, 'who perceived them as a vehicle for restoring their own dominance'.[4] These elites had never been reconciled to Weimar and the democratic constitution; they hated the left and trade union power; they wanted to scrap, or radically revise, the Treaty of Versailles and looked forward to a point when Germany would once again play a leading (and indeed dominant) role within Europe. Their aim for Germany was similar at key points to that of the Nazis and, whilst they might disagree over the extent, methods and speed of such a transformation, there was much in common between the ambitions of these elites and Hitler. Later, however – post 1945 – many of their members would be in denial about their own responsibility in making the Nazi disaster possible.[5]

Furthermore, given the way in which many other European countries developed in the 1920s and were continuing to do so, in the face of the depression of the 1930s, this drift into dictatorial, militaristic, right-wing government was part of a growing trend and would not have seemed particularly unusual. Germany seemed to be travelling on the same road as Italy, Poland, Latvia, Estonia, Lithuania, Hungary, Romania, Bulgaria, Portugal and Yugoslavia. And it was a road that, after 1933, would be followed by Austria and Spain and would be admired by right-wing groups across Western Europe (even in countries such as France, which remained democracies) before the outbreak of the Second World War.[6]

Even those who feared the Nazis could console themselves with the thought that this Hitler government was only a temporary arrangement. Sebastian Haffner, a Berlin lawyer and journalist opposed to Nazism, in January 1933, could conclude: 'All things considered, the government was no cause for concern. It was only a matter of what would come after it . . .'[7] But this hope was misplaced.

Gleichschaltung: bringing Germany into line

Hitler was in a vulnerable position in January 1933. He was not a dictator. At any time, he could be dismissed by President Hindenburg, just as recent chancellors such as Brüning, von Papen and von Schleicher had been before him. More than this, when Hitler became Chancellor only two major offices of state were held by Nazis: Hitler was Reich Chancellor and Wilhelm Frick was Minister of the Interior.

However, Hermann Göring was appointed Reich Minister Without Portfolio and Acting Prussian Minister of the Interior, which gave him direct control over the police in most of Germany. So, in fact, the Nazis were in a potentially more powerful position than their allies realized. With this latter government position under their control it would be possible to ensure that the police system ran to their advantage and to unleash the SA on their enemies. As the French ambassador noted (referring to the conservatives and nationalists who believed they were using Hitler): 'They have believed themselves to be very ingenious, ridding themselves of the wolf by introducing him into the sheepfold.'[8]

However, at first, it seemed that there had been a return to democratic government within Germany since the Chancellor was no longer dependent on the President passing emergency decrees. This Chancellor could actually command a majority in the Reichstag when Nazi votes were added to those of their allies and likely allies amongst the other nationalists.

Hitler, though, had no intention of remaining in this dependent position. His aim was *Gleichschaltung* (coordination). This German word can also be translated as 'bringing into line'. It was a phrase borrowed from the electrical industry and described a situation where all the switches in an electrical circuit were coordinated, so that one master switch would make all the electrical circuits active. It was also used where alternating current was changed to direct current, allowing electricity to flow in one direction only.[9] What this really meant, as the Nazis used it, was the Nazification of German politics and society. Their aim was to create a situation where the whole of German society would respond to the orders and instructions of the Nazi leadership embodied by Hitler.[10]

This process of 'coordination' and of 'bringing Germany into line' would not just be something imposed from above. Instead, all over Germany, enthusiastic Nazis set about infiltrating and taking over their local communities. This included areas as non-political as local singing clubs, orchestras[11] and women's groups. Nothing would be allowed to have an existence independent of Nazi control and at variance with Nazi ideas. This aim extended from dominating government in Berlin, through taking over government in the *länder* (states) of Germany, down to controlling every club and institution in the smallest town and village. In education, it affected the whole spectrum, from kindergarten to university.[12]

Whether this would be possible only time would tell, but it was a key characteristic of the Nazi plan for the transformation of German society. In time, they hoped that this would create a *Völksgemeinschaft* (a racial community) in which class divisions and 'racial impurities' would be removed. Such a German nation would, in the Nazi view, be a truly united and harmonious society, entirely geared to Nazi values and aims. It would exclude the Jews and others who were considered by the Nazis as not being members of the racial community, such as the mentally ill and those with severe learning difficulties and genetic disorders.

The Nazi leadership described their government as a 'national uprising' and this described both the legal manner of Hitler's appointment as Chancellor and the revolutionary seizure of control of Germany by ordinary Nazis that followed. This feature of Nazi rule is important to understand. Ordinary party members and their allies actively participated in this transformation and the conservative elites who had brought Hitler to power soon found that they had unleashed a flood of activity, which they were quite incapable of stopping. And, once the flood had started, many non-Nazis also decided it was safest to actively cooperate in this Nazi takeover.

Building a dictatorship

As February 1933 progressed, attacks on the Communist Party were extended to the Social Democrats too. Their meetings were broken up and people assaulted and killed. With the police and the army now firmly working against them it was almost impossible for these groups to defend themselves. If they had fought back they would have been bloodily crushed and, even faced with defeat, the Communist Party and the Social Democrats would not work together to defend democracy.

It was with the aim of crushing opposition that Hitler persuaded President Hindenburg to call another Reichstag election. Before it took place, the Nazi leadership set in motion three important developments. First, on 3 February, Hitler met the leaders of the German military. He promised them money to rearm Germany, the reintroduction of conscription, the end of the Treaty of Versailles and their independence from politics. Furthermore, he enticed them with the future prospect of invading Eastern Europe and 'Germanizing' it by expelling millions of the native Slav inhabitants. He also promised that the government would deal with the 'threat' of the communists. Second, on 20 February, he met the leaders of German industry. He promised them he would bring about the end of the communist threat and would ensure the security of German capitalism. In return, they promised 3 million marks to help pay for the Nazis' election campaign. After Hitler had left the meeting, Göring promised those present that the forthcoming election would be the last, not just for four years but probably for the next hundred years. There is no record of anyone present being shocked at this statement. Finally, on 17 February, Göring, in his capacity as head of the police, urged the police to cooperate with the SA and to use whatever force was considered necessary against communists. Chillingly, he promised: 'Police officers, who in the execution of their duty, use their firearms, will be supported by me without regard to the effect of their shots.'

Göring went even further on 22 February, when 50,000 SA, SS and Steel Helmets (First World War veterans) were actually brought into the police as auxiliary support units, to break into the offices of the Communist Party and trade unions. Despite the Nazis' reputation for street violence this fusion was relatively easy to establish because Nazi violence had traditionally been directed at communists and then Jews and Polish workers; it had rarely been directed against the police.[13] The police were being turned into a branch of the Nazi organization, but such political use of the police did not start with the Nazis. In 1932, von Papen had begun to sack senior police officers who were politically unacceptable to him, indicating the way politics was going even before Hitler became Chancellor. Nevertheless, the Nazis radically accelerated the trend.

On 23 February, the police launched a massive raid on the Communist Party's headquarters in Berlin and claimed to have found evidence of plans for a revolutionary uprising. It was almost certainly faked. While the communists seem to have made plans for a long period of illegal, or semi-legal, activity under government persecution and had probably hidden a large number of weapons, they do not seem to have been planning a revolt. Under orders from Moscow, their official stance was that the Nazis were the last expression of capitalism in crisis and would soon collapse – to be followed by the victory of communism in Germany.

Then, on 27 February, the Reichstag building was set on fire.[14] The police arrested a Dutch ex-communist, Marinus van der Lubbe. Immediately, the Nazi leaders claimed that this was the start of a communist uprising. The argument still rages as to whether this event was a total Nazi set-up or whether they simply made maximum use of a fortuitous act by this mentally unstable Dutchman.

On one hand, fires seem to have been started all over the building, suggesting that it was the work of several people. The communist leadership were taken completely unawares by the event, despite the fact that the Nazis held them responsible for the crime. In fact, the communist leader in the Reichstag surrendered himself to prove that no revolution was being planned. The lack of danger posed by the communists is revealed in the fact that the Communist Party was not banned until some time after its so-called 'revolution' had been crushed. All of this suggests that it was a Nazi set-up.

One the other hand, van der Lubbe was a genuine arsonist. On 25 February, he had attempted to set fire to a welfare office, the town hall and a former royal palace in one area of Berlin. Regarding the likelihood of one man causing such a widespread blaze, there is a possibility that the dome above the Reichstag chamber acted as a chimney, helping the fire to spread and enabling one man to cause so much damage. And van der Lubbe had sufficient materials on him to start several fires. While there is no evidence that he was ordered to burn the Reichstag by the Communist Party, he carried communist leaflets and the Nazis seized on this; but it seems to represent no more than his own anti-Nazi campaign. As if this was not complex enough, Rudolf Diels, head of the Prussian Political Police, interrogated van der Lubbe and in his memoirs, published in 1950, recalled how he was sure that the Dutchman acted alone. Interestingly, von Papen entertained exactly the same opinion.[15]

Whatever the exact circumstances, the key point lies in how the Nazis made use of the event. Hindenburg was persuaded to pass an emergency decree on 28 February, 'For the protection of people and state'. Paragraph one of this decree restricted personal liberties, freedom of expression, freedom of the press, the right of assembly and the privacy of postal services. Paragraph two gave central government power to overrule regional governments. This decree provided the legal basis for the subsequent suppression of opposition. By the end of April, about 25,000 opponents of the Nazis had been arrested in Prussia alone as a result of this emergency decree. Temporary prisons, the forerunners of the concentration camps, were set up and torture was used on many of those arrested. In these ways, the decree was the first major step towards outright dictatorship.

The last Reichstag election, March 1933

Hitler's government had all the advantages in the run-up to the March 1933 election. Its propaganda campaign, organized by Joseph Goebbels, used all the resources of the state, and the police were used to intimidate communist opponents. The Communist Party was not actually banned but the police and SA attacked huge numbers of individual communists and their offices and homes. By allowing the Communist Party to remain in existence, Hitler hoped to avoid a violent reaction by its supporters and also hoped to reduce the number of votes that might otherwise go to the Social Democrats.

SA violence, over which Hitler and his immediate leadership group had no direct control, exploded across Germany. This was very much in keeping with the methods of Nazi leadership developed since the 1920s. The upper leadership called for violent action in general terms, and the party activists and SA and SS understood the cue and put it into specific, violent practice in their own areas as they decided. It was a form of leadership that deliberately initiated extreme violence, but which tried not to be too closely implicated in the brutality that actually took place on the ground. It also allowed party activists to let loose their own anger and to experiment with different ways of putting violent orders into practice. This was later seen most clearly in Nazi policy towards Jewish people, but to start with it was felt by the communists.

There certainly was a national fear of a communist uprising in the aftermath of the Reichstag fire. Yet, despite this, the Nazis only gained about 44 per cent of the votes cast. Hitler was well short of the 66 per cent needed to change the Weimar constitution. But added to the 8 per cent of votes cast for the Nazis' allies, the nationalists, Hitler's government had 52 per cent of the vote and an overall majority in the Reichstag.

Amazingly, the Communist Party, despite having most of its candidates arrested, or in hiding, won 12.3 per cent of the vote and the Social Democrats won 18.3 per cent. This meant that just under a third of the German electorate were still prepared to vote for strongly anti-Nazi parties, despite the violence and intimidation. The Catholic Centre Party took 11.2 per cent of the vote. Even in what was by now a semi-dictatorship, the Nazis and their nationalist allies had only won 20 million votes in a country whose electorate numbered 45million in 1933. At no time did the Nazis win over the majority of the electorate.

Nevertheless, the Nazi success was enough to unleash a wave of violent action across Germany. The brutality of the SA increased dramatically. Nazis seized control of local and city governments, knowing they could not be stopped. Between 6 and 15 March, Nazis in the police and auxiliary units of the SA and the SS raised the swastika flag on all official buildings across Germany. Ministers who objected were forced to resign, or were put under house arrest. Nazi state commissioners were appointed, with the power to replace all non-Nazi local police chiefs and government ministers with their own appointees. The federal system of German government had now been replaced by central control.

As the repression increased, Heinrich Himmler, commander of the SS, took charge of the police in Bavaria and accelerated the process of arresting political opponents. On 22 March, the first concentration camp was opened at Dachau, near Munich. Those considered enemies of the new Nazi state were held without trial and subjected to torture. Many were murdered. Soon makeshift camps were being established across Germany. At least 100,000 people were arrested in 1933 and 600 were murdered.

In the middle of this unrest, the Nazis realized that it was necessary to reassure their conservative allies that order was not totally breaking down. On 12 March, the black, red and gold flag of the Weimar Republic was officially replaced with the black, white and red of the pre-1919 imperial German flag. It was a gesture designed to wipe away all official traces of the Weimar years and to suggest that the 'old' (pre-1919) Germany and the 'new' Nazi Germany were one and the same thing.

On 21 March, President Hindenburg joined Chancellor Hitler in a service of national reconciliation and renewal at Potsdam, near Berlin. Occurring on the first day of spring, the Nazi-dominated press was quick to draw parallels with the beginning of a new 'season of growth' in the life of the German nation.[16] As one Bavarian newspaper put it: 'What is taking place in Germany today is the struggle not only for the renewal of the idea of the state, but also for the reshaping of the German soul . . .'[17] The event was followed by the spontaneous planting of hundreds of 'Hitler-oaks' across Germany, as local communities competed to show their Nazi loyalty.

Potsdam had a special place in German history as it was closely associated with the famous 18th-century German king

Frederick the Great (king of Prussia, 1740–86). Frederick the Great had inherited a small, northern German kingdom and then, during his reign, he had turned it into a powerful European state, mostly through his military achievements. It was an image of power and transformation that most Germans looked back to with approval. By holding the event at Potsdam, the Nazi government was sending out two important signals: first, it too was set to revive German greatness and, second, it was in line with the hopes of traditional German society and its elites in government, the military and industry.

The Enabling Act: the end of democracy

On 23 March, the new Reichstag met for the first time after the March elections. Due to the Reichstag fire, it met in the Kroll Opera House in Berlin. With the election secure and the Potsdam Memorial service over, the Nazis now acted to secure their hold on power. The Reichstag passed the 'Law for the Removal of Distress from the People and Reich', which is better known as 'the Enabling Act'. Under the Enabling Act, the Reichstag transferred its power to Hitler as Chancellor for four years. Hitler could now rule without the agreement of the Reichstag or the President. The Weimar Republic had collapsed. Democracy was over.

Even with many Communist Party Reichstag deputies in prison, and therefore unable to vote on the Enabling Act, Hitler had still needed the support of the Centre Party for the necessary two thirds majority to pass the law. They gave it. They hoped that by so doing they would preserve the influence of the Catholic Church in Germany. It was an appalling miscalculation by people who had failed to grasp just what Hitler intended for Germany, despite the evidence all around them. It is an indicator of how far to the right politics had shifted in Germany by 1933 and how unstoppable the Nazi advance seemed. The old parties of the Weimar Republic were confused and exhausted by the storm that had overwhelmed them since 1929. The Centre Party was also influenced by a trend being seen in the Catholic Church across Europe in the 1930s. Many Catholics were prepared to support authoritarian governments, and even dictatorships, in order to prevent the spread of communism. Earlier, in 1929, the Catholic Church had been prepared to accept the fascist regime in Italy through a 'concordat'; an agreement that guaranteed the independence of the Church. In 1933, the Vatican put pressure on the Centre Party to agree to Nazi demands in the hope of guaranteeing something similar in Germany. And Catholic politicians were later to support authoritarian governments in Austria and Spain. As a result of this support from other parties, the Enabling Act was supported by 444 Reichstag deputies. The only people to vote against it were 94 Social Democrats, and few of them would remain free for much longer.

The Enabling Act was officially a temporary measure that needed renewing every four years. But once it was in place the dictatorship was permanent. An emergency piece of law became the foundation for the end of German democracy. It was renewed again in 1937 and in 1939. It was made permanent, by decree, in 1943.

The fate of the other parties

On 1 May, in an attempt to preserve themselves, trade unions took part in Nazi-organized May Day marches. On 2 May, SA and SS took over every Social Democrat-affiliated trade union office in Germany. This showed that no gesture of acceptance would be enough to ensure the survival of an independent trade union movement. On 4 May, the Catholic trade unions voluntarily put themselves under Nazi control. From this point onwards there were no independent trade unions in Germany; all labour organizations were part of the Nazi state.

On 10 May, the property and funds of the Social Democratic Party were seized. On 21 June, they were banned. Many of its leaders had already fled abroad and its headquarters were now in Prague, in Czechoslovakia. Thousands of its members were arrested and many were killed.

On 1 July, the Nazi government agreed a concordat with the Roman Catholic Church. This promised the freedom of the Catholic Church and its organizations from state interference and the full participation of Catholics in German government and society. The price was the end of the Catholic Centre Party itself. The concordat was therefore quickly followed by the formal dissolution of the Centre Party on 5 July. It was a crushing end to a party that, so recently, had had two of its leading members as Chancellor – Brüning and von Papen.

On 14 July, the Communist Party was officially banned. The parties of the left were now totally crushed. But what about the nationalist allies of the Nazis? The answer was that they too had no future. The nationalists were officially allies but could not escape the intimidation that targeted all non–Nazi groups. Hugenberg, a member of the government, even found himself banned from speaking by the police and attacked by the Nazi press. On 26 June, he resigned and soon his party was no more. The law that banned the Communist Party specifically also outlawed all non-Nazi political parties. Germany was now officially a one-party state.

Next, it was the turn of the First World War veterans' group the Steel Helmets. After Hitler came to power, they had ceased to have any independent influence. On 26 April, its leadership placed it under Hitler's direct leadership; it was absorbed into the SA and was finally dissolved by the Nazis in 1935. This was an organization that, in 1930, had contained 500,000 members. Yet within four years it had vanished, overwhelmed by the Nazi tide.

President Hindenburg made no attempt to oppose what Hitler was doing and he only ever objected to one Nazi law. On 7 April, the Reichstag passed a law for the 'Restoration of the Professional Civil Service', which called for the immediate sacking of all Jewish civil servants. Hindenburg refused to accept this law until it had been amended to exclude all Jewish veterans of the First World War, Jewish civil servants who had served in the civil service during the First World War and those

Jewish civil servants whose fathers were veterans of the First World War. Hitler, who believed that no Jews had actually fought in the war, changed it to satisfy Hindenburg's objections. It is important to note that Hindenburg was not objecting to Hitler's anti-Semitism; rather he only wanted to protect those Jews linked to the German war effort. That the law, when changed, would still destroy the careers of large numbers of Jewish people clearly meant little to the President. It is a disturbing insight into how many Nazi beliefs fitted into existing German prejudices in the 1930s. As the historian Richard Evans reminds us:

> the speed and enthusiasm with which so many people came to identify with the new regime strongly suggests that a large majority of the educated elites in German society, whatever their political allegiance up to that point, were already predisposed to embrace many of the principles upon which Nazism rested.[18]

It is a disturbing thought, but was Hitler securely in power? By July 1933, Hitler did seem to be in an unassailable position. The Reichstag was irrelevant, Nazis were swarming all over local government and institutions, the police were dominated by the party, the communists were crushed, other political parties banned or dissolved and anyone who opposed the government was held in one of the new concentration camps. From 13 July, it was compulsory for all public employees to greet each other with the 'Hitler Salute'. An addition to this law promulgated two weeks later allowed the physically disabled to use their left arm. The power of the Nazis had been transformed in approximately six months. Those elite politicians such as von Papen, who had thought they could manipulate and control the Nazis, had been totally outmanoeuvred and overwhelmed by events. As for von Papen, 'His effete drawing-room Machiavellianism [had] underestimated Hitler's rat-like cunning.'[19]

Yet, Hitler was still not as secure as he needed to be if he was to hold dictatorial power in Germany. There were still three major danger areas for him: first, the President had the power to remove Hitler as Chancellor. Second, the army had the power to remove him. Third, the SA was a real area of weakness for Hitler. Its members were becoming uncontrollable now they had experienced power and they were ambitious. Under Röhm, they still hoped to overturn German middle-class society, challenge the power of the traditional German elites and take control of the army: in short, to put in place a violent Nazi revolution. Their behaviour was stirring up opposition amongst significant sections of society. Many middle-class Germans were shocked at the rude violence of the SA. More importantly, the army feared losing its power to the SA and, as the only force that could – if ordered by President Hindenburg to remove Hitler – end Nazi rule, the army was a dangerous group to alienate.

In addition, over 50 per cent of the electorate had never voted Nazi and their loyalty could not be taken for granted. There was also still a need to keep conservative nationalists on board since, for all those who enthusiastically supported Hitler, there were many more who did so, 'with reluctant and calculated complicity' or 'from fear that the alternative might plunge the system backwards . . .'[20] Institutions such as the Christian churches were not fully under Nazi control, either. The powerful industrialists seemed content to support the Nazi government so long as it provided the security and opportunity for personal wealth-creation that they valued. But their support was conditional. In the summer of 1933, Hitler's dictatorship was not as unassailable as it first appeared. If he was to secure his dictatorship he would have to act in order to put his position beyond challenge.

5

THE REVOLUTION EATS ITS OWN CHILDREN: THE DESTRUCTION OF THE SA

Karl Ernst was an SA *Gruppenführer* (group leader). This was a high rank within the SA (and from 1930 within the SS also). Considered within the SA to be the equivalent of an army general, such an officer commanded a large number of SA units. Ernst was, from early 1933, the leader of the SA in Berlin and a senior member of the Nazi organization. But, like many in the SA, his career had a complex back-story. Before joining the Nazis, he had been a bell-boy in a hotel and a bouncer at a gay nightclub.[1]

Ernst was nicknamed 'Frau Rohrbein', due to his intimate friendship with Paul Rohrbein, Berlin's first SA commander. Ernst had first met Rohrbein at the El Dorado, a favourite meeting place of Berlin's homosexual community and, in 1931, Rohrbein had introduced Ernst to an old comrade: Röhm, the overall commander of the SA. By April of that same year, Ernst was promoted to a command within the SA and, by 1932, was elected to the Reichstag as a Nazi deputy. Such string-pulling gave the SA the reputation of being a homosexual fraternity.[2]

Ernst has been accused of being part of an SA detachment

that set fire to the Reichstag building on the night of 27 February 1933. However, despite his place at the centre of Nazi politics, Ernst was not to survive the internal feud that led to the destruction of the SA leadership by Hitler and his closest associates in the infamous 'Night of the Long Knives' in 1934. This event saw the destruction of the power of the brutal, disorderly and scandal-dogged SA and its replacement by Hitler's bodyguard organization, the black-uniformed SS.

On 30 June 1934, Ernst – despite his earlier homosexual associations – had just married, and was in the port of Bremen with his new wife, on his way to their honeymoon in Madeira. When an SS arrest-squad swooped, Ernst's wife and chauffeur were wounded, and he himself was taken back to Berlin. Some 150 SA leaders, including Karl Ernst, were stood against a wall at the Cadet School at Lichterfelde and shot by SS firing squads. The death of Ernst, along with many other SA leaders who had well-known homosexual connections, removed both Hitler's political rivals and potential sources of scandal in one violent bloodletting. Clearly, it was political rather than sexual factors that led to the execution of the one-time bell-boy and gay nightclub bouncer, along with the rest of the SA leadership. But the life and death of Karl Ernst reveals something of the complex factors that led to the Nazi revolution devouring some of its most ardent 'children' in June 1934.

The history of the SA

The brown-shirted SA (short for *Sturmabteilung*, literally Storm Division – the Storm Troopers) had its roots in the earliest years of the Nazi party.[3] Its characteristic brown uniform was the result of the purchase of a large quantity of cheap army-surplus uniforms in the early 1920s. These light-brown uniforms had originally been produced for the German army serving in the African colonies, before these were taken from Germany in 1919.

Its early members were ex-soldiers and, even though its ranks would later be flooded by a younger generation, it was these older men, with their experience of the imperial army and of trench combat (and with better educational qualifications), who would make up the highest ranks of the SA. Of these highest ranks, 76 per cent were veterans of the First World War and 73 per cent had seen combat.[4] From early in the life of the Nazi party, such men were formed into a group designed to defend Nazi meetings and break up the meetings of rival organizations. In 1920, this unit began to be called the 'Hall Defence Detachment' and, in August 1921, it was reorganized under the misleading title of the 'Gymnastic and Sports Division' of the Nazi Party. From September of that year, it began to use the SA name and, after a particularly violent beer-hall brawl in November (in which a small group of SA routed opposition fighters), this became its official title. The name was derived from that of elite army units formed during the First World War and designed to storm and penetrate enemy defences. One of the early SA's leading members was the ex-army officer named Captain Ernst Röhm.[5]

Following Hitler's failed attempt to seize power in Munich in 1923, the SA was banned. While Hitler was in prison, Röhm rebranded the SA in an attempt to get around its ban but soon differences arose between him and Hitler over matters of organization and tactics. It was the start of a troubled relationship, which would eventually culminate in the execution of Röhm, on Hitler's orders, in 1934. But all this lay in the future when, disillusioned with politics, Röhm left Germany in 1925 to work abroad as an advisor to the Bolivian army. Heinrich Himmler (later commander of the SS) temporarily took over the running of the SA but the storm troopers proved a difficult organization to control.

In 1927, the Munich SA rebelled against their leader, Franz von Pfeffer (who had been appointed its commander in 1926). Hitler spoke to the SA members concerned, shook hands with each and secured their personal loyalty. This crisis had been defused but it would be followed by others. In 1931, there was the so-called Stennes Revolt, in which SA units in eastern

Germany revolted under the leadership of Walther Stennes. Reasons for this revolt included disputes over pay and problems with the local Nazi Party leaders, the Gauleiters, over control of the SA. Another factor was resentment that Hitler had recently set up a rival organization to the SA in the more disciplined and obedient SS. In Berlin, one SA unit even attacked the office of Joseph Goebbels and beat up the SS men on guard outside. In the end, these Berlin SA men had to be removed with the help of the police and Hitler rushed to Berlin to stop the revolt. He convinced the SA to return to duty by promising them more pay and more power within the Nazi movement. As a response to these problems, Hitler took over the direct SA leadership himself and, in January 1931, recalled Röhm as the SA Chief of Staff. Under Röhm's leadership, the SA expanded rapidly. In about a year its membership grew from 70,000 to 170,000 members. By 1934, the SA membership stood at 4,500,000.

The problems posed by the SA after January 1933
The SA had always been a difficult group to control. The revolts of 1927 and 1931 illustrated this point. The members were bred on violence and turmoil and this had become their reason to exist. During the long and violent road to power, however, this had served its bloody purpose in attacking rival groups and in undermining Weimar society. This violence on the streets had generally worked to Hitler's favour. As a result, it had been possible to overlook the fact that the SA's primary loyalty lay to its own interpretation of Nazism, rather than to Hitler's supreme leadership. Furthermore, its dream of destroying the existing German society and replacing it through a Nazi revolution was a desire dear to the hearts of many rank-and-file Nazi Party members.

The accession to power of Hitler as Chancellor in January 1933 subtly changed this situation. At first, the explosion of SA violence that followed this event served his purposes. Political rivals were arrested or intimidated; non-Nazi organizations were brought into line with the new political realities or broken up. But soon the SA extremism began to become counter-productive. In June 1933, three members of the Berlin SA were shot as they attacked a young member of the Social Democratic party. In retaliation, the local SA rounded up some five hundred local men and tortured ninety-one of them to death. Whilst Hitler showed no concern for the fate of members of opposition parties, the extent of this SA violence was beginning to prompt criticism from those Hitler wanted to keep on-side. The Reich Justice and Interior Ministries felt that they were losing control of policing and sentencing and they also protested at the arrests of civil servants and lawyers by the SA; the Reich Economic Ministry complained that the appearance of unrest on the streets discouraged foreign investors. Even more worrying was the increased power that Röhm gained from the rampaging tactics of the SA. For him, the 'Nazi Revolution' had only just started and would not be complete until the radicals of the SA had been rewarded for their years of struggle. In May, he asserted that 'Whether declarations of loyalty come every day from "co-ordinated" beekeeping or bowling clubs makes no odds'![6] What was needed was a real transformation of German society. And, increasingly, it was Röhm who felt he should decide the character of that transformation.

However, Hitler and his closest associates had no intention of allowing the SA to dictate the terms of their victory. In July, Hitler unambiguously declared that the time of upheaval was over: 'Revolution is not a permanent condition . . . it must be channelled into the secure bed of evolution.'[7] In August, in an attempt to roll back the policing powers of the SA, Hermann Göring stopped the enrolling of SA as auxiliary police officers in Prussia and soon other German states followed this line. In a related move, the SA lost its control of the improvised prison camps it had established. Increasingly, these came under the control of the central power of the state. This is a reminder that it was not the brutally repressive nature of the SA that was in question, rather the government's aim was to carry this out in a more regulated manner under government control.

Nevertheless, while these actions reduced the role of the SA, they did not reduce its size or its potential for causing trouble. Whereas in May 1933 recruitment to the Nazi Party had been stopped, as a response to the flood of opportunists who had joined the party since January 1933, recruitment to the SA continued and was increased when the First World War veterans' association – the Steel Helmets – was incorporated into the SA. By early 1934, the total strength of the SA and associated groups stood at 4,500,000; this was in stark contrast to the regular army with its cap of 100,000 men set by the Treaty of Versailles (1919). This huge group of paramilitaries expected jobs and perks as a reward for their efforts and resented attempts to resist their demands. They also resented the way in which jobs went to more respectable right-wing politicians who now threw in their lot with the Nazis. From early 1934, street violence involving drunken and bored SA men increased. And, at the same time, Röhm made a number of speeches at SA rallies in which he criticized the leadership of the Nazi Party and the conservative and upper-class leadership of the army. Secret reports for the Sopade (the name of the Social Democratic Party in exile in Prague, 1933–38, in Paris 1938–40, and in London until 1945) recorded grumbles within the SA 'that Hitler does not want any socialism'.[8] Röhm also continued to demand that the SA should be regarded as a national militia, which would eventually replace the army. Evidence mounted that he had ambitions on the post of Minister of Defence, a job held by the army representative, General von Blomberg.

Threatening the independence of the army was a mistake. Although the military had gone a long way towards accommodating the Nazis – for example, using the swastika in army insignia and banning Jews from the armed forces – it still regarded itself as relatively independent. The head of the army, General von Fritsch, was a Prussian officer of the old school and regarded the Nazis as vulgar upstarts. He was supported by President Hindenburg who, as President and army Commander-in-Chief, still had the power to dismiss Hitler as Chancellor if he so chose. In February 1934, in an attempt to keep the army happy and muzzle the SA, Röhm was forced to sign a declaration promising to respect the independence of the army. Röhm clearly had no intention of keeping to the agreement, which had been forced on him by that 'ridiculous corporal' (Hitler), as he admitted to his men following the signing of the agreement. Furthermore, if the Chancellor proved inflexible, Röhm boasted: 'We'll manage the thing without Hitler'.[9] Some SA units began seizing army weapons as if preparing for a coup. There is no evidence that this was more than local initiatives by some disgruntled SA leaders but it further increased the *impression* that the SA were planning to seize power. Whilst Röhm never went so far as actually saying this was his aim, other SA leaders were less discreet. In April, Hitler, Blomberg and other senior army officers went on a four-day cruise off the Norwegian coast and it seems that some kind of deal was done to reduce the power of the SA. Overall though, the evidence suggests that, as spring turned to summer in 1934, there was no 'SA revolution' being planned: Röhm went on holiday to Bad Wiessee, near Munich, and the SA were sent on leave for the whole of July. If a revolution was being planned it was a rather inept one. Instead, it seems clear that, although tensions were rising, the SA leadership had no coherent plan for where its restlessness was heading.

The Night of the Long Knives

The SA might have lacked a clear plan of action but others were stirring the pot and would soon bring it to the boil. Vice-Chancellor von Papen still seems to have deluded himself that he could influence events and this sense of self-importance was encouraged by the fact that President Hindenburg was clearly gravely ill – von Papen clearly hoped to benefit from any crisis following his death. Consequently von Papen became the centre of complaints against the government and members of his inner circle were in contact with disgruntled army officers. In June 1934, von Papen made a speech at Marburg university in which he attacked the idea of a 'second revolution'. Hitler was furious at von Papen's criticism and denounced him as a 'little worm'. But the attack could not be ignored because it resonated with too many important people. When Hitler met the dying Hindenburg four days after von Papen's speech it was clear that Hindenburg was considering putting the country under military rule and removing Hitler if the crisis over the SA was not swiftly resolved. And this was not the only incentive to take decisive action; leading Nazis were also encouraging Hitler to act. Goebbels confided in his diary that Hitler must act or risk being removed from office. In Prussia, the Nazi leader, Göring, handed over control of the police to the leader of the SS, Himmler. Although still nominally a part of the SA, the SS was fast developing into a separate police organization of the Nazi state, which was unquestioningly loyal to Hitler. Göring's action meant that, from this point, the ex-chicken farmer was in charge of the political police for the whole of Germany. Whilst this countered the threat posed to Göring by militant SA in the areas under his control, it also encouraged Himmler to further free himself and the SS from SA interference and influence. Himmler's political police, in close collaboration with the SS Security Service (the SD) under Himmler's deputy, Reinhard Heydrich, began the manufacturing of evidence to accuse Röhm of treason. It was an example of the vicious infighting between the big beasts of the Nazi leadership jungle that would so characterize the government of the Third Reich. Looking back after 1945, Field Marshall von Kleist described how, in 1934, warnings of SA preparations caused the army to go on alert, which caused the SA to feel *themselves* under threat. It was a mutual suspicion, which was being encouraged by the SS. To senior army colleagues, he confided at the time: 'I have the impression that we – the army and SA – are being egged on against each other by a third party', by which he meant the SS.[10]

As the campaign against Röhm mounted, the army expelled

him from the Officers' League and put the army on full alert. Hitler next ordered the SA leadership to meet him at Bad Wiessee (where Röhm was on holiday) on 30 June. That night, alarmed members of the SA went on the rampage in Munich, threatening to meet any attempt to crush the SA with violence.

Early the next morning, Hitler and units of the SS and police headed to the hotel where Röhm and other SA leaders were staying.[11] The SA leaders were still asleep and the first SA leader to be dragged out of bed was still in the company of his eighteen-year-old blond boyfriend. Similarly unprepared was Röhm, who clearly had not yet grasped the seriousness of his situation, as he ordered coffee from the barman when escorted into the hotel vestibule by two detectives.[12] Shortly afterwards, all the SA leaders were hauled off to nearby Stadelheim prison. Hitler meanwhile, went to the Nazi Party headquarters in Munich where he announced that Röhm had been in the pay of the French. Hitler's loyal follower Rudolf Hess volunteered to personally shoot the SA leader. Instead, Röhm was given a revolver and told to kill himself. He declined. An SS delegation was sent to give him a second opportunity but, on returning to the cell, found that he had still not shot himself. Consequently they shot him dead. Other SA leaders were killed at the same time.

While matters were being brought to their bloody conclusion in Munich, Göring had been sent to Berlin to oversee the killing there, assisted by the SS and Secret State Police (the *Gestapo*). The killing in Berlin and across Germany had the code-name 'Hummingbird'. Clearly enjoying himself immensely, Göring strode about his room in white tunic and white high-boots, shouting 'shoot, shoot' in a grotesque caricature that one police officer described as looking like a murderous 'Puss in Boots'.[13] It was a settling of scores that ranged beyond the SA. Indeed, in Berlin, the killing particularly targeted conservative rivals and both von Papen's secretary and speech writer were murdered by SS and Gestapo units. Von Papen himself was considered too high profile to kill. General von Schleicher – who had been Chancellor before Hitler, had opposed Hitler's appointment and whose addiction to conspiracy had caused him to engage in communications with both the French ambassador and Röhm since January 1933 – was gunned down, along with his wife. Similarly repaid for past rivalry was Gregor Strasser, who had once led the Nazis in northern Germany, had proposed a more left-wing version of Nazism than Hitler and had negotiated with von Schleicher for a post in the government in late 1932. He had long been bitterly at odds with Himmler and Göring – and so was another victim of the Nazi leadership jungle.

Across Germany, SA leaders and old political rivals were murdered. Memories were long. In Bavaria, the old conservative politician von Kahr was hacked to death with axes for suppressing Hitler's Munich Putsch of 1923. For successfully prosecuting Hitler in 1921 and for breaking up a meeting at which he was speaking,[14] another old Bavarian politician, Ballerstedt, was gunned down. A defrocked priest, Father Bernhard Stempfle, was found near Munich with a broken neck, almost certainly because he knew too much about the suicide of Hitler's niece, Geli Raubal, who had been driven to despair by the obsessive control of her uncle. Then there were personal vendettas: two senior SS officers took the opportunity to have rivals killed and at least five Jews were murdered. And there were mistakes, such as the Munich music critic Willi Schmid, who was killed because his name was confused with that of a local SA commander. And there were those whose category defies definition, such as a Waldenberg municipal engineer who had proved uncooperative on the subject of building licenses. Many of the SA who died did so without knowing why they were being shot. Karl Ernst – the ex bell-boy and gay nightclub bouncer – died calling out, 'Heil, Hitler'.

The aftermath

The official death toll stood at seventy-four, but Göring alone had arrested over a thousand people and the final number killed remains a matter of debate. To the cabinet and to the

Reichstag, Hitler explained that his actions had been necessary to foil a treasonable plot. Goebbels broadcast to the nation that the plot had involved the SA and dissident members of the old conservative elites who were unreconciled to the Nazi government. Using his control of the press (see Chapter 14), Goebbels went on to record the gratitude of Hindenburg and the army for the removal of the SA leadership. It seems they were willing to overlook the fact that the victims of the purge had included two senior army officers. Public opinion was further appealed to by lurid tales of the homosexual excesses of the SA. The complete illegality of the action was soon remedied by the passing of a retrospective law.

Public reactions to the purge were initially mixed. There were expressions of concern as many members of the public struggled to understand what the bloodletting meant. Over time, though, this seems to have been replaced by general approval of the events. The SA violence had been unpopular and their disorderly conduct had alarmed many ordinary Germans as well as the army. Their destruction seemed to promise a greater stability. And it was this, after all, that had been the reason for many Germans voting Nazi in the first place.

Some, such as Victor Klemperer, a Jewish professor at the University of Dresden who, not surprisingly, opposed Hitler, hoped it might weaken the Nazis. He wrote in his diary in July that: 'No sympathy at all for the vanquished, only delight, a) that they are eating one another up, b) that Hitler is now like a man after his first major heart attack.' But he had to admit disappointment too that the crisis did not escalate: 'I was depressed when everything remained calm during the days that followed.' He was quick to note with dismay that other Germans approved of the events and supported Hitler. Furthermore, he noted how much prominence was given to the sexual activities of the SA leadership and how this further encouraged approval, 'as if Hitler were a moral cleanser. But after all he knew what the inclinations of his intimate friend

and chief-of-staff were . . .'[15] The future failed assassin of Hitler
– Claus von Stauffenberg – likened the purge to the lancing of
a boil. A secret Gestapo report from Harburg-Wilhelmsburg
noted, in July 1934, that 'Among the population at large, confidence in the Führer has been consolidated by his energetic
action.' It went on to report that many in the population
wanted the purge to go further in the Nazi Party and root out
the petty dictators found there.[16] A report based on comments
made at Bavarian labour exchanges in July noted the admira-
tion expressed regarding Hitler and condemnation of Röhm. A
Gestapo report from Cologne mentioned 'a massive increase in
the confidence in the Führer'.[17]

The same mixed interpretations can be seen in foreign
responses. The British cartoonist David Low, on 3 July 1934,
pictured terrified SA men with hands raised in surrender,
before Hitler who was holding a smoking gun and Göring, in
barbarian Germanic costume, holding a spear dripping with
blood. His satirical caption read, in a parody of the well-known
Nazi salute, 'They salute with both hands now'. But the *Daily
Mail* presented a more approving account in its earlier report
of 2 July 1934:

> Herr Adolf Hitler, the German Chancellor, has saved his
> country. Swiftly and with exorable severity, he has delivered
> Germany from men who had become a danger to the unity of
> the German people and to the order of the state. With lightning
> rapidity he has caused them to be removed from high office, to
> be arrested, and put to death.
>
> The names of the men who have been shot by his orders are
> already known. Hitler's love of Germany has triumphed over
> private friendships and fidelity to comrades who had stood
> shoulder to shoulder with him in the fight for Germany's future.[18]

The events of the Night of the Long Knives had other implications too within the Nazi Party. Röhm was replaced as Chief
of Staff of the SA by Victor Lutze. Under Lutze, the SA lost its
power and many members were eventually absorbed into the

army. Indeed, its membership dropped dramatically after June 1934 as many disillusioned brown shirts left the organization. On the other hand, the SS, under Himmler, replaced the SA as the armed wing of the Nazi Party and it was officially separated from the SA following the death of Röhm. Its loyalty and usefulness had been proved on 30 June. Ahead of it lay eleven years of increasing power as it came to control the police forces within Germany and eventually within the occupied countries after 1939. Such would be its influence that Nazi Germany would eventually become, in many respects, an SS state. Its black-uniformed forces would develop many roles and agencies in a virtual empire of racially motivated repression, exploitation and mass murder. As such, Himmler was one of the main beneficiaries of the destruction of Röhm. But it was Hitler himself who would gain most in the immediate aftermath of the killings.

The death of Hindenburg and the creation of the position of 'Der Führer'

Hindenburg remained President until his death, aged 86, from lung cancer at his home at Neudeck in East Prussia, on 2 August 1934.[19] The day before Hindenburg died, Hitler flew to Neudeck and visited him. Hindenburg, old and senile, thought he was meeting the old Kaiser, Wilhelm II, and called Hitler 'Majesty'. With Hindenburg dead, Hitler declared the office of President to be permanently vacant and, in effect, united it with the office of Chancellor under the title of Der Führer. Hitler held a plebiscite on 19 August 1934, in which the German people were asked if they approved of Hitler merging the two offices of state. The national 'Yes' vote was 84.6 per cent. Given the state of Nazi intimidation, it is noteworthy that the vote dropped to this level and in some working-class areas the 'Yes' vote dropped as low as 66 per cent. Clearly not everyone approved of increasing Hitler's power.

Hitler had become both Germany's head of state and its head of government. He also became supreme commander of the military, which now swore an oath not to the state, or the constitution, but to Hitler personally. With the SA's power broken, the military were prepared to offer Hitler their personal loyalty. The leader of the army and Defence Minister, Colonel-General Blomberg, took the initiative in this; it did not originate with Hitler. Later, Blomberg would claim, 'We swore the oath on the flag to Hitler as Führer of the German people, not as head of the National Socialist Party.' However, far from making Hitler dependent on the army, 'the army chained itself to the Führer'.[20] Soon the Nazi badge of the eagle grasping a wreathed swastika would appear on military uniforms and swastikas would appear on medals, flags and equipment. In addition, there was no military opposition to anti-Jewish legislation affecting the armed forces after 1935, or the establishment of a military high command for the armed forces (the OKW) under Hitler's direct authority in 1938.[21] Blomberg himself was rewarded when, in 1935, he became Minister of War and Commander-in-Chief of the armed forces and, in 1936, the first field marshal appointed by Hitler. Not for nothing would those in the military who wanted to stand up to the Nazis call him Hitler's 'rubber lion'. The greatest potential threat to the Nazi dictatorship – the army – had been reconciled to the government. The process of 'bringing Germany into line' had taken another huge step forward.

6

ECONOMIC TRANSFORMATION, OR SMOKE AND MIRRORS? THE NAZI IMPACT ON THE GERMAN ECONOMY, 1933–9

Fritz Thyssen, of the Thyssen mining and steelmaking company based in the Ruhr city of Duisburg, was born in 1873. Joining the army in 1914, he was soon discharged on grounds of ill health. After the First World War, Thyssen's conservative nationalism was clearly seen when the French and Belgians occupied the Ruhr in 1923. He refused to cooperate and was arrested, imprisoned and fined. As a result he became a national hero. Unusually, Thyssen donated large sums to the Nazi Party before 1933, at a time when many German industrialists regarded the Nazis with suspicion. In November 1932, he was one of a number of leading industrialists who wrote to President Hindenburg, urging him to appoint Hitler as Chancellor. In 1933, Thyssen joined the Nazi Party. He approved of Hitler's suppression of the Communist Party, the Social Democrats and the trade unions. Although not an active anti-Semite, he went along with Nazi discrimination against the Jews and dismissed Jews who worked for his firm.

However, in time he began to have his doubts. In 1937, he

wrote to Hitler complaining at Nazi intimidation of the Catholic Church and Christians generally. In 1938, he protested at the violence towards Jews on *Kristallnacht* ('Crystal Night', the night of broken glass). By 1939, he was vocal in his condemnation of the state's subjection of the whole economy to the needs of war. That same year he left Germany for Switzerland. From there he moved to France and was intending to emigrate to Argentina. However, he was visiting his mother in Belgium in 1940 when the Germans invaded. Arrested, he spent the war imprisoned in concentration camps, first, at Sachsenhausen and, then, at Dachau. He was joined in prison by his wife who refused to escape to Argentina; together they survived the war. Tried for complicity in the Nazis' crimes, he admitted supporting Hitler until 1938. He was acquitted of the charges against him but paid compensation to victims of his actions. In 1950, he emigrated to Argentina and died in 1951.

Fritz Thyssen was unusual. He had supported the Nazis when most other industrialists stood apart from them. And then he had rejected the Nazis when most other leading industrialists had come to support them and were benefiting financially from heading industries under the Third Reich. However, his story raises the question of what the impact was of the Nazis on the German economy and what the relationship was between the leaders of industry and Hitler.[1]

The Nazi aims for the German economy

The Wall Street Crash of 1929 – with its attendant banking collapse and worldwide depression – had thrown six million German workers into unemployment. It was essential that this be addressed by the Nazi government, as offering a solution to crushing unemployment had been one of its central promises. German economic recovery was essential in order to create stability at home, reduce opposition from workers (many of whom had been supporters of either the Social Democratic Party or the Communist Party, before 1933) and provide the basis for German rearmament and territorial expansion. The

Nazi propaganda machine made great claims about the positive impact of the new government on the German economy. But how successful was the Nazi economic transformation? And was it only sustainable if eventually accompanied by a war of conquest and seizure of raw materials? In order to decide, it is necessary to examine exactly what the Nazis did for the German economy and then explore how substantial and sustainable these changes really were.

Given the Nazi promises that they were the only party that could rescue Germany from the depression, it is noticeable that they were remarkably short of detailed economic plans. This was consistent with Hitler's general approach to issues of setting broad goals and then leaving the detail to later. The Nazi Party programme promised limitations to the monopoly powers of big businesses, limitations to the powers and profits of financiers, assistance to small business through the abolition of department stores and assistance to farmers. As the depression deepened, these goals from the early 1920s were added to with promises of job-creation in order to put the German unemployed back to work. At the same time, Hitler rowed back on the anti-capitalist aspects of Nazism. Whilst his personal outlook typified the resentments of the German lower middle classes towards the wealthy and powerful, his personal dislikes were tempered by the need to reassure German business leaders, distance the party from the socialists and communists and ensure that nothing got in the way of his rearmament goals. These were important constraints on Nazi radicalism.[2]

The principal aims of Nazi economic policy that emerged in the 1930s were, first, increased political direction of economic planning whilst still allowing considerable freedom of manoeuvre for German capitalists to prosper; second, to create *autarky*, which aimed to make Germany self-sufficient and independent of the international system of trade; third, to establish a war-economy whereby the overall aims of the economy were ultimately geared to winning a future war. However, just listing these aims gives them the appearance of being part of a coordinated and coherent plan. Nothing could be further from the truth. As with so much else in the Third Reich, Nazi economic policies would be a complicated mass of, at times, contradictory policies.[3]

Perhaps the most famous achievement of the Nazi regime was a reduction in German unemployment figures from about six million in 1933 to under one million by 1938. This, unsurprisingly, made a great impression on Germans at the time and was loudly trumpeted by the Nazi propaganda machine. To many international observers the replacement of dole queues with armies of determined workers engaged in building projects would be one of the most striking characteristics of the Third Reich. It was achieved by government investment in public-works programmes designed to employ large numbers of the unemployed, even if this was in labour-intensive schemes that were not necessarily the most efficient way to get a job done. The most famous and conspicuous form of these could be seen in the new system of *autobahns* (motorways), overseen by Fritz Todt, who was appointed to this task in June 1933. By 1938, a total of 2,170 miles (3,500 kilometres) had been built despite the fact that Germany had few cars.[4] Companies were given tax-relief if they took on more workers, and, in addition, there were many public-building projects, draining marshes, bringing moorland under cultivation and increased spending on armaments. The first two had been planned under Weimar governments but the Nazis took the credit for implementing these schemes. In the same way, the Nazis were assisted by a worldwide economic recovery that was slowly under way.

The role of Dr Schacht
Between 1933 and 1937, economic policy in Germany was greatly influenced by Dr Hjalmar Schacht, who was 'an ingenious, pragmatic banker, not a theoretical economist'.[5] Schacht was not a Nazi but instead was a well-respected conservative who was made President of the Reichsbank in 1933 and

Economic Minister in 1934. Under Schacht, interest payments on foreign debts were frozen. Whilst this was widely condemned by creditor countries, they failed to take a united stand against this German action and instead allowed their own self-interest to dominate their reactions. Therefore, instead of a united approach to Germany, what followed was a series of trade agreements between Germany and individual countries (bilateral agreements), which resulted in Germany importing most of its raw materials from South-Eastern Europe and from friendly South American states. The aim of this was twofold. First, it ensured that Germany was not dependent on countries that might prove hostile in a future war. The memory of being starved of resources by the British naval blockade in the First World War was a constant shadow over Nazi planners.[6] Second, it built on traditional pre-Nazi German ambitions to dominate Central and South-Eastern Europe (see Chapter 15).

This idea of a German-dominated Central and South-Eastern Europe was described in the word *Mitteleuropa* (literally 'middle Europe' or central Europe) and implied a German control of Central Europe accompanied by economic exploitation of this region alongside territorial seizure, settlement of German colonists, expulsion of non-Germans from areas seized and eventual 'Germanization' of a series of puppet states, which would be created as a buffer between Germany and Russia. Whilst this had been a traditional geographical area of German influence for generations, the radical plan took concrete shape during the First World War and influenced the later thinking of Weimar politicians after 1930, as well as Nazi leaders.[7] By 1938, Germany overshadowed the economies of South-Eastern Europe. As a massive buyer of food and raw materials Germany dominated this trade from the Balkans. In return these countries had to accept payment in German currency, which then had to be used to buy German goods, or invested in industries that produced goods required by Germany.[8] Whilst this was not actually autarky, it did create a situation in which Germany largely controlled the key resources from those countries it considered in its sphere of influence and it lessened Germany's dependence on British merchant shipping.[9]

At the same time more of the German economy was devoted to rearmament. As a result the percentage of the German economy engaged in producing consumer goods fell from 25 per cent in 1935, to 17 per cent in 1937. The German government faced two main problems in this huge rearmament programme. First, it was banned by the Treaty of Versailles (1919), which aimed to reduce Germany's military power. Second, there was a legal interest rate limit of 4.5 per cent. Borrowing extra funds by offering a better rate of interest was problematic because of this interest rate cap and because it would attract international scrutiny at a time when the Nazi government wanted to disguise its rearmament programme. Clearly, a large government borrowing programme, creating a deficit, would have given the game away. Consequently, to help pay for this rearmament programme and to get round these problems, Schacht introduced something known as *mefo bills*. These were credit notes issued by the government under the guise of the Metallurgical Research Corporation (abbreviated in German to MEFO). This was a cover organization. So-called mefo bills were issued by the government as payment to armaments manufacturers. These could be converted into Reichsmarks when necessary but firms were encouraged to delay conversion through gaining interest on the bills they held. Consequently, they disguised the real extent of government spending as the total number of mefo bills issued was kept secret, without an obvious paper trail. No more were issued after 1937, since Schacht feared they would have an inflationary effect on the economy. By 1939, there were some 12 billion Reichsmarks of mefo bills in circulation – some figures suggest a total of 21 billion was eventually reached – compared with the 19 billion Reichsmarks the government raised through official government bonds. As well as hiding the government deficit and the real extent of rearmament, these mefo bills also

paid for other goods and services, which the government rein-
vested in the economy.

At the Nuremberg War Crimes Trials, Schacht would later
claim that he opposed the gearing of the whole German economy towards war and that his resignation in November 1937
was due to his realization that Hitler was determined to force
the economy to support his war plans regardless of economic
consequences. The reality seems to have been that Schacht and
Hitler disagreed over the speed and sustainability of the build-
up rather than its objective, Hitler being committed to rapid
preparation and Schacht to a more sustainable and slower build
up.[10] The Nuremberg prosecutor summed it up in his statement that Schacht broke with the Nazis 'over tactics, not
principles'. Schacht was, though, a strange mass of contradictions: he helped establish the Nazi economy yet defended Jews
and attended a church whose pastor was an anti-Nazi; he
assisted in rearming for war but was eventually imprisoned in
a concentration camp towards the end of the Second World
War for opposition. Acquitted at Nuremberg, he died in
Munich in 1970 at the age of ninety-three.

But what is clear is that, by 1936, a number of Nazi leaders
– notably Hermann Göring – were expressing impatience at
the speed of rearmament. Despite its impressive achievements,
these Nazis believed that Schacht was too concerned about the
dangers of inflation and that this was slowing down the drive
to rearm. And to accompany this there was a crisis in the availability of imported raw materials. These prices were increasing
just as German reserves of gold and foreign currencies were
running low. As a response to this, a 'Four-Year Plan' was set
up under Göring.

The Four-Year Plan
Hermann Göring knew nothing about economics but he was
one of the 'big beasts' in the Nazi jungle and a bigger player in
politics than Schacht could ever be. The aim of the Four-Year
Plan (inspired in part by the Five-Year Plans of the USSR in

the 1930s) was to make Germany self-sufficient in food and raw materials and ready for war by 1940.

The incentive to set up the Four-Year Plan had been caused by a contradiction in Nazi economic policy. By 1935, Germany had insufficient reserves of foreign currencies to purchase both the raw materials it needed for rearmament and food. This was made worse by the fact that German farmers could not keep pace with food demands within Germany. And the organization responsible for agriculture (the Reich Food Estate, under Richard Walther Darré) had discouraged agricultural expansion in order to keep farm prices high, so as to please farmers. What was to be done? Rationing would be bad for morale and an embarrassment to the government. Darré instead had demanded that Schacht divert more of the foreign currency reserves to purchase foodstuffs and animal fodder. Schacht refused. This was because such a move would cause a reduction in imported raw materials needed for rearmament. Hitler, typically, could not make a decision and gave Göring the job of sorting out the contradiction. Göring backed Darré because he feared popular discontent if food prices increased, but this was no long-term solution. One answer would have been to export more German goods to increase funds of foreign currencies and to then use these to buy the much-needed raw materials. But this was unacceptable for two reasons. First, foreign countries were not keen on buying more German goods as the Nazi obsession with autarky and tough import controls had not won friends abroad. Second, it would mean diverting energy within Germany towards export industries when the priorities of the Third Reich were on armaments. The Nazis were caught in a fix of their own construction.[11] Schacht characteristically complained that the obsession with autarky was 'cutting our own throats'.[12] But Hitler was unmoved, and was implacably opposed to any reduction in the building of weapons. This was a policy of 'guns before butter'. And it was as a result of this crisis that he instructed Göring to set up a Four-Year Plan in August 1936.

The Four-Year Plan set out a number of radical goals: reduction of imported raw materials; their replacement by synthetic products (e.g. 'buna rubber'); incentives to farmers to increase food production. The setting up of the Four-Year Plan undermined the position of Schacht – and he knew it – and is a clear illustration of the way in which the Third Reich was riddled with competing and overlapping agencies, which undermined its coherency and efficiency. In January 1939, Schacht wrote to Hitler complaining that the 'overstretching public expenditure' was 'bringing the finances of the state to the edge of ruin'.[13] Hitler sacked him from his post as President of the Reichsbank and he was replaced by Göring's man Walther Funk, who ensured that henceforth the Reichsbank was subservient to the Four-Year Plan. And what of the Four-Year Plan?

There were successes. By 1939, Germany was self-sufficient in bread, potatoes, sugar and wheat; and there were significant increases in production of aluminium, coal, coke, artificial fibres and synthetic fuel. But, overall, the Four-Year Plan failed in its aim of autarky by 1940. In 1939, Germany was still importing about 15 per cent of its food[14] and about 33 per cent of its overall raw materials. It was particularly dependent on imported oil (66 per cent), copper (70 per cent), rubber (85 per cent) and almost all the raw materials needed for the production of aluminium. Something much more radical would be required. But first, the energy of German capitalism needed to be successfully harnessed.

The role of German capitalists under the Nazis

Far from being eclipsed by the arrival of the Nazis, as many disgruntled SA and lower-middle-class Nazi voters had hoped, capitalism played a vital part in putting government plans into action. This was particularly the case regarding the drive towards war. Although German industrialists were harnessed to Nazi goals, they still retained the freedom to make enormous profits if they pulled in the same direction as the state. The clearest winners were the largest industrial complexes.

Many of these increased their size as larger monopolies made it easier to meet the demands of the state for rearmament. For directors of such companies profits rose enormously. In these companies, managers' salaries rose considerably, at a time when suppression of independent trade unions ensured that workers found that their wages remained static and many even experienced a reduction in their purchasing power. At the top of this pyramid of businesses stood the huge industrial giants such as the chemical monopoly of IG Farben, the steel giant Thyssen and the arms manufacturer Krupps.

The corrupting effect of compliance with the Nazi state was seen at all levels of business and banking.[15] For example, the Deutsche Bank, Germany's largest financial institution, played an important role in the expropriation of Jewish-owned enterprises both in Germany and in the areas seized by the German army during the Second World War. It benefited from the Aryanization policies of the Nazi regime, whereby Jewish banks and businesses were taken over by Aryan (non-Jewish) Germans and their assets seized. From 1938 onwards it became even more radically involved as the Nazis seized Jewish assets in occupied countries. The bank played an important role in gold transactions and in the financing of the construction of Auschwitz. Important work on the relationship between the banks and the Nazis has been carried out by Harold James, Professor of History at Princeton University, USA,[16] and reveals the alarming complicity of these pillars of the community in Nazi crimes.

However, things were not all plain sailing for capitalists under the Nazis. By the mid 1930s it was clear that failure to comply with government demands could lead to major problems for industrialists. This was seen most clearly in 1937 in the government's handling of a confrontation with the iron-making industry in the Ruhr. Here companies had been reluctant to expand their capacity by processing uneconomic German iron ore. The government though was determined to reduce dependence on better quality iron ore from abroad and reacted ruthlessly. It was also determined to make it clear who made the ultimate decisions in Germany. In response to reluctance from the Ruhr capitalists a huge state-run plant was established at Salzgitter. Called the 'Reich-Works-Hermann-Göring' it operated in direct competition with the iron works of the Ruhr valley and was given priority in allocations of both labour and raw materials. It was clear who would win in any showdown between the Nazi state and capitalism. As Göring remarked, 'The programme of munitions production and armaments must not be jeopardized, in the event of war, by a shortage of ore. Everything possible must be done by the firms, and the State must step in where the firms are clearly no longer in a position to do so.'[17] While German capitalists found it could be economically advantageous to fall in line with Nazi economic policies they were riding a tiger. And it was a tiger that was easier to mount than dismount.

Restrictions in many areas reduced the independence of industrialists. They were controlled with regard to their imports, use of raw materials, wages paid and prices asked, employment regulations, what to produce and how much of it, where new factories should be built, the amount of profit to take. Some who had earlier supported the Nazis became disillusioned. One such was Fritz Thyssen. But there was no united opposition to this Nazi interference, or to the kind of society created by the Nazis, because there was no common experience of the impact of the Nazis. Whilst some industrialists suffered financially and struggled with the demands of state control, others made fortunes and had no intention of rocking the boat. IG Farben, for example, saw its net profits rise from seventy-four million Reichsmarks in 1933 to two hundred and forty million Reichsmarks in 1939. It showed its gratitude in its contributions to the Nazi Party. These contributions in 1939 stood at 7,538,857 Reichsmarks for the year. When war came, the chemical giant's role would only grow and it would eventually build a vast industrial site within the Auschwitz complex and work it by slave labour. When the panzer divisions rolled into Poland, in September 1939, they used tyres made from IG Farben's synthetic rubber and their engines ran on IG Farben's synthetic fuel. About 35 per cent of a German foot soldier's equipment was made of IG Farben materials and even the keys on the Enigma coding machines were made of IG Farben's plastic. Furthermore, the company supplied materials for the racial mass murder carried out at the extermination camps.[18] But IG Farben was not alone in the advantage it gained from being both compliant with the Nazis and operating in a militarily useful area of production. Overall, the profits of big business rose from 1.3 billion Reichsmarks in 1928 to 5.0 billion Reichsmarks in 1939. For some, business under the Nazi economy was indeed booming.

Further down the social scale though the promises made by the Nazis to small businesses failed to materialize. Whilst some gained from the Aryanization policy, which saw Jewish businesses taken over by 'Aryan' (racially acceptable) Germans, many of these small business people experienced at best mixed gains from Nazi policies and at worse major problems. Department stores were not banned (although Jewish ones were expropriated) and the pressure to create bigger, more coordinated and more efficient industrial units worked against small businesses. There was some increased protection for skilled workers through increased regulation of craft qualifications. Overall though, this mixed middle-class experience was particularly striking, given the noticeably lower middle-class origins of many in the Nazi Party (see Chapter 8).

The same mixed experiences applied to farmers. On one hand, prices paid for agricultural products increased by 20 per cent between 1933 and 1937; and the Hereditary Farm Law (1933) protected farms from being mortgaged or sold due to debt. On the other hand, the drive towards autarky caused a sharp upward hike in the cost of imported animal feed and hit those producing for the export market hard; the outlawing of selling a family farm meant farmers were tied to the soil; the ban on raising a mortgage on a farm made it hard to raise loans;

the drive for rearmament meant that many labourers or younger children found the wages offered in industrial enterprises highly attractive and caused something of a flight from the land. In this way the Nazi ideologies of Germanic peasants on hereditary farms and rapid industrialization conflicted with each other. This was a common feature in the chaotic jungle of Nazi government. By the end of the 1930s the main beneficiaries of Nazi agricultural policies were the biggest landowners and commercial farms. This was not what the majority of German farmers had voted for.

Economic Miracle? Or smoke and mirrors?

The world was amazed at the sight of Germany put back to work after 1933. A nation without hope appeared to have been transformed into one of activity and construction; it seemed to be a nation in which unemployment was a thing of the past. A stagnant economy appeared to have been replaced by one of dynamic action and growth. Clearly, though, despite the apparent achievements of the Nazis, there were real problems in the German economy, and as the 1930s progressed, these problems increased. The Nazi 'economic miracle' was not due to improved efficiency. Nor was it due to increased exports to the wider world. Nor was it sustained by increased consumer spending because the policy of 'guns before butter' meant that consumer goods were not a high priority.

The economic growth was primarily due to the huge expansion of arms production and the public works programme – but the cost of this, as we have seen, was hidden in a world of mefo bills. In the long term, this cost would need to be met by either increased taxes or increased German trade with the international community. However, the former was unacceptable because it would be unpopular (as would be the option of rationing foodstuffs). The latter was not going to work because the drive for autarky was reducing German trade with the rest of the world, not expanding it. Inflation too was a real challenge. This problem was masked by the government policy of freezing prices and wages during the 1930s but, in the long term, it would not be possible to sustain this.

In short, the German economy under the Nazis was highly abnormal. By the end of the 1930s it had reached a situation where a series of wars were almost inevitable, in order to meet the needs of the imbalanced German economic system through theft and the control of European resources, markets and populations, particularly in the East.[19] Germany simply did not possess enough gold and foreign currency reserves to buy these products legitimately, given the huge expansion of armaments it had undertaken. This preparation for war made war almost inevitable, not that this would have disturbed Hitler. As he had noted in the directive of August 1936, which established the Four-Year Plan as a reaction to the conflicting demands of importing raw materials and rearming: 'The final solution lies in extending our living space, that is to say, extending the sources of raw materials and foodstuffs of our people. It is the task of the political leadership one day to solve this problem.'[20] Hitler, then, would solve his economic problems by invasion and plunder. But this was hardly surprising, since he had created the problem in the first place by racing to gear Germany for war. There was a chilling circularity in the processes involved and in their outcome.

7

RELUCTANT SUPPORTERS, OR SULLEN OPPONENTS? THE GERMAN WORKERS

Josef Amediet and Josef Nösler were two miners employed by the massive Krupps metalworks. When they discovered in 1936 that they had won a holiday to the Portuguese island of Madeira on an all-expenses-paid cruise organized by the Nazi workers' leisure organization 'Strength through Joy', they at first thought that someone was pulling their leg. But it was no joke. Once there they were amazed at the island's lush vegetation, banana trees and flowers. But they appreciated more than just the luxury of their holiday destination. They also saw the poverty of the locals and concluded that such a situation would never be tolerated in the Germany of the Third Reich. Because, as they noted in the report they wrote for the *Krupps Magazine*, in Germany the Führer really understood the needs of workers. After all, where else but in the Third Reich would two working men have experienced the holiday of a lifetime to a place of sun, sea and sand? And, before the Nazi era, such an experience was only reserved for the middle classes and the rich. Amediet and Nösler were grateful.[1]

In 1934, the US sociologist Theodore Abel was permitted to

organize an intriguing essay competition in which Nazi Party members explained why they had joined the party. In all, some seven hundred people took part and the study provides a fascinating insight into the mindsets of German supporters of Hitler. One worker wrote:

> Faith was the one thing that always led us on, faith in Germany, faith in the purity of our nation and faith in our leader. Holy was our battle and holy our victory ... Some day the world will recognize that the Reich we established with blood and sacrifice is destined to bring peace and blessing to the world.[2]

This may have been how the committed saw things, but for most working-class Germans, however, this was a qualified faith and deeply connected to the hope that the coming to power of Hitler would bring both national unity and economic prosperity to those whose lives had been blighted by unrest, uncertainty and unemployment since the Wall Street Crash of October 1929. As such, it was a 'faith' that depended on the Nazi ability to deliver economic security and improved living standards. As early as 1930, the German pacifist journalist and politician Helmuth Gerlach, who was a consistent opponent of German nationalism, wrote: 'If the sun shines once more on the German economy, Hitler's voters will melt away like snow.' Or, as the historian Michael Burleigh has put it, 'Nazi support was a mile wide but, beyond a hardcore of fanatics, only an inch deep.'[3] If this was true – and the overall evidence suggests that it was – then the extent to which German workers supported the Third Reich would rest entirely on its ability to deliver.

But one thing *was* clear: the German working class was both large and complex. A study of the 1925 German census by the German analyst Theodor Geiger, in 1932, suggested that even before the Wall Street Crash of 1929, whilst the number of those classed as workers was 25 million, actually some 45 million people 'were living – during a period of increasing prosperity nearly five years before the depression – on proletarian incomes'. This constituted about 75 per cent of the German population. However, whilst the commonly defined working class made up about 46 per cent of those actively involved in the economy when Hitler came to power – some research suggests as high as 52 per cent in 1933[4] – and was the largest social class in Germany, it was not a united group. Only about 30 per cent worked in large unionized industries and had a strong tie to the Communist Party or the Social Democrats. About 60 per cent of workers were not even members of a trade union. As a result the working class did not have one experience, set of allegiances or outlook.

For all the lower-middle-class origins of the Nazi Party, a surprising number of workers had supported the Nazis before 1933. Complex analysis of voting data has shown that some 40 per cent of Nazi voters were from the working class and this same percentage appeared in Nazi Party membership figures. Amongst the brown-shirted SA this figure rose to 60 per cent. This was far less apparent within the better-educated and more middle-class SS but, even there, the working-class representation was noticeable.[5] Clearly then, for all the complexity of the German working class, there were still many whose hopes were riding on the Nazis. Up to three million Nazi voters between 1928 and 1932 were former Social Democrats. They were attracted to Hitler by both the promise of national revival and the apparent egalitarianism of the Nazi Party, which promised a national comradeship regardless of class. For many German workers in the industrial centres of the Ruhr and Saxony, this 'solidarity' may not have had the racial intensity that it had for the middle-class Nazi voters of Bavaria, for example, but its sense of national/racial solidarity was attractive to many who felt looked down on by the political elites and even by those a little higher in the social ranking.

Breaking the power of the trade unions
Unemployment had greatly weakened the power of the German trade union movement. In the economic crisis following the 1929 Wall Street Crash, strikes were difficult to use as a

tactic since striking workers could easily be dismissed and replaced from the army of the unemployed. This made it easier for the new Nazi government to break the trade unions. It was seen as a necessary step in order to dominate the German working class and to break the power of the Communist Party and the Social Democrats. The same applied to the Catholic working-class organizations too, despite the fact that the Catholic Centre Party had not opposed Hitler since he came to power in January 1933.

The prelude to this attack on the trade unions was a grand gesture on 1 May 1933, which appeared to show a commitment by the new government to the working class: Nazi leaders attended May Day rallies. This contrasted with the attacks on rival organizations since March, which had seen trade unions come under increasing pressure and left-wing parties struggling to survive. However, on the day after the May Day rallies the Nazi police swooped. Trade union offices were raided and their activities wound up. In place of these long-established defenders of working-class rights the Nazis set up their own organization – the German Labour Front.

The German Labour Front, or simply the Labour Front, replaced the earlier National Socialist Factory Cell Organization, which had not been popular with employers and – with its links to the SA and a tendency to cause trouble in the work-place – it was no longer acceptable to the Nazi leadership either. Bringing it under control was part of the same trend that was to also see the destruction of the SA (see Chapter 5). The leader of the Labour Front was Robert Ley. Ley was a complex character, to put it mildly. The son of an impoverished father, who had been convicted of arson for setting fire to his own farm to escape debt, Ley had been injured in aerial combat in 1917, which had left him with deteriorating brain damage, causing his behaviour to become increasingly erratic. His personal corruption, womanizing and drinking grew to epic proportions. In 1937, while hosting a visit by the Duke and Duchess of Windsor, he was so drunk that he drove their

Mercedes through a locked set of factory gates. He was reputed to have once torn off his wife's clothes at a social engagement in order to show guests how beautiful she was. His corruption was part of a widespread feature within the Third Reich. German comedians in the 1930s would mimic customers at suit-fittings at their tailor's asking for 'wide-open pockets in the current style'.

The aim of the Labour Front was to have one single body to represent all workers in negotiations with employers regarding wages, hours, overtime, conditions, etc. Its dominant philosophy was that there would be a new harmony in the workplace instead of class conflict. This turned out to be a sham, as the Labour Front suppressed worker unrest and created a system of industrial relations that was favourable to the employers. This state of affairs accelerated after the more radical ex-leader of the old Factory Cell Organization was shot dead in a pub-brawl in September 1933. Consequently, the end of independent trade unions had a very negative effect on the freedom of German workers to defend their interests and to negotiate improved wages and conditions of work. However, the attack on the unions had less of an impact than it otherwise might have had if more German workers had actually been members of trade unions in the first place. As we have seen, only about 40 per cent were members in 1933. Nevertheless, with wages suppressed, hours cut to soak up more unemployed and rising prices, the lack of independent representation in bargaining with employers hit workers. And any attempts to challenge this were met with the force of the state. Even the Nazi radicals of the Factory Cell Organization were dismissed at the time of the crushing of SA independence in 1934.

Despite this brutal suppression of opposition, there were isolated acts of resistance. Alma Stobbe, an underground communist activist in Hamburg, reported how, 'In October 1936 five large crates labelled "machine parts" – but actually containing brand-new field howitzers – were sunk in the harbour. Two more crates were smashed on the wharf and two officials were seriously injured. The Gestapo arrested several dockworkers but could not work out who was responsible.'[6] It is interesting to note that, amongst the few attempts on Hitler's life that had any chance of success, one was made by a worker: Johann Georg Elser, in November 1939. Angry at the Nazi suppression of trade unions and attacks on the Christian Church, Elser left a bomb in a Munich beer hall at which Hitler was due to speak. But Hitler left early and the explosion missed the Führer. Elser was imprisoned in a concentration camp and eventually executed in April 1945 (see Chapter 20.) However, this attack was not part of any wider network of working-class resistance, which had seen its leadership brutally crushed since 1933.

And then there was humour. In a recent study based on contemporary literature, diaries and interviews, the German author, film director and screenplay writer Rudolph Herzog has catalogued the way in which humour was used in response to Nazi dictatorship. A Berlin munitions worker, identified only as Marianne Elise K., was convicted of undermining the war effort 'through spiteful remarks' in 1944 for telling this joke: 'Hitler and Göring are standing on top of Berlin's radio tower. Hitler says he wants to do something to cheer up the people of Berlin. "Why don't you just jump?" suggests Göring.'

A fellow worker overheard her telling the joke and reported her to the authorities. She was executed.[7] But such jokes, even though they showed the survival of an independent spirit, were clearly no real threat to the leadership of the Third Reich. And yet for all the grumbles, at least there was work.

The impact of job creation

For all the complaints about loss of negotiating power and collective bargaining under the Nazis, an undoubted gratitude did exist for the provision of work. The crushing unemployment of the early 1930s and the *threat* of unemployment that hung over the heads of many workers was clearly alleviated by the job-creation policies of the Third Reich.

In January 1933, some six million people were registered as unemployed in Germany. In addition to these, about three million people (mostly women) had vanished from the employment statistics completely. As well as those without work, there were others suffering from short-time work, or who had been forced to accept cuts in their wages or hours.

It was this that Hitler was committed to redress. In Hitler's first radio broadcast of February 1933, he declared that: 'Within four years unemployment must be finally overcome.'[8] The official statistics appear to show that this aim was remarkably successful. By April 1933, the numbers of unemployed had fallen by 500,000. By 1934, unemployment was below three million; by 1935, it stood at 2.2 million; and by 1937, it was less than one million. Nazi propaganda trumpeted this achievement and many workers were obviously grateful.

However, the situation was more complex and, as the British historian Richard Evans has concluded, the 'regime was indeed far from averse to cooking the books'.[9] This occurred in a number of ways. Men drafted into the Labour Service were counted as employed, as were unpaid farm helpers who had never previously been registered. In addition, occasional workers were counted as fully employed. Taking these scams into account, when the Nazis said in 1935 that there were only 2.2 million unemployed, the figure was really closer to four million.

The final end to unemployment only came with the huge expansion of armament production and then the reintroduction of compulsory military service in May 1935; it was the drive to war then that achieved the much-vaunted Nazi ending of unemployment.

Conditions at work within the job-creation schemes were also problematic. Resistance to 'voluntarily' joining the Labour Service in its programme of construction and rural work was punished by loss of welfare payments, or even prison. Protests at the poor working conditions and poor-quality food on some road projects escalated into acts of open rebellion and the destruction of barracks. Some of those who protested were sent to concentration camps. This reminder of the realities that lay behind the statistics for new jobs counterbalances the official propaganda image. The same is true of the wages and living standards of many workers in other areas of employment too; for, whilst the state focused on numbers of jobs, the workers were also concerned at the lifestyle that accompanied them.

Wages and living standards in the Third Reich

In order to pull more workers into employment, regulations cut working hours in a number of industries. This led to real wage reductions overall and a fall in the standards of living of those already in jobs. The destruction of trade unions meant that there were no independent workers' organizations to resist this pressure to reduce wages. The reduction in purchasing power helps explain why the production of consumer goods in 1935 was still 15 per cent below what it had been in 1928. As wages were held down in the middle 1930s the prices of food and clothing rose. To increase their real wages it was necessary for workers to put in excessive amounts of overtime and any improvement in wages was offset by shortages, which had pushed up prices yet further. And, anyway, the ersatz nature of many goods lowered their quality and desirability.[10]

The rearmament campaign had set the priorities as 'guns before butter'. Göring himself was associated with the phrase in 1936 when, in a radio broadcast, he claimed: 'Guns will make us powerful; butter will only make us fat.' Goebbels, earlier that same year, had commented: 'We can do without butter, but, despite all our love of peace, not without arms.'[11] The realities of life reflected these priorities. By 1939, access to butter, fat, fruit and coffee was restricted. Disappointing harvests and foot-and-mouth disease amongst cattle did not help. The imbalanced Nazi economy meant there was insufficient hard currency within Germany for importers to bring foreign goods into the country. This reduced the availability of coffee, bananas and oranges well before the outbreak of the Second World War in September 1939. And where these luxuries were available they commanded high prices, despite the ineffective attempts of the state to control these. As a result, ordinary German workers could not afford them and even eggs and cheaper cuts of meat were hard to come by. The reality of life fell well short of the promise.

Similarly, the government's attempt to promote car owner-ship raised expectations only to dash them. Workers had been persuaded in large numbers to set aside a proportion of their wages to buy one of the promised 'People's Cars' (the Volkswagen). The contract for producing this car went to Ferdinand Porsche. The cost per worker, via a savings scheme, would be 990 Reichsmarks, when an average income was around 32 Reichsmarks per week. The car's official name was the 'KdF-Wagen', where the initials stood for *Kraft durch Freude* (Strength Through Joy), the Nazi leisure organization. The look of the vehicle copied the Czech Tatra car and a lawsuit followed but was ended when Germany invaded Czechoslovakia in March 1939. By the outbreak of war in 1939, about 270,000 workers had contributed 110 million Reichsmarks to the scheme, but not one of them got a single car. It was not until after the Second World War that the famous 'Beetle' appeared as a civilian car. During the war the factories had made vehicles for the military.

Other attempts to win worker support were more success-ful. Most notable was the 'Strength through Joy' movement. Founded as part of the Labour Front in November 1933, it aimed to provide leisure activities for workers. This had a double benefit: first, it would make workers appreciative and second, it would make them more dependent on the Nazi state. It would add National Socialist content to activities wherever possible, as part of the control of ideas. The end product was massive. By 1936, about 35 million people were members and huge numbers took part in its subsidized activities including sports (both playing and learning new skills), attendance at the theatre, concerts and art exhibitions. Furthermore, hundreds of thousands took part in its heavily subsidized holidays, both inside Germany and abroad. The organization even had its own fleet of cruise ships. In February 1941, Hitler entertained a passing fantasy of using this fleet to forcibly transport Jews to Madagascar.[12]

On the 1930s cruise ships it was made clear that the aim was cultural improvement, not excess or sexual promiscuity. However, not everyone took these instructions on board. One joke, which parodied official propaganda, stated: 'In the fields and on the heath, I lose strength through joy', in a thinly veiled reference to sexual promiscuity. And many quiet country areas were less than appreciative of the invasion of subsidized Strength through Joy holiday parties. But its overall impact was huge.

Its activities have been explored in detail by the US historian Shelley Baranowski, who has shown that it was the most popular institution in the Third Reich, both in the activities it promoted and in the promises it made about future prosperity once Germany had won 'Living Space' in the East. It developed mass tourism and subtly reinforced the Nazi message, as it rewarded productive but uncomplaining workers, excluded 'undesirables' from its rewards, reinforced racial stereotypes as German tourists visited poorer destinations in Southern Europe and North Africa, supported the growth of the armaments industry and the idea of future expansion. In short, it was part of the whole Nazi concept of creating a mass-base that was loyal and compliant. As Baranowski suggests: 'Although aesthetically pleasing workplaces and smiling tourists appear tangential to emergency decrees, concentration camps, and genocide, Strength through Joy exposed Nazism's fusion of pleasure and violence.'[13]

Linked to Strength through Joy was the allied 'Beauty of Labour' organization. It aimed to improve conditions in the workplace. This was designed to assure the German workers of their importance within the Third Reich and to compensate for lower wages and long hours by attempting to improve the experience of work itself. Focusing on better toilet facilities, washrooms, lockers, noise reduction and other workplace improvements it offered tax incentives for compliant firms, along with national certificates of improvement signed by Hitler himself. The achievements of this organization were limited by its voluntary basis and by the fact that many employers who did take part deducted the costs of improvements from workers' wages or expected them to take part in the decorating themselves.[14]

On final analysis

Workers had a very mixed experience under the Third Reich. Many were reluctant members of the Nazi state anyway and their treatment in the 1930s was a complex cocktail of repression and bribery; this was reflected in the opinions that they expressed about the government. As the Security Service of the SS (the SD) reported of workers' conversations it had investigated in central Germany in 1938: 'They often complain about the fact that they earn much less now than in 1929, but at the end of the day they always say: "At least we have work". But even now – although they know there is a shortage of workers – they are all scared of losing their jobs. The years of unemployment have not been forgotten.'[15]

Secret agents working for the Sopade noted a similar, though more calculated ambivalence. Workers were prepared to feign enthusiasm, they found in 1934, in return for access to Strength through Joy holidays. Another, more worried agent noted in 1938 that, over time, such middle-class pleasures could lead to genuine gratitude. By 1939, some Sopade reports were commenting that these benefits were actually reconciling significant numbers of workers to the regime, to some extent, despite the real disappointments in other areas of working-class life.

Reactions to the Nazis also varied according to the workplace. In the once strongly unionized docks at Bremen, the Gestapo struggled to monitor the workers and it was dangerous for any docker to show signs of Nazi loyalty. However, in the hi-tech aeronautical factories of Focke-Wulf, more highly skilled employees gained from the benefits on offer and were more easily assimilated into working for the system. The case of the dockers at Bremen was not an isolated instance of left-leaning solidarity surviving under the Nazis; illegal union networks also survived in other areas too, such as amongst railwaymen and merchant seamen. There is even evidence suggesting that, in some enterprises, worker-manager negotiations were officially overseen by representatives of the Labour Front, while in reality they were organized by well-established union representatives.[16] However, even *within* an enterprise worker solidarity was often undermined by differential pay and sickness benefits given to different workers on the basis of factors such as individual productivity and length of service.[17]

This complexity was compounded by the fact that there was no viable alternative to the Nazis and no surviving organizations that could articulate worker grievances. When coupled with grandiose attempts by the state to secure loyalty, the line between coercion and cooperation blurred. This was a process accelerated by the seeming success of the Nazis in foreign policy and a rebuilding of national pride. And so many workers adapted and made do. They adjusted to the new political realities. They reinvented themselves. A Nazi-era joke summed up this survival mechanism as it affected one imaginary group of German industrial workers:

> Robert Ley (leader of the German Labour Front) to the manager of a factory:
> Ley: Tell me, have you still got any Social Democrats with you?
> Manager: Oh yes, about half the workforce.
> Ley: How dreadful! But surely no Communists?
> Manager: Oh yes, about a third of the men.
> Ley: Really! What about Democrats and so on?
> Manager: They make up the remaining 20 per cent.
> Ley: Good gracious! Haven't you got any Nazis at all?
> Manager: Oh yes, of course, all of them are Nazis![18]

8

THE BETRAYED MIDDLE CLASS?

Ernst Selbac was a hotel worker and Nazi Party member from the Ruhr but he had a craft skill. He made a violin. Sending it to Hitler, he attached a note that included these lines: 'To Mein Führer Adolf Hitler, Reichs Chancellor! After many long hours, I succeeded in making this violin for you. Work that mirrored the rebuilding of the nation under your leadership . . . I built it by hand and decorated it with ivory and ebony . . . The inlaid swastikas alone have 245 pieces of ivory. If God wills it, I would like to hear my Führer play it just once in this life!' We have no record of whether Hitler ever played his violin but he sent a hand-written note to Selbac assuring him of his Führer's 'sincere thanks'.

Selbac was not the only craftsman who wanted to dedicate his skills to the Nazi leader of the Third Reich. Thousands of letters poured into Hitler's office assuring him of love and devotion. Many were from solid middle-class members of German society, like the master-barber who enthusiastically offered to walk 400 miles from his home town to the Chancellery in Berlin to cut the Führer's hair.[1] They were not alone in their devotion but what they eventually made of the Nazis is unknown. Surely the barber would have appreciated the law of May 1933, which forbade department stores from offering hairdressing services (and so protected self-employed barbers). But what would the violin maker have made of the fact that, by the end of the 1930s, violin making in the Mittenwald was in crisis?[2] It faced increasing competition from the very factories that many middle-class craftspeople expected the Nazi government to protect them from.[3] And competition for raw materials in a rearming Germany, combined with the increasing controls of the Four-Year Plans, meant that violin manufacturing was not high on the priorities of the Third Reich. Clearly, the passage of time would show that some middle-class hopes had been badly misplaced.

The social class that had the most to hope for from the Nazis was that group of people described by German historians, economists and sociologists as the *Mittelstand*. This word is often translated as 'middle class' and it describes a wide range of different groups who found themselves socially between the industrial workers on the one hand and the owners of large businesses and large landowners on the other. As a consequence, their experiences, hopes and fears were not unified and they included many different kinds of people who were employed in many different jobs. These included: small shopkeepers, skilled craftspeople running their own businesses, lower civil servants, teachers, self-sufficient peasant farmers. Nevertheless, they had a number of things in common: a fear of being forced down into the ranks of less skilled workers, a resentment of those socially and economically more prosperous than themselves, a strong nationalist tradition (not unique to this group of course), a tendency towards resentful anti-Semitism, social conservatism, and a fear of the threat of modernization and change. Anxiety was a prominent feature of their outlook. Shopkeepers feared being undercut by department stores, craftspeople resented the competition of the factories, peasant farmers objected to the cheaper products of the bigger estates.

As the US historian David Schoenbaum has shown, groups who had increased in prosperity under the Kaiser were suffering under Weimar. Most notable in this group were the retail traders, 'a bumper crop sown by the imperial order and in constant fear of being mowed down by the economics of the Republic'.[4] To right-wing politicians the middle class were an independent and hard-working section of society who were 'the healthy core of the German People'.[5] Standing apart from the class war raging between workers and capitalists they seemed to offer a unifying middle ground. They regarded themselves as providing a repository of the virtues of honesty, reliability and hard work. In many ways they wanted government protection from wider social forces, which, in reality, governments could not control.[6] For such people, the Nazis seemed to offer not simply what their class required but more fundamentally, 'an escape from class and sectional politics altogether'.[7]

Many of these middle-class people supported the Nazis and joined the party in the uncertain days of the early 1920s. Experiences of wartime defeat, trade union unrest, communist uprisings and then the hyperinflation of 1923 made these people very open to Nazi appeals. In fact, it is clear that the early Nazi membership lists were dominated by skilled workers and lower-middle-class men. The two founding members in 1919, Anton Drexler and Karl Harrer, were a locksmith and a sports journalist respectively. Other founding members were skilled workers from the Munich locomotive works. Hitler himself came from a lower-middle-class background, as his father was a customs officer. These were all from a vulnerable section of society, which feared downward mobility and felt powerless in the face of the seismic changes shaking Germany after 1918. Their resentments and ambitions were revealed in details of the 25–Point Programme issued by the party in 1920, with its calls for: the 'first duty of every Citizen to carry out intellectual or physical work' (Point 10), 'abolition of all income obtained without labour or effort' (Point 11), 'confiscation of all war profits' (Point 12), 'large-scale development of old-age pension schemes' (Point 15), 'the creation and maintenance of a sound middle class; the immediate communalization of the large department stores, which are to be leased at low rates to small tradesmen. We demand the most careful consideration for the owners of small businesses in orders placed by national, state, or community authorities' (Point 16); 'abolition of ground rent and prevention of all speculation in land' (Point 17) 'education at the public expense of specially gifted children of poor parents' (Point 20).[8]

While other points, such as profit sharing and nationalization, reveal the influence of working-class members, the anxieties of the lower middle class are clear in these demands. As the 1920s progressed, the drift of the middle class towards the Nazis increased at the expense of the traditional liberal and conservative parties.[9] When Hitler came to power in January 1933, these members of the party expected to be the main beneficiaries of the newly won power. To these should also be added the white-collar workers – described by German sociologists as 'the new Mittelstand' – who in the years since 1929 had felt their status under threat and feared being pushed down into the ranks of the manual labourers. For them a defence of their status was a top priority.

If the middle class lacked a clear definition, they nevertheless made up a significant proportion of the German working population. In 1933, the self-employed made up 20 per cent of the working population and white-collar workers and civil servants made up 18 per cent of this same section of society. Together, therefore, they constituted 38 per cent of the total working population. In addition, the self-employed themselves provided jobs for a further 11 per cent. Whilst this was still a minority compared to the 52 per cent classified as 'workers', it was still a very large proportion of those at work in Germany.[10] And it should be remembered that the German working class was not itself a united or homogenous group either socially or politically, so this 52 per cent did not constitute a coherent social or political bloc either. In short, the middle class were a social and economic force that could not be ignored.

A lower middle class revolution?

During the process of 'bringing Germany into line', which occurred after January 1933, the lower middle class members of the SA and the party went into overdrive. These tradesmen, shopkeepers and artisans believed that the moment had come to eliminate rivals. The most active group were the Combat League of Middle Class Tradespeople. Resentful at competition from department stores and consumer cooperatives they organized boycotts of these enterprises. But they soon found that – whatever Point 16 of the '25–Point Programme' promised them – they were not going to be allowed to carry out their middle-class revolution. Instead, as disruption to the economy grew in the early months of 1933, the Nazi government stepped in to control their activities.

A directive from the Reich Commissioner for the Economy made it clear that ordering direct action was 'the sole responsibility of the *leadership* of the Reich Combat League'. There would be no spontaneous disruption of shopping. And, furthermore, it was made clear that there would be no 'influence on prices or direct influence on business activity'.[11] It would be the state that would decide these issues and not the activists of the Combat League of Middle Class Tradespeople. This clearly did not go down at all well with these grass-roots Nazis. They wanted department stores broken up and quickly. They were going to be disappointed. In July, a senior Nazi, Rudolf Hess, told them: 'Its solution will follow at the appropriate time . . . In view of the general economic situation, the Party leadership considers action intended to paralyse department stores and similar institutions to be inadvisable for the time being.'[12] In case the point had not gone home, in the summer of 1933, the Combat League was dissolved and replaced by a new organization that was more closely controlled and mostly geared to political education. The shopkeepers had been taught an important lesson; in the Nazi state it was the party hierarchy that decided direction, not the grass-roots radicals. A year later the SA would learn the same lesson.

Anticipating the will of the leadership and developing it as local activists saw fit was a key feature of the Third Reich. But the leadership would slap down any misinterpretation of the leadership will and certainly any interpretation that challenged the authority of the leadership. It was a tightrope that Nazi activists had to tread carefully.

Successes and disappointments

The Nazi leadership was aware of middle-class supporters and sympathetic to some of their aspirations. The Law for the Protection of Individual Trade, of May 1933, stopped chain-stores from expanding or opening new branches. They were also banned from having self-contained departments that would compete with local small businesses. The resentment directed at department stores led to the government ordering the closing of all restaurants in these stores. It went on to ban a range of other activities in department stores from sausage making to watch repairing. Prices were also controlled in an attempt to stop the undercutting of local small businesses. The party organization procured its uniforms from small businesses and government work creation assisted plumbers and carpenters as well as others in the building trade. As a result, when in 1938 overall retail trade reached 93.7 per cent of what it had been in 1928, that of department stores only reached 70.1 per cent.[13] Whilst these stores had not been destroyed, they had been significantly curtailed. In May 1933, the Law for the Protection of Retail Business controlled the establishment of new businesses and so kept competition under control.

In an attempt to protect the skills of artisans, guilds were set up from June 1934 to regulate their work. All craftspeople had to join in order to open a workshop and the guilds supervised qualifications and the awarding of the status of 'master'. This was an important victory in the battle against factory-based production that these craftspeople were waging and one in which the Nazi administration was receptive to their demands.

One terrible advantage gained by some small businesses

came with the increasing 'Aryanization' of German society, as Jews were forced out of business from the mid-1930s onwards. Competitors with close connections to the Nazi party could make the most of this opportunity to eliminate rivals and to take over Jewish businesses (see Chapter 9).

However, for all these successes and advantages there were many areas of severe disappointment. We have already seen how the shopkeepers learned that change would not be on their terms. The same disappointment affected Germany's white-collar unions. Non-Nazi leaders of their main professional associations were swiftly arrested in early 1933 and imprisoned in concentration camps. Changes to their organizations swiftly followed. Instead of being represented by a distinct association, these white-collar workers found themselves merged into the German Labour Front (see Chapter 7), along with manual workers. This was definitely not what they wanted. A Sopade report (for the Social Democratic Party in exile) in 1936 found that, while many white-collar workers were pleased at the crushing of the Communist Party, they themselves were mostly apathetic in their general attitude towards the new regime. They grumbled at the party but admired Hitler. They had been neutralized by the state and were consequently incapable of any organized action to defend their interests.

University-educated professional groups experienced mixed effects from Nazi programmes. Support for the Nazis was high amongst many in the teaching professions. And yet the Nazi emphasis on military service and anti-intellectualism meant that many in these professions soon felt downgraded, if not overshadowed by Hitler Youth and SA in their classrooms and lecture theatres, who now felt that they were the arbiters of what was acceptable in the New Order of the Third Reich. Civil servants and lawyers too found themselves pilloried by a regime that was both increasingly lawless and that despised many in the old German elite professions. Engineers though did find a rapid expansion of projects calling for their expertise, although this often did not translate into higher rates of pay. Doctors too found that their status was mixed. On one hand the Nazi obsession with 'racial hygiene' meant that medical examinations and health were high on the agenda. Many doctors benefited from an enhanced role as they took part in the regime's programme of sterilization and they also benefited from taking over the practices of Jewish doctors. This was accompanied by increased salaries and by career opportunities on offer within the military and the SS. On the other hand it was, of course, 'health' as the Nazis defined it. Patient confidentiality was overridden if it conflicted with the regime's campaign to remove those suffering from hereditary diseases, sexually transmitted diseases and congenital disabilities. Attendance at courses on 'racial hygiene' was compulsory.

In the long term many of those who had initially benefited from government action in 1933 and 1934 found they lost out once the rearmament programme really got off the ground after 1936. This was because rearmament favoured larger industrial enterprises and centralized control. They were discovering that any hope that the recovery in these early years would settle down into stability and normality was illusory; 'the Third Reich was incapable of settling into "normality".'[14] The upward spiral of change geared to war would see to that. The fixed prices and regulations of the Four-Year Plan clashed with the hopes of the independent middle class of shopkeepers and small-scale producers. Even when small artisan workshops were provided with employment making component parts for larger enterprises (and weapons systems in the Third Reich often involved a staggeringly large number of such sub-contractors) it was at the cost of their independence. Increases in the numbers of artisan workshops, which occurred between 1933 and 1936, went into reverse after the latter date. In 1939, the output from these workshops was lower than it had been in 1926.

This was not what such lower-middle-class people had expected in 1933. Such small businesses could not compete in the purchasing of raw materials and soon found government regulation irritating and an obstruction to business. Passing guild exams, keeping records of income and expenditure and being governed by leaders chosen by the state soon made the guilds anything but the self-regulating protection that had been envisaged in 1934. And the more attractive wages paid by larger firms caused a chronic shortage of labour for small businesses, a problem that could only be rectified by employing more family members. By 1939, some 44 per cent of soap and brush shops were run by women, and where there was a male owner, over 50 per cent were aged over fifty years of age.[15] Even the Aryanization of Jewish businesses only benefited a tiny number of German enterprises. It has been estimated that, of the 10,000 Jewish craft workshops shut by the end of 1938, only about 3.4 per cent were actually taken over by other businesses and continued in production. The rest were very small units and were simply shut down.

By 1939, the needs of the military economy meant that increasing numbers of skilled craftspeople were drafted into large-scale military enterprises. Guilds were instructed to identify businesses that were not viable, so that their owners could be redeployed into higher-priority industries. As if this was not enough, the suppression of wages meant there was not enough spare cash around to spend on the consumer goods produced by sweet makers, or cabinet makers. Guns did not only come before butter. Furthermore, government price controls suppressed profits and taxes were going up as the rearmament drive increased in pace after 1936. And then there were the contributions to the party and the corruption, which led to local party members being given management positions in many cooperative stores that small shopkeepers had wanted closed down entirely.

All of this led to much bitterness. One Sopade report recorded the complaint of a shopkeeper: 'What didn't they promise us before? The department stores were going to be closed, the co-operative societies were going to be destroyed, the one-price shops were going to disappear. Nothing has happened! We've been lied to and betrayed!'[16] Foreign policy successes could only take people's minds off their problems for so long. No sooner had the public euphoria over the reoccupation of the Rhineland in 1936 died down, than middle-class grumbles over prices and economic problems joined those of other sectors of society: workers complaining about low wages and working conditions; farmers unhappy with the pressures put on them by the government.[17] Another Sopade report noted, in July 1939, that: 'The small businesses are in a condition of gloom and despondency. These people, to whom the present system to a large extent owes its rise, are the most disappointed of all.'[18] The reasons cited were price controls, shortage of raw materials, obligatory production of detailed accounts, tensions with customers tired of shortages and, finally, forcible redeployment to other industrial sectors. And in the countryside farmers found that in return for increased stability and a favourable treatment in the Nazi ideology of 'Blood and Soil', they were more tightly controlled than ever in the drive for self-sufficiency. This was not all; labourers left for better pay in armaments factories; animal feed went up in price and they could not pay for improvements by raising mortgages on their farms any more, since that had been banned.

But things were better than in the depression. Like the grumbling workers, the German middle class had much to complain about but also reasons to put up with it. It had once been worse, was a general conclusion. As a consequence, the grumbles did not coalesce into anything resembling a political challenge, as Sopade reports noted in 1939. Significantly too, despite disappointments, much of the Third Reich in the late 1930s still resonated with the German middle class. Sympathy for nationalist expansion and expropriation of the Jews was strong in this sector of society, a characteristic that had long predated Hitler coming to power. And so this nuanced support for the Nazi government expressed a great deal of middle-class opinion by 1939. It had not been as expected . . . but it could have been worse. A betrayal of previous hopes . . . but not entirely so.

9

THE PERSECUTION OF GERMAN JEWS IN THE 1930S

Nazi anti-Semitism impacted on Jewish people's lives in many ways. One of the strangest effects was on the life of the young Sigmund Tobias. Fleeing Germany with his family in 1938, the six-year-old ended up in Shanghai, China. With so many doors shut to desperate Jews, this unlikely place of refuge allowed in Jewish refugees without a visa. In all, some 17,000 Jews eventually settled in the area of the city known as Hongkew, which was administered by the Japanese. As his later account describes it, the city was indeed a 'Strange Haven' for those fleeing Nazi brutality. Struggling to survive wartime conditions in an environment vastly different to their native Germany, the Jews of Shanghai illustrate the terrible impact of Nazi persecution, which scattered those that it did not succeed in killing. But, hard as life was in wartime China, it would have been more disastrous if the family had remained in Germany. For the period 1933 to 1939 saw an escalating persecution of the Jews of Germany, which was itself a prelude to something even worse.[1]

The Nazis were an unashamedly racist party and their ultimate aims for Germany were based on this racism. In the Nazi *Weltanschauung* (worldview) there was a hierarchy of races.

At the top were those termed 'Aryans', who were regarded as the ultimate in human development. At the bottom were those regarded as inferior races, whose culture and way of life was regarded as debased. Furthermore, this worldview was a kind of bastardized Darwinism, which saw all human history as a struggle for dominance between these antagonistic races. This outlook was central to Nazi beliefs and Hitler's worldview. It viewed existences as 'a cosmic racial struggle'.[2]

In this pecking order of humanity, Slavs, Gypsies, people of African and Asian origin were all regarded as inferior. But the fiercest hatred was reserved for the Jews.

The nature of Nazi anti-Semitism

The anti-Jewish ideology of Hitler and the Nazis drew on a centuries-old tradition of scapegoating and persecution of an identifiable minority. Throughout the Middle Ages, Jewish people in Europe had been a recognizable religious minority. As such, they were easy targets for any problems in society. They were frequently stereotyped and accused of the most incredible and imaginary crimes. Added to this was the fact that, as the only community allowed to lend money at interest, they were resented despite the fact that they performed a valuable service in funding developments in the economy. As a result, they were the targets of periodic violent attacks and frequent acts of discrimination. In fact, there is strong evidence that, by the nineteenth century, economic anti-Semitism was far more prevalent than the traditional religious antagonisms. Jews were accused of manipulating trade and banking to their advantage and to the detriment of German society.

This then was the reservoir of racism that Nazism tapped into. But during the nineteenth century this persecuting outlook had taken on a significantly different complexion. The medieval persecutions – although conveniently described as 'racist' – were fundamentally a matter of religious antagonism and economic resentment. However, during the nineteenth century this gained a new pseudo-biological complexity.

Attempts to categorize human communities led to the assertions that instead of a common humanity there were instead competing races. With the acceptance of Darwin's Theory of Evolution this racial outlook gained a new twist. Amongst a large number of writers on 'race' across Europe it became fashionable to designate some groups in this human competition for 'survival of the fittest' as being fitter than others. Not surprisingly, those who advocated these theories always decided that their – white, Western European – group was the pinnacle of human racial evolution. And other groups were labelled inferior because, it was argued, their culture was based on biological inferiority.

Groups of people who had faced traditional hostilities and persecution now faced the added indignity of being classified as not fully human. This air of scientific respectability to racism was found across a wide range of European writers. In Germany, from the 1870s, some political parties developed anti-Semitic policies influenced by this new biological racism.

It should though not be imagined that this was a solely German phenomenon. Far from it. Given the German-led mass murder of the Jews of Europe in the 1940s it can be tempting to conclude that there was something peculiarly German in this anti-Semitic hatred. But the reality was far more complex. In the 1880s, the most violent anti-Semitic pogroms occurred in Russia and Romania. There were no similar outbursts in Germany. In fact, as anti-Semitism seemed on the rise in France between 1894 and 1906 it seemed to be declining in Germany.[3]

In the turmoil and anxieties of the early years of the Weimar Republic it was easy for extremist parties to label traditionally stereotyped groups as being in some way to blame for the defeat of Germany in 1918 and for the failures of the German economy in the 1920s. To those seeking scapegoats the German army – apparently undefeated in the field and still fighting outside the borders of Germany in 1918 – had been betrayed at home by the 'November Criminals' of socialists, communists and Jews. And it was these enemies of Germany, it was claimed, who were continuing to corrupt the nation. This outlook was more appealing than the alternative one of taking personal responsibility for the disaster that had befallen Germany in and after 1918. Particularly within Bavarian society these *völkisch* (racist) groups had a receptive audience where anti-Jewish political parties had traditional support. This then was the breeding ground of Nazism and it would influence the south German party even more virulently than the party in other areas of Germany, once it had become a national force.

To this, Hitler added his own personal and Austrian ingredients. Personally bitter and fiercely nationalistic, his German chauvinism was also deeply affected by the anxieties and fears of his formative years in a pre-war Vienna that was losing control of its non-German empire and was resentful of east European immigrants fleeing the pogroms of Russia. Hitler possessed a virulent hatred for the Czechs and Slavs, although most of all for the Jews.

During the 1920s, this cocktail of resentments had rearranged itself within Hitler's outlook. What eventually emerged was a commitment to a *Volksgemeinschaft* (racial/national community) that excluded Jews and that consisted only of so-called racially pure 'Aryan' Germans. It would be a community in which race transcended class and which contrasted with the classless and international society associated with communism. By the mid 1920s, Hitler's identification of Jews with capitalists and 'profiteers' was giving way, in his speeches, to a greater focus on Jews as responsible for the horrors of Russian Bolshevism and this was linked to the idea of an eventual war to ensure German domination of Eastern Europe. As a result, Hitler held the mutually contradictory opinions that both capitalism and Marxism were weapons used by the international Jewish community to dominate the world. There was an attractive simplicity in this outlook for those seeking to find one tangible origin for all that they feared and hated.

In this way the struggle against the Jews was always the core component of Hitler's worldview and the outlook of the Nazi

Party. This is not to say that Hitler had a blueprint for how Jews were to be neutralized, or removed from German society. But there was, from the mid-1920s, an unshakeable commitment to removal of Jews from Germany, a war of conquest to gain *Lebensraum* (living space) for the German people in an Eastern European empire and to populate that empire with 'racially pure' Germans. Furthermore, the building of this racist empire would accompany the destruction of so-called Jewish Bolshevism. In this sense at least, 'Auschwitz was latent in the anti-Semitic obsessions of Hitler and his party'.[4] Latent but perhaps not inevitable; it would take wider events to create the context, the opportunity and the Nazi justification for the genocide of the 1940s.

Jews in German society before the Nazi assault

What is so puzzling, given the virulent Nazi hatred for Jews, is how few Jewish people there were in Germany. In 1933, there were only about 500,000 Jews in Germany, or 0.55 per cent of the total population. The Jewish population was both ageing and declining in numbers. After 1925, numbers of deaths exceeded that of births. In addition, they were highly integrated into German society. Such a community had little in common with Jews from the East 'who seemed like the incarnation of some earlier embarrassing self'[5] and assimilated German Jews were often very concerned about immigration from the East.

Of this Jewish population, most lived in the major cities and almost 50 per cent were self-employed. Jews were strongly represented in the clothing trade, in medicine and in the legal professions. In the countryside many cattle dealers were Jewish. But all regarded themselves as German. This explains why many did not leave Germany, even in the face of Nazi persecution.[6]

The assumption that anti-Jewish feeling was an active ingredient in support for the Nazis[7] has been challenged by other research and, even amongst many early Nazi Party members, it may not have been the prime motivation for joining the party.[8] Instead, within German society there seems to have been a fairly common low-level sense of antagonism towards Jewish people but it was not a high priority for most German voters.[9] As late as 1936, a Munich police report complained at the numbers of women shoppers attending the annual sales at a large Jewish clothes shop. Once in power, the Nazis would both be assisted by the background noise of racism and also frustrated by the lack of popular enthusiasm for turning it into radical action, particularly if it threatened order and routine.

Putting racism into practice: Nazi racial policy 1933–39

Despite their hatred of Jews, the Nazis had not put together a programme of what they intended to do once they achieved power. Clearly, they wished to exclude Jews from German society, but little thought had been given to how to achieve this. It was not until the 1940s that a total strategy (or 'Final Solution') would emerge to solve what the Nazis called 'the Jewish problem'.[10] But what was clear from the start was that Nazi hatred would explode into action once the government was in their hands. As soon as the Nazis came to power in 1933, acts of violence erupted against Jewish people. These were not, at first, the result of coordinated government action, since there was no preconceived programme. Instead, they were led by long-time Nazi Party members, along with the SA and the SS, who had long been promised a showdown (as they saw it) with German Jews. The American consul in Leipzig, Ralph Busser, reported how uniformed Nazi thugs raided a synagogue in Dresden, smashed windows of Jewish shops in Chemnitz and forced Jews to drink castor oil, while some Jews had their beards forcibly shaved.[11]

Strangely – given the well-publicised anti-Semitism of Hitler – these voluntary actions by Nazi enthusiasts were not approved of by the government. This was not due to any compassion for the Jews but rather to avoid offending the more law-abiding members of the coalition government and public opinion, which frowned on lawlessness and anarchy. The leadership was content with the aims of the Nazi radicals but not their methods.

However, as a response to demands by the Nazi grass-roots membership, an official boycott of Jewish businesses commenced on 1 April 1933. This was also a response to calls by Jews abroad for boycotts of German goods following widespread violent attacks on many German Jews by Nazis.[12] SA members stood outside shops to intimidate customers, windows were covered with offensive posters or painted with slogans. The boycott was not a great success. Many ordinary Germans seem to have objected to the disruption of their shopping routines and the action was condemned by the international press. In May, the Munich police that reported public resentment at a Nazi demonstration that had disrupted Saturday shopping. Even some party members were, rather surprisingly, disapproving. Richard Sneider, from Frankfurt am Main, complained at how elderly shoppers, 'who had made the greatest sacrifices fighting for four years for their Fatherland' had to run the gauntlet of 'half-grown boys . . . rascals and scallywags . . . a vulgar pack of people . . .'[13] It should though be noted that his complaint was prompted by disrespect for elderly war veterans and lack of public order – not by concerns about effects on Jewish people generally. But, despite these misgivings, the scene had been set for the steady expulsion of Jews from the economy and their isolation from German society.

Laws in April 1933 introduced the so-called 'Aryan Clause', which led to the dismissal of Jewish civil servants, academics and teachers. An insight into the faltering steps of these early policies can be seen in the reaction of President Hindenburg, who insisted on the exemption of Jewish war veterans and relatives of war dead. But this again was due not to compassion, but to a wish to honour the veterans of the First World War who were so closely associated with traditional German nationalism. And even into the early days of the genocidal Final Solution, Jewish holders of the Iron Cross First Class were temporarily exempted from the worst treatment. Such an exemption did not last but shows the bureaucratic and convoluted way in which this vicious Nazi anti-Semitism was put into practice. In 1933, the Nazis were caught out by how many Jews were exempted through war service, or war sacrifice; at first, only 47 per cent of Jewish judges were dismissed and 30 per cent of Jewish lawyers. These same statistics also remind us of how many German Jews had suffered for their nation in the First World War. It reveals just how fictional was the Nazi propaganda that said Jews lacked German patriotism. But the lie would soon swamp the truth.

So important a part was played by Jews in the national life that Hitler was initially forced to specifically exempt Jewish doctors from the Aryan Clause. But Nazi officials simply ignored this and local authorities dismissed Jewish doctors anyway. As a result, the central government responded by adjusting the law to reflect what was happening in reality. This is an example of the unplanned nature of Nazi government policy towards the Jews, which was often made more radical by enthusiastic Nazis further down the chain of command. As Joseph Bürckel, local Nazi leader in the Rhineland commented: 'We old Nazis don't give a damn about the remarks of some Nazi bigwig. As far as we are concerned, all we have to do is fulfil the Programme as the Führer wishes'.[14] Not that the central government was unsympathetic to their enthusiastic anti-Semitism.

Slowly, Jews were squeezed out of the economy. When the Nazis came to power, about 100,000 businesses were owned by Jews. While some were large concerns, most were very small-scale enterprises. By June 1935, the number had fallen by 25 per cent, and by mid-1938, the original figure had collapsed by almost 70 per cent. By the end of that year, Jewish businesses no longer existed. All had been 'Aryanized' – taken over by non-Jewish Germans at knock-down prices or at no cost at all. Minor Nazis on the make did very well from these seizures. And major industrialists joined in the feeding frenzy by seizing vulnerable – but desirable – Jewish businesses.

In 1933, there were about 60,000 Jewish children up to the age of fourteen years and, whilst the exclusion of adults from society took several years to implement, these children faced a faster deterioration in their treatment at school and by non-Jewish friends. The 'Law against the Overcrowding of German Schools' of April 1933 fixed a general limit of 1.5 per cent of a school's population for Jews. However, where Jews made up more than 5 per cent of the local population, the ceiling could go as high as 5 per cent. Children exempted from this discrimination included those whose fathers had served during the First World War, children from mixed marriages (but with no more than two Jewish grandparents) and those Jewish children who had foreign citizenship. The number of pupils exempted in this way was about 75 per cent of Jewish children in 1935–6. The number surprised the Nazis, who had expected an immediate effect on almost all children they regarded as Jewish.[15] It was hard for Jewish children to defend themselves against bullying from teachers and from other children who soon adopted the racist outlook of the poisonous Nazi children's books published in association with the rabid paper *Der Stürmer* (*The Stormer*). Here, ugly Jews – made unrealistically recognizable by hooked noses, sidelocks and beards – seduced pure Aryan girls and undermined German society.

In 1935, the Nuremberg Laws organized racial discrimination through two pieces of legislation. The 'Law for the Protection of German Blood and German Honour' banned marriages and also extra-marital intercourse between Jews and 'Germans'. The judgement being that no true German could be a Jew. It was also made illegal for a Jew to employ a 'German woman' aged younger than forty-five. The sexual obsession of the Nazis with Jewish men seducing Aryan women and the protection of so-called 'German blood' from adulteration was central to these regulations. In one German town the local Nazi officials removed housemaids from Jewish households on the very night the law was passed. But this was an isolated act of enthusiasm; elsewhere the law was put into force over the following weeks. A second law, 'The Reich Citizenship Law', stripped those no longer considered to be truly German of their citizenship. Henceforth, there would be two categories of Germans: 'Reich citizens' (Aryans with full rights) and 'nationals' (who were subject to the racial discrimination of Nazi policy). In twelve years of Nazi rule, the Reichstag only passed four laws and the Nuremberg Laws constituted two of these.[16]

The laws themselves were thrown together in a hurry. Attacks on Jews and boycotts of Jewish businesses by disgruntled party members were disrupting the economy and once again prompting international condemnation. These attacks were, it seems, encouraged by local party leaders and some national figures such as Goebbels and Julius Streicher (the party leader in Franconia, an ex-elementary school teacher and publisher of *The Stormer*) who were frustrated by the slow pace of the persecution of the Jews. Other members of the government, such as Hjalmar Schacht, the conservative Minister of Economics, protested about the illegal behaviour of these Nazi Party members, which was disrupting economic activities and attracting negative attention from foreign journalists. But, at a hastily convened conference of government ministers, the party representative argued that only strict action against Jews would satisfy the Nazi rank and file. It was once again a reminder of how chaotic and disorganized a regime the Third Reich could be, despite its dictatorial rhetoric and the undeniable venom of its racism. The resulting laws were hastily put together in time for presentation before the Nazi Party at its annual Nuremberg Rally. The first law was written overnight by officials hurriedly flown in from Berlin, and the Reich Citizenship Law was later drafted in half an hour and was scribbled on the back of a hotel menu card, due to a lack of available paper.

Hitler, in a rare speech to the Reichstag, justified the new laws with the bizarre assertion that they had been prompted by provocative behaviour by Jews. The regulations, he suggested, were necessary in order to stop outraged Aryan Germans from taking the law into their own hands. The laws, he claimed, were designed to contain 'a problem' and to create a basis from which Germans could have a 'tolerable relationship with the Jews'. If this legal strategy failed, he threatened, it would be necessary to refer the matter to the Nazi Party 'for final solution'. It was typical of the way in which Hitler presented controversial policy. First, fictional outrages were presented; these were then contrasted with the pressing need to defend the German people; finally, destructive threats were made against those who were the objects of these fictional accusations.

The next year saw a relaxation of anti-Semitic propaganda to avoid offending visitors to the Olympic Games in Berlin. When a Nazi activist, Wilhelm Gustloff, was murdered in Switzerland in February 1936 by a young Jew, the German government insisted there should be no reprisals. However, exclusion of Jews from national life had already impacted on German sport. As early as April 1933, the German Boxing Association had expelled the Jewish amateur champion, Eric Seelig. Gretel Bergmann, a world-class high jumper, was thrown out of her sports club, and Germany's top-ranked tennis player, Daniel Prenn, was expelled from Germany's Davis Cup Team. Needless to say, no Jews represented the Third Reich in 1936. Although, as a result of pressure from the Olympic leadership, German officials allowed Rudi Ball, who was half-Jewish, to compete as part of the German ice-hockey team at the Winter Olympics held in the Bavarian Alps. Other victims of Nazi racial prejudice were also driven out of sport. In June 1933, the Sinti boxer Johann 'Rukelie' Trollman, the German middleweight boxing champion, was banned from boxing. This politicization of sport provoked calls in the USA to boycott the 1936 games, but to no avail. And when the USA decided to send a team, all other major nations followed suit. The only state that boycotted the games was the USSR but it boycotted all Olympics until the 1952 Helsinki Games and was not prompted by concern for Jews.

The year 1938 saw a steady radicalization of Nazi Jewish policy. It accompanied a period of increased risk taking by the regime and increased confidence as each gamble was successfully pulled off.[17] In the spring, the Anschluss with Austria was achieved with no significant reaction by the international community. In the autumn, the Sudetenland area of Czechoslovakia was occupied, with the cooperation of the Western democracies. The fact that, in November, there occurred the most radical and brutal attack on Jews since Hitler came to power should not be considered a coincidence. This is not to suggest any coherent blueprint or plan but it was in keeping with a year of ratcheting up the radicalism of Nazi ambitions. The immediate prompt for the outrage that would later be called *Kristallnacht* (Crystal Night, the night of broken glass) was the assassination of a German diplomat in Paris by a seventeen-year-old Jewish refugee of Polish extraction, Hershel Grynszpan. This itself had its origins in the German police action of 28 October, which had seen 18,000 Jews of Polish nationality expelled from Germany. Refused access by the anti-Semitic Polish government, they found themselves trapped in the zone between the German and Polish borders. Amongst those in this tragic situation were the family of Grynszpan. Ironically, the man he shot – Ernst vom Rath – was himself under surveillance by the Gestapo. When vom Rath eventually died of his wound, the Nazi leadership used it as the excuse for an outpouring of violence that targeted the German Jewish community. On the night of 9–10 November, every synagogue (some 400) was set alight. In addition, 7,500 businesses still in Jewish ownership were ransacked, along with many Jewish homes. About 25,000 Jews were arrested and sent to concentration camps and about 100 were killed in the violence of the night, with hundreds more badly injured.[18] The only people punished for their part in these acts of violence were members of the SA who had raped Jewish women, their crime being an infringement of the Nuremberg Law banning sexual intercourse between Aryans and Jews.

The way in which this act of widespread violence was organized gives a revealing insight into the way in which the Nazi leadership guided the course of anti-Semitic policy in the 1930s.

The actual organizer of the attack was Goebbels, not Hitler. In fact, Hitler was careful to distance himself from too close an association with the order. This was a strategy that was to be seen in this area of Nazi policy on various occasions. The general approach seems to have been as follows: Hitler set the broad agenda; others improvised the methods; Hitler gave approval for significant changes in gear, or direction, but was careful to keep this approval secret, in order to avoid too close an association with radical policies that might backfire on him, or attract criticism. This has led to suggestions that Hitler was not really in the driving seat of the anti-Semitic policies of the Nazi state. Nothing, in fact, could be further from reality. Time and again the evidence trail leads back to Hitler, even when no written orders were issued (as indeed was the norm in the chaotic jungle-politics of the inner echelons of the Third Reich). But the enthusiastic way in which party and government operatives threw themselves into this process of 'working towards the Führer' reminds us that there was active and energetic involvement of huge numbers of people, at all levels, in the persecution-politics of the Third Reich.[19] This is a theme we will return to again when we explore how popular Hitler's dictatorship really was (in Chapter 16) and how the mass murder of the 'Final Solution' finally emerged as official policy and the extent to which it was approved of by the German population (in Chapter 18).

But to return to the events leading up to Crystal Night: Goebbels was out of favour with Hitler due to an affair with the Czech actress Lída Baarová. Attending a meeting of old Nazis in Munich on 9 November, he saw a chance to gain Hitler's favour and increase the tempo of anti-Jewish action. After Hitler had left the meeting, Goebbels told local party leaders that Hitler felt that attacks on Jews were not to be organized by the party but should not be stopped either. Clearly, having detached himself from any direct blame, Hitler had left Goebbels to hint at what was expected of loyal party members. The hint was enough. A later secret report from the

Nazi Party Supreme Court recorded how telephone messages were rapidly made to local party organizations to set up the violence but not to appear responsible. From this callous combination of Hitler's ingrained racism, Goebbels's personal ambitions and the enthusiasm of party activists came the worst example so far of Nazi race hatred. Other Nazi leaders disapproved of Goebbels's actions. Göring resented Goebbels's influence and the economic damage, while Himmler (though lending SS units to support the attacks) preferred a more systematic approach. The competing big beasts in the Nazi jungle rarely saw eye to eye. More surprising is the evidence of significant popular condemnation of the violence, revealed in the Sopade reports. It may have been this lack of popular support that forced Hitler to reject demands by Nazi radicals, after November 1938, that Jews should be forced to wear distinguishing badges. And when, one year later, on the anniversary of the event, there was an attempt on Hitler's life, the government prohibited a retaliatory attack on the Jews. Clearly, the Third Reich was not yet ready for the kind of radical action that would eventually occur as the Second World War progressed.

Nevertheless, the aftermath of the November attacks saw the final and complete exclusion of Jews from the German economy. They had barely maintained a significant economic presence there by 1938 but what presence there was now ended. All remaining Jewish businesses were either closed or Aryanized – transferred to state-approved owners. Half the property was seized by the state. In addition, a collective fine of one billion Reichsmarks was levied on the Jewish community. Those Jews who remained in Germany survived on the edge of society, relying on what funds survived in the hands of Jewish community organizations or was supplied by individuals. When, after 1941, these people were finally deported to their deaths in the extermination camps in Eastern Europe, the Gestapo paid for their transportation by stripping the last assets from these remaining funds.

What fate had the Third Reich decided for Jews by the end of the 1930s?

The clear answer was not genocide. This was not due to any moral scruples but simply because the methods and circumstances simply did not exist in the 1930s. And neither, of course, were the Jews of Europe in Nazi hands. The Third Reich, by 1939, consisted of a Greater Germany that was made up of Germany, Austria, the once-Czech Sudetenland and the Protectorate of Bohemia-Moravia, which along with the area of the Sudetenland made up the Czech half of the once-independent state of Czechoslovakia.

For those Jews living in these areas the preferred policy that had emerged by the late 1930s was emigration. Between 1933 and the first transports to death camps in October 1941, some 66 per cent of Germany's Jewish population either emigrated or died (most from natural causes at this stage). Göring had, in the aftermath of Crystal Night, gained Hitler's approval that he should coordinate Jewish policy. But under the umbrella of Göring's authority it was actually Himmler's SS organization that was increasingly taking the reins into its own hands. In newly annexed Austria it was the SS, under Adolf Eichmann, which had pursued a ruthless policy of forced emigration. So, in January 1939, Göring delegated responsibility for forced emigration to Himmler's deputy, Reinhard Heydrich, the chief of the SS Security Service (the SD). With Himmler, Heydrich and Eichmann in command the murderous trio who would later implement the Final Solution were in place. Though nominally still under the authority of Göring, henceforth it would really be the SS who would be the leading force in implementing Jewish policy. The future was bleak for those Jews under Nazi control but, for now, emigration was still the policy of choice. It would remain so until the outbreak of war, in September 1939, led to the consideration of more radical and lethal options.

Between 1933 and 1939, the Nazi government had succeeded in totally isolating the Jewish population in the territories under its control. Through a torrent of propaganda and through discriminatory laws this once vibrant and assimilated community was reduced to poverty and desperation. The diaries of Victor Klemperer reveal the demoralizing effects of curfews, of being banned from public parks and the use of libraries, having his driving license withdrawn and on and on . . . Desperately, he recorded his feelings in December 1938: 'All peace of mind is lacking . . . this absolute uncertainty'.[20] In these ways the Jews had been marginalized and depersonalized in the eyes of many of their neighbours by the determined stereotyping of laws, posters, films and school textbooks. One German schoolgirl, Melita Maschmann, later reflected on how propaganda had led her to feel that she had to cut off ties with Jewish friends, since one could 'either have Jewish friends or be a National Socialist'.[21] It was on this foundation that the 'Final Solution', or 'Holocaust', would be constructed during the years of the Second World War. As the historian Ian Kershaw put it, in a much-quoted and debated phrase: 'The road to Auschwitz was built by hate, but paved with indifference.'[22] Whilst this applied to the particular events of the 1940s, this sense of an Aryan German population that had become morally indifferent to a whole section of the community[23] was well on the way to being established by 1939.

In a speech to the Reichstag on 30 January 1939 (to which we will return in Chapter 18), Hitler summed up his unfinished business with the Jews of Europe: 'If the international Jewish financiers in and outside Europe should succeed in plunging the nations once more into a world war, then the result will not be the Bolshevizing of the earth, and thus a victory for Jewry, but the annihilation of the Jewish race in Europe'.[24]

10

'RACIAL HYGIENE' IN THE 1930s

One of the most terrible aspects of the Third Reich started with the appeal to Hitler, in 1938, by the father of a child since known to historians as 'Baby Knauer'. The child's father requested that his son be killed because he had been born blind, with severe learning difficulties and was missing an arm and a leg. Hitler turned the case over to his personal physician, Karl Brandt. Meeting the family in Leipzig and discussing the case with the baby's doctors soon led to the conclusion that there was no justification for keeping the child alive. The baby's doctors were informed that there would be no legal consequences for what was considered a 'mercy killing'. As a result, the father's request was granted and 'Baby Knauer' was killed.

This was the first death in a euthanasia programme that would claim tens of thousands of lives and that, with its experimentation with lethal injections and poison gas, would develop an expertise in killing that would feed directly into the genocide of the Final Solution, or Holocaust.

The meaning and origins of 'racial hygiene'
The Nazi persecution of the Jews in the 1930s (Chapter 9) was part of a wider outlook that sought to remove from German society all those who were thought to be threatening the purity

of the German race. This is sometimes described as 'racial hygiene' and the chilling reality is that it was not invented by the Nazis but had a long history. It was part of a general interest in eugenics, the idea that selective breeding of humans can be used to 'improve' the human species. Furthermore, many aspects of it were enthusiastically supported by highly educated academics, doctors and nurses. Indeed, doctors played a curiously intimate role in Nazi atrocities.[1]

The roots of German interest in eugenics and 'racial hygiene' stretch back into the nineteenth century. The rapid growth in German industry and cities by the 1890s had brought with it all the familiar problems associated with industrialization and the breakdown of traditional society. The spread of tuberculosis, alcoholism and sexually transmitted diseases did not go unnoticed by German doctors and lawmakers. The same trends caused anxieties across many Western European nations. In Britain, in some towns, 90 per cent of recruits to fight the Boer War (1899–1902) were rejected as physically unfit. As a result, a government-sponsored 'Committee on Physical Deterioration' was established in Britain in 1903. And this in turn fed into Liberal health and social reforms after 1906. The same kind of concerns were gripping Germany and there was a kind of 'healthcare race' going on before the First World War, alongside the more familiar arms race, as these rival nations struggled to reach the goal of creating a healthier, fitter and more productive population. This had both positive and negative aspects. On one hand, it encouraged reforms dedicated to improved healthcare; on the other, it singled out those thought responsible for weakening the nation's health and productivity. In Germany, there were suggestions that marriage should be restricted to the hereditary healthy and that the whole population should be screened for signs of serious disease and issued with 'health passports'.[2] Some of those putting forward these theories were also anti-Semitic, but others were Jewish, which demonstrates that this interest in eugenics had not yet taken on the clear racial undertones that would later dominate so many aspects of it.

By 1912, government medical officials in Germany were exploring the extent to which a declining birth rate was caused by hereditary 'degeneration' of the population. Now the state as well as doctors was getting closely involved in the whole eugenics debate and this would only increase as a result of the First World War, with its slaughter of many of the physically fittest members of German society. Some eugenics experts argued that the government needed to put more effort into improving the birth rate by radically improving the reproductive powers of the German people; at the same time, others argued that only conquering more land and population would make up for the loss. Both these strands would later come together in the domestic and foreign policies of the Third Reich as it fought its two-front biological struggle for 'race survival' both at home and abroad. During the Weimar years (1919–33), experiments were carried out in Prussia and in Saxony collecting data on health and heredity in the hope than this could, in the future, positively affect national health and crime-prevention policies. However, under Weimar democracy, there was a limit as to how far such speculations could go. But there were those taking in these findings who would apply them very radically in the future, even if it was not yet clear what might be done with such ideas. Two young students studying these theories were Heinrich Himmler (later to head the SS) and Joachim Mrugowsky (who would later be in charge of the racial purity of the *Waffen SS*, the fighting regiments of the SS). Himmler was studying agricultural science at Munich and would later, for a short time in the late 1920s, be an unsuccessful chicken farmer. Mrugowsky, on the other hand, was studying natural sciences and medicine at the University of Halle and he achieved doctorates in medicine and botany in 1931. In 1933, he became an assistant at the Hygiene Institute at Halle and, in 1930, had joined the Nazi Party. In 1931, he joined the SS, rising to the rank of colonel and, in 1937, he joined the sanitary department of the SS with special responsibility for the health of the Waffen SS. During the Second World War, he saw active service as a member of the SS Division Das Reich. In 1948, he was executed for medical experiments carried out on concentration-camp prisoners. Both Himmler and Mrugowsky demonstrate the way in which eugenics and 'racial hygiene' *could* develop when all moral constraints were removed after 1933. An interest in selective breeding and species 'improvement' could then be applied to people with murderous results. This was by no means inevitable but its seeds were always dormant in the more extreme ideas of the movement for racial improvement.[3]

In 1920, two respected academics, Karl Binding (a law professor) and Alfred Hoche (a doctor), published a book entitled *Permission to Destroy Life Unworthy of Life*. Those aiming to 'improve' the race by removing those thought to be polluting it had two main theoretical methods. One was to prevent reproduction through sterilization. The other was – as Binding and Hoche suggested – to remove those whose lives were thought unworthy of continuation, through euthanasia.

Euthanasia was clearly even more controversial than forced sterilization, since the latter (whilst massively infringing personal freedoms) did not involve killing anyone. So it is not surprising that euthanasia was not practised until the Nazi dictatorship was well established. Sterilization, on the other hand, was adopted by a number of countries in the early twentieth century. A number of US states experimented with sterilization to combat the reproduction of those defined as 'mentally retarded' and 'mentally ill' after 1907, and the incidence of forced sterilization increased after 1927. Sweden passed a sterilization law in 1934 aimed at preventing mental illness and disease and sanctioning force to achieve this. Forced sterilizations occurred in Switzerland in the 1920s and increased in number at the same time as such practices were being introduced in the Third Reich. This list is by no means exhaustive and gives a clear indication of the acceptability of such medical procedures in a number of countries in the 1920s and 1930s. Germany was by no means alone.[4] In the social and economic crisis following the Wall Street Crash in 1929, scientists at

Berlin's Kaiser Wilhelm Institute for Anthropology, Human Heredity and Eugenics suggested welfare assistance for healthy families, alongside sterilization of those of less 'value'. Until 1933, these calls did not translate into policy but the issues were being publicly aired even before the Nazis came to power.

From theory to practice: 'racial hygiene' under the Third Reich

The arrival of the Nazi government in January 1933 gave the green light to suggestions that, prior to this, had been simply theoretical. Now they could be put into practice under a government that embraced the idea of racial purity and the concept that some lives were 'worthless'. These, in Nazi terminology, were the so-called 'useless mouths', who consumed resources but who were considered to make no useful contributions to society. As such they were expendable.

As early as July 1933, the Law for the Prevention of Genetically Diseased Offspring – frequently called simply the Sterilization Law – came into force. This legalized the compulsory sterilization of any citizen who, in the opinion of the newly established Genetic Health Court, suffered from any of a list of alleged genetic disorders. The list of these 'genetic disorders' included: 'mental deficiency', schizophrenia, manic depression, epilepsy, Huntington's chorea, hereditary blindness and deafness. The boundaries of who was to be included in this target group proved very elastic. In time it would encompass those suffering from alcoholism, 'habitual criminals' and, in 1937, 400 of the so-called 'Rhineland Bastards' were sterilized. These were mixed-race Afro-Germans who, in popular prejudice, were thought to have been conceived when French colonial troops occupied the Rhineland in 1919. In fact, most were children of German settlers and missionaries who had married African women in the Kaiser's empire. As a result of the accusation of collaboration levelled against these particularly unfortunate people in the Rhineland, only these particular Afro-Germans were targeted for sterilization.[5]

In order to carry out these decisions force was sanctioned, if necessary. Under the Third Reich, somewhere in the region of 400,000 people were sterilized against their will. Shocking as this is, it should be remembered, as we have already seen, that in the contemporary USA there was already compulsory sterilization of certain inmates in psychiatric hospitals. The Third Reich was not alone in this draconian policy.

Sterilization was not the only outcome of the desire to purify German society. In November 1933, the 'Law against Dangerous Habitual Criminals' gave the police powers to arrest so-called 'asocials'. These included Gypsies, prostitutes, beggars, chronic alcoholics, and homeless vagrants. Those arrested were held in the growing number of concentration camps.

There were, of course, more positive aspects to 'racial hygiene'. The promotion of fitness and sport was an important aspect of the drive to improve the German community. This played a major role in programmes for workers, as part of the 'Strength through Joy' organization (see Chapter 7), and in the outdoor activities and sporting competitions put on for young people (see Chapter 11). Vaccination programmes too were expanded,[6] though there were public disputes between proponents of vaccination and some in the Nazi leadership who favoured so-called 'natural therapies'.[7] It is an irony that the success in eradicating typhus from Germany actually increased the risk of German troops and civilians contracting the disease following the invasion of the USSR in 1941, since natural immunity had not been increased through contact with the disease at home. Indeed, during the Second World War, countering threats of typhus and cholera epidemics in occupied Eastern European territories (made more likely by the Nazi policy of crowding Jews into ghettos) was one of the undercurrents flowing into genocidal experiments. In this, both the medical and 'racial currents' of Nazi 'racial hygiene' flowed shockingly together.[8] Amongst the crimes of Mrugowsky was that of testing typhus vaccines on prisoners at the concentration camp of Buchenwald and then infecting them with this deadly disease. He also, in a different range of experiments, tested the use of different types of bullets by having them fired into live prisoners – a chilling insight into scientific experimentation that was no longer restricted by moral restraints.

From sterilization to murder: the 'T4 Programme'

Sterilization was controversial. Euthanasia was more so. One was a savage infringement of human rights. The other, as practised under the Third Reich, was murder, since it was inflicted against the will of the individuals concerned (though it was often dressed up as 'mercy killing'). Those who would feel this the most were the patients in Germany's mental asylums. During the 1930s, pressure grew from Nazi radicals to do something about these 'useless mouths'. As part of the Nazi education of SS members, some 6,000 SS in training visited Munich's Eglfing-Haar asylum. The aim of the visits was to convince them of the necessity of finding a permanent solution to the problems posed by the severely mentally ill.

Accompanying this was a reduction in resources devoted to the care of the patients in asylums. In some hospitals the ratio of doctors to patients rose to as high as 1:500. Food rations were also cut. Nazi administrators were placed in charge of many asylums and many of the psychiatrists became SS members, with psychiatric nursing posts being increasing filled with Nazi party members escaping the unemployment queues.[9] In such circumstances the 'care' of the patients became increasingly brutal.

However, it was requests for 'mercy killing' that moved the brutal treatment up a gear into actual killing. The most infamous was that of 'Baby Knauer', but this was by no means an isolated case. In asking for action in these cases the families of severely disabled or injured people were pushing at an open door. Hitler was personally very sympathetic and assigned the examination of these cases to the Reich Chancellery. It was this arm of government that received such requests directed to the Führer and, by authorizing them to make decisions, these actions could take place secretly. Following the case of 'Baby Knauer', a Reich Committee for the Scientific Registration of Serious Hereditary and Congenital Illnesses was set up. At the same time the registration of such conditions was made compulsory. So the killing became institutionalized. At special paediatric clinics the children involved were killed by a mixture of starvation and the use of strong sedatives. It is important to remember that all the doctors involved were volunteers.

On the outbreak of war in 1939, the euthanasia programme was extended to adult psychiatric patients by a direct Führer order. In addition, SS units began the systematic shooting of psychiatric patients in occupied Eastern Europe. This escala- tion became systematic over a very short period of time and became known as the 'T4 Programme'. The name was derived from the address from which this secret programme was directed: Tiergartenstrasse 4. At six secret locations, specially selected teams of doctors, nurses and SS men drawn from the concentration camps killed over 70,000 people between 1939 and 1941. Most of the killings were done by gassing. Experience gained from this method of killing would feed directly into the murder of Jews from 1942.

Registration forms were sent to asylums across the Reich to be processed in order to assess patents' suitability to be dealt with by the T4 teams. When some asylums refused to comply they were visited by teams of assessors. The T4 Programme graphed its progress on what it termed 'disinfections' and calculated the money it was saving the Reich by closing these 'useless mouths'. A small number of asylums tried to protect patients by discharging them but this depended on the willing- ness of families to take in these people. Many were not willing to do so. The Mariaberg asylum records contain the letter writ- ten by one particular man who refused to take in his brother, Otto, but who promised, instead, a 'little something' in the post for Christmas. Otto did not survive until Christmas, as he was gassed on 13 December.[10]

In August 1941, the T4 Programme was ended. It had killed

its target quota and protests were mounting against its activities. The most public of these condemnations were sermons preached by Archbishop Galen, the Catholic Archbishop of Münster.[11] The T4 Programme had always been a secretive operation without any formal legal existence. The secrecy surrounding its operations gives an insight into the complex working of the Third Reich, which – while openly brutal in the extreme – still was reluctant to go public on its most striking atrocities. Clearly, the prime motivation was not to be too closely associated with actions that even the Nazis had to admit would shock a significant number of Germans. However, the impossibility of keeping such activities secret was revealed in the criticisms of the programme that Galen voiced.

The operatives who had gained experience from T4 continued their murderous work in other fields. Some were redeployed to the killing of 'sick' concentration-camp prisoners; there are suggestions that some operated behind the lines on the Eastern Front, dispatching seriously wounded German soldiers; some SS 'experts' were used to murder the Jewish population of the Warthegau, around the city of Posen, in an area annexed from Poland; others were sent to Lublin to begin the mass murder of Poland's two million Jews. But their story then became part of another chapter in Nazi history: the genocide of the Jews. Meanwhile, in the asylums within Germany (both in the Germany of pre-1939 and in the lands annexed since the start of the war), the killing of mental patients continued through starvation and neglect.

Gypsies in the 1930s

The Nazi classification of peoples thought to pollute German racial and social purity also included the Gypsies. Amongst those that German racial 'experts' classified as Gypsies were groups who described themselves as Roma and Sinti. But no such differentiation was used by the governments of Germany in the 1920s and 1930s. To many Germans, these were people who lived on the margin of society, were associated with petty criminality and were generally considered outsiders. In this, of course, they were not alone, for as we have seen, many groups were consigned to the fringes of German society in the 1930s.[12]

However, discrimination against Gypsies pre-dated the Third Reich. A law of 1926, in Bavaria, allowed for the two-year imprisonment of Gypsies in workhouses if they could not prove they had regular employment. By 1929, this practice had been adopted across Germany. After the Nazis came to power, discrimination against those classified as Gypsies intensified but, at first, it was not supported by any specific laws. When a number of towns – sensing the mood of the times – confined travelling groups to insanitary 'Gypsy camps', they were working on their own initiative. The same applied to sterilization and the arrest of Gypsies as 'asocials' after 1933. This was because early racial and race-hygiene laws targeted Jews, the hereditary ill and those classified as 'asocial', but there was no specific mention of Gypsies. However, this began to change after 1935. In November of that year, the Ministry of the Interior sought to clarify what was meant in the Nuremberg Laws when they stated that the right to marriage would be denied if the resulting children were 'a threat to the purity of German blood'. Clearly, this affected Jews but, what of other ethnic groups? The point was duly clarified. The law – a later decree stated – also banned marriage between Germans and 'Gypsies, Negroes and their bastards' (i.e. those of mixed race).[13]

From this point onwards, policy became more sharply focused. In June 1936, a Central Office to 'Combat the Gypsy Nuisance' was opened in Munich, Bavaria. This office soon became the headquarters of a national data bank, collecting information on Gypsies. From here researchers toured Germany, measuring the racial profiles of Gypsies as part of the 'scientific' side of Nazi racial policy. Much of this collecting of racial data was coordinated by Dr Robert Ritter, who had a special interest in genealogical and genetic research.

In July 1936, the Berlin police arrested about 600 Gypsies ahead of the Berlin Olympics and moved them to an internment camp near a sewage dump in Marzahan, located in the suburbs of the city. The conditions in the camp soon deteriorated since it had only three water standpipes and two toilets. It was a pointer to worse things to come. In December 1937, a crime-prevention drive led to further mass arrests by the police. Further actions took place in June 1938, when around 1,000 German and Austrian Gypsies were deported to concentration camps at Buchenwald, Dachau, Sachsenhausen and the women's camp at Lichtenburg. Further mass arrests, followed by confinement in concentration camps, occurred a year later. In the camps, Gypsies were identified by being made to wear either black triangular patches (the symbol for 'asocials') or green ones (the symbol for habitual criminals), and sometimes the letter 'Z' (for 'Zigeuner', the German for Gypsy) was sewn onto their prison uniforms.

In December 1938, the SS leader Himmler issued a circular to police authorities on the 'final solution of the Gypsy Question'. All Gypsies and all those vagrants classified as living a 'Gypsy-like existence' were ordered to register with their local police, whose records would go to the Reich Central Office for Combating the Gypsy Nuisance. The registration applied to all those over the age of six. The decree further stated that: 'Treatment of the Gypsy question is part of the National Socialist task of national regeneration' and 'the aim of measures taken by the State to defend the homogeneity of the German nation must be the physical separation of Gypsydom from the German nation, the prevention of miscegenation, and finally, the regulation of the way of life of pure and part-Gypsies'.[14]

The bitter irony of this was that – with an original medieval home in western India and a language related to Sanskrit – the Roma and Sinti people were part of that ethnic group that the Nazis regarded as 'Aryan'. The reality, of course, was that the Nazis had no intellectual rigour, or consistency, in their pseudo-historical and pseudo-archaeological research methods. For all their pretended 'scientific' racism, they were, in reality, possessed by a highly subjective cultural and national race outlook. As a consequence, they moved their terminology about as it suited them. Whatever the genetic origins of the Gypsies, the simple and brutal reality of the Third Reich was that culturally they did not fit the norm that the Nazis had dictated to be acceptable. This fact was clear in the vague Nazi terminology of who was a Gypsy. Himmler's 1938 circular referred to: 'All persons who by virtue of their looks and appearance, customs or habits, are to be regarded as Gypsies or part-Gypsies'. In the final analysis, 'Gypsies' were whoever Nazi officialdom decreed them to be.

Until March 1941, Gypsy children were still allowed to attend school. As with Jewish children, they suffered from the racist taunts of teachers and other school students. However, many were seized from their families and placed in special homes. Any who infringed school attendance rules were placed in special juvenile schools.

The most radical application of this anti-Gypsy doctrine would not be seen until after the outbreak of the Second World War. Two Gypsy internment camps were then opened in Austria: one at Salzburg in October 1939 and another at Lackenback in November 1940. This second camp was situated in the Burgenland, the eastern Austrian state bordering Hungary. The conditions at this second concentration camp were particularly appalling. In October 1939, Eichmann, the senior SS officer in Vienna, supervised the transportation of thirty-four wagons of Gypsies from Vienna to resettlement in Poland. They accompanied a transportation of Austrian Jews. But this left unsettled the fate of those Gypsies living in Germany itself (the so-called 'Old Reich'). In September 1939 and again in January 1940, German government conferences produced plans to expel 30,000 German Gypsies from Germany and to resettle them in occupied Poland. This expulsion process started in May 1940. Even worse was to follow: by the end of the war somewhere in the region of 250,000 European Gypsies had died at the hands of the Nazis, victims of roving SS units in the USSR after June 1941 and in the extermination centre of Auschwitz. By this time, the fluctuations of Nazi definitions had moved from persecuting those *socially* defined as 'workshy', to killing those *racially* defined as marked for murder. Along this route there had even been times when Himmler considered sparing those he classed as 'pure Gypsies' since he approved of their Aryan racial credentials.[15]

The persecution of homosexuals

Despite the high incidence of homosexuals in the early SA, the Nazi state had a clear policy of discrimination against homosexuality. But this ambiguity has led to sharp debates about the actual stance of the Nazi government towards homosexuals.

Controversially, it has been argued that, despite the number of homosexuals killed in the camps, Nazism was itself deeply defined by a militaristic homo-eroticism.[16] The cult of uniformed male youths and the homosexual camaraderie of the SA could be said to have pointed this way. Yet, in February 1937, Himmler ordered that any homosexuals discovered in the SS were to be expelled, imprisoned and shot 'while escaping'. And, earlier, Hitler had made Röhm's homosexuality a partial justification for his death. However, even at the time this was regarded as being unconvincing and a contemporary joke queried that, if that was what Hitler did when learning of Röhm's homosexuality, what would he do when he discovered Goebbels's club foot? The reality, as this jibe suggested, was that the sexual orientation of the SA leader was an open secret and one that Hitler had been able to tolerate until the SA became a political liability. And the vast majority of the SA were heterosexual. The reality of the situation seems to have been that, whilst there was a surprisingly large homosexual element within the macho world of the SA, Hitler's position had been to tolerate this and not approve of it. This was in line with his general approach towards ignoring Nazi members' personal lives, so long as they did not cause him trouble. Overall though, there was no sympathy for homosexuality amongst most of the Nazi leadership and their sexual orientation doomed homosexuals, since they would not contribute to the Nazi drive for expanding the German population and were regarded as deviants. As such they were targets for action.

The Nazis revised Paragraph 175 of the Criminal Code, which already made homosexuality illegal. This revision expanded the definition of criminal acts, increased police powers and led to the arrest of about 100,000 homosexual men, of whom 50,000 were imprisoned. Analyses of the actual number of homosexual victims of the Nazis have faced the problem that, since their sexual orientation continued to be a crime after the war ended, they were not always included as victims of Nazism in early studies. Furthermore, they were not eligible for compensation for their term of concentration-camp imprisonment.

Those arrested under the revised Paragraph 175 could be imprisoned for up to ten years, but in reality faced being held in prison indefinitely. In concentration camps, they were differentiated by a pink triangle sewn onto their uniforms. In these camps, they were particularly targeted for abuse and a number were also castrated. Some became victims of crude medical experiments designed to 'cure' them of their sexual orientation. Targeted by both guards and other prisoners, the death rate amongst homosexual prisoners was thus very high.[17] An example of homosexuals' treatment at the hands of the Nazis is provided by Friedrich-Paul von Groszheim. He was arrested in January 1937 at the age of thirty-one as part of a crackdown by the SS, which included the arrest of 230 men in Lübeck. Held for ten months, he was tortured and humiliated. Eventually, in 1939, he agreed to be castrated as the price of release.

'Racial hygiene' in the overall context of the Third Reich

The long-term consequences of these experiments in 'racial hygiene' are well summed up by the historian Henry Friedlander: 'Nazi genocide did not take place in a vacuum. Genocide was only the most radical method of excluding groups of human beings from the German national community. The policy of exclusion followed and drew upon more than fifty years of scientific opposition to the equality of man.'[18] As Friedlander reminds us, these policies grew out of a wider intellectual culture that affected more than the Germany of the Third Reich. But the idea of removing those thought to be threats to the biological and cultural 'purity of the German race' was galvanized by Hitler coming to power in 1933 and then grew in many directions and used many methods. And it tied together many different strands in the repressive and murderous activities of the Nazi state. Escalating from discrimination and disorganized violence to sterilization and mass murder, its tentacles would eventually draw in so-called 'aliens' (most notably Jews, Gypsies and Slavs) and those classed as 'asocials' (the mentally and physically ill or disabled, homosexuals, habitual criminals, alcoholics, the 'workshy' and vagrants).[19] This was a vast group, who had nothing in common except that the Nazis had consigned them, together, to the rubbish heap of history due to their categorization as enemies of the purity of the national racial community. This was the underlying theme that defined these very different groups as unworthy of life. As Nazi power increased – and as restraints on the exercise of this power decreased – this outlook would grow more lethal. This was a direct consequence of what Nazism stood for, even if it took a complex web of unforeseeable (and unplanned) events to make its most murderous applications possible. The so-called purification of the national racial community, as defined by the Nazis, was always a road leading to mass killing.[20]

11

THE NAZI IMPACT ON SOCIETY: YOUNG PEOPLE AND EDUCATION

In the ruins of the French town of Falaise, Normandy, in August 1944, sixty battle-tested teenage soldiers of the 12th SS Panzer Division *Hitler Jugend* (Hitler Youth) held out against advancing Canadians for three days. The only two SS soldiers captured alive were wounded.[1] Other young SS soldiers – wounded and captured – revealed a similar depth of fanaticism. One Allied nurse recounted how a sixteen–year-old SS soldier had torn off his bandages and declared he wanted to die for Hitler; another flung the food she gave him in her face; a third was only silenced by the threat of giving him a transfusion of Jewish blood.[2] What is particularly shocking is how young these fanatical Nazis were. When 12th SS Panzer Division was first formed in 1943, many of its Hitler Youth recruits were so young that they were supplied with sweets instead of the standard tobacco and alcohol ration. But what had created such a fanatical group of young Nazis?

The Nazi aims for young people

At the Nuremberg Rally in 1935, Hitler outlined his aims for young people: 'In our eyes the German youth of the future must be slim and slender, swift as the greyhound, tough as leather, and hard as Krupp steel. We must educate a new type of man . . .'[3]

In 1938, he expanded this general aim with more details, chillingly explaining how they would: join the Nazi youth movement at ten years of age and at fourteen go into the full Hitler Youth; at eighteen they would graduate into the party, the Labour Front, the SA or the SS; if after two years they were not committed Nazis they would go into the Labour Service; then for two to four years in the army; and once out of that, they would go back into the SA or the SS 'and they will not be free again for the rest of their lives'.[4] However short of this controlling ideal the system actually fell, the intentions were clear: German young people would be owned by the Nazi Party. As the leader of the Nazi Teachers' League put it: 'Those who have youth on their side control the future.'

Nazi youth groups and their impact on society

Since before Hitler came to power there had been a youth wing of the Nazi Party. But in the years up to 1933 it was comparatively small and faced competition from a range of other organizations in Germany. These included youth groups organized by the Protestant and Catholic churches and youth wings of the Social Democrats and the Communist Party. In 1930, there were only 18,000 in the Hitler Youth and by the end of 1932 it had grown no larger than 20,000. But all this changed after Hitler came to power in January 1933. Pressure then mounted on all young people to join the Hitler Youth and those who did so realized that they were part of the tidal wave of 'Bringing Germany into line', which gave them added encouragement to ostracize and bully those who refused. This spontaneous pressure soon had the force of law behind it. From July 1936, only the Hitler Youth could organize sporting activities for those under 14. This was soon extended to encompass those aged up to 18. Membership was still not compulsory but it had a tremendous impact. By early 1934, there were 2.3 million between the ages of 10 and 18 in the Hitler Youth; by 1936, this figure hit 4 million; by early 1939, it reached 8.7 million young people. This covered 98 per cent of all those aged between 10 and 18 years of age.[5] From 1936, the Hitler Youth was, via its leader Baldur von Schirach, accountable directly to Hitler himself. And, after March 1939, membership was finally made compulsory for children aged 10 and above. Parents who did not register their children could be fined up to 150 Reichsmarks, or even imprisoned.

This law introduced the so-called 'duty of youth service'. According to the details of Article 1.(2), this duty involved:

In particular,
1. the boys aged 10 to 14 in the German Young People (DJ).
2. boys aged 14 to 18 in the Hitler Youth (HJ).
3. girls aged 10 to 14 in the Young Girls League (JM).
4. girls aged 14 to 18 in the League of German Girls (BDM).[6]

Within each age group of the movement there was a set syllabus of indoctrination into Nazi ideas, accompanied by fitness training and, eventually, military training. The results of this 'investment' were seen in May 1940, as the US reporter William L. Shirer followed the victorious German army marching into Belgium. He noted 'the contrast between the German soldiers, bronzed and clean-cut from a youth spent in the sunshine on an adequate diet, and the first British war prisoners, with their hollow chests, round shoulders, pasty complexions and bad teeth . . .'[7]

For girls, the programme included exercises and the training that was necessary to turn them into fit and healthy bearers of the next generation of German babies. In this they were part of the drive for 'racial hygiene' (see Chapter 10). They were being groomed for the Nazi ideal of racially pure women, just as the boys were being drilled to become the warriors who would carry out the war of Germanic conquest and territorial expansion that was at the heart of the Nazi worldview of racial struggle and German survival.

However, the impact of the Nazi youth programme had a greater effect on the mind than on the body. The Hitler Youth motto was 'Führer command – we follow!' and the vow sworn on joining included such quasi-religious phrases as: 'The Reich is the object of our struggle; it is the beginning and the Amen' and 'You Führer, are our commander! We stand in your name'. The 1937 syllabus for a fortnight's camp included such daily mottos as: 'Hitler is Germany and Germany is Hitler', 'To be one nation is the religion of our time', 'It is not necessary for me to live, but certainly necessary for me to do my duty', 'Let struggle be the highest aim of youth' and 'Germany must live, even if we have to die'. These were the sentiments that had moulded the young minds of those who fought to the death in the 12th SS Panzer Division Hitler Youth in Normandy in 1944. Such indoctrination was designed to replace all family and religious loyalties and to bind children completely to the Nazi ideology and to personal devotion to Hitler. It was a factor that caused the SS to see the Hitler Youth as one of its key recruiting grounds.[8] One former member of the Hitler Youth later recognized what had been the aim of this relentless propaganda: 'We were drilled in toughness and blind obedience'.[9]

Concerned agents of the Social Democratic Party in exile noted in their secret Sopade reports the cases of children from socialist families who abandoned the ideals of their parents. 'I despise you,' taunted one such teenager to his father, 'because you don't possess a shred of heroism.' And another agent reported how all the children spoke of was 'heroes and heroism'.[10] It goes without saying that the heroes were Nazi heroes and the heroism was the racially focused defence of Germany and its new aggressive ideology. Some parents despaired: 'It is extremely difficult for parents who are opponents of the Nazis to exercise an influence on their children.' And another – aware of how children were encouraged to denounce anti-Nazi parents – sadly commented: 'You've got to watch yourself in front of your own children.' And yet another reported, 'I feel as if my lad is the spy in the family.'[11]

But it was not only in the home that such children could feel an exhilarating sense of power over adults. At school they could threaten teachers who seemed to lack Nazi zeal; on public transport they could threaten ticket collectors who did not 'Heil, Hitler' every passenger. Their Hitler Youth uniforms signalled to all observers their power, their confidence and their solidarity. As a Sopade report noted in 1934, 'The fact that school and the parental home takes a back seat compared to the community of young people – all that is marvellous'[12] However, it was not only images of power and violence that captured the attention of young minds. Along with a view of a world purged of what they had been led to believe were those polluting it, was a manipulated enthusiasm that the new Germany would create lasting peace. A young Nazi activist, Melita Maschmann, would later look back on the Berlin Olympics of 1936 and those foreign young people who would return home with a new outlook because they had competed in the Third Reich: 'In all of us there was the hope in a future of peace and friendship.'[13]

The limits of dictatorship

Despite the massive impact of the campaign to organize and influence young people, there were still those who slipped through the controlling 'net' of Nazi efforts. And the Nazis knew it. By the mid-1930s there were complaints from Nazi local organizers about young people failing to turn up to meetings on a regular basis. Many were more interested in the sport than the ideology. Others resented the dragooning and the boring lectures. Long hours hiking rapidly lost appeal. Brutal discipline on Hitler Youth camps[14] might have been designed to make the subjects 'tough as leather, and hard as Krupp steel' but it left many determined not to return the next summer for another brutalizing. The same Sopade reports also contain (more heartening to the Social Democrat agents) news of young people not paying their membership fees and skipping training and evening parades; telling anti-Nazi jokes and commenting on how boring they found the camp-fire sing-songs; resenting the way the camping trips were being militarized; consequently, many were becoming merely paying members. This was not what was expected of the 'new type of man'. Even a Hitler Youth leader might begin to find 'the compulsion and the requirement of absolute obedience unpleasant' and might begin to resent the way in which the Hitler Youth 'was interfering everywhere in people's private lives'.[15]

The constant demands of the party began to be reflected in wry humour, of the kind collected and published in a recent German study. In one example, a girl is asked about the Nazi credentials of her family by a friend. She replies: 'My father is in the SA, my oldest brother in SS, my little brother in the HJ, my mother is part of the NS women's organization, and I'm in the BDM.' 'Do you ever get to see each other?' asks the girl's friend. 'Oh yes, we meet every year at the party rally in Nuremberg!'[16]

The Nazi impact on education

A German maths textbook of the late 1930s carried the following test question: 'A modern night bomber can carry 1,800 incendiaries. How long (in kilometres) is the path along which it can distribute these bombs if it drops a bomb every second at a speed of 250 km per hour?'[17]

Clearly, the school and university system allowed the Nazis an opportunity to manipulate the formative learning experiences of young people. This offered them the chance of countering the influences of the home and giving young people a Nazi outlook. Even more than the provision of the youth organizations (which as we have seen were not compulsory until 1939) school gave access across the board to the children and youth of Germany.

From July 1933, the central government laid down guidelines on history textbooks, which ensured that in future they would stress the role of heroism and leadership. As a result much of German history teaching became the celebration of German cultural superiority since the Stone Age, emphasized the nature of history as being rooted in struggle and insisted that racial identity was the defining characteristic of the Germanic past. This kind of manipulation affected all ages and all subjects. The picture books used with young children portrayed Jews as evil and cunning, associated with dark places and obsessed with the corruption of Germans and Germany. The outlook of a generation was being moulded and corrupted. Secondary-school subjects were all affected by a Nazi angle. Biology became focused on matters of race; physics became occupied with military themes such as the study of ballistics; arithmetic involved calculations related to the proportion of blond-haired people in Aryan society or the cost of feeding patients at lunatic asylums or calculating the destructive capacity of a bomber; geography examined the need for Lebensraum for the German people. On graduating from school, any student wishing to attend university had to (after 1934) complete six months' labour service. It was one more attempt to imbue young people with the Nazi doctrine of 'blood and soil' and to try to break down barriers of class through a comradeship based on service to the Third Reich.

In order to achieve the Nazi goals for education it was necessary to control the teaching profession and to purge it of any teachers who opposed the new Nazi state. In April 1933, the Reich Law for the Re-establishment of a Professional Civil Service led to the establishment of investigative committees to drive 'unreliable' teachers out of the profession. These were initially set up by Bernhard Rust, the Nazi Minister of Education in Prussia. This led to the dismissal of almost 16 per cent of headteachers (male and female) in Prussia but only about 2.5 per cent of teachers. Almost all Jewish teachers were sacked and those who survived in post were finally removed in 1935. In addition, about 60 per cent of lecturers in Colleges of Education were dismissed.[18] The pressure on school teachers to conform to Nazi expectations was increased by a directive issued in 1934, which insisted that schools should educate their children 'in the spirit of National Socialism'. Some teachers put up a subtle resistance to this; their Hitler salutes were clearly half-hearted or they raised questions about the material they were passing on to their students. But this was dangerous and laid them open to the threat of being denounced to the authorities with the attendant loss of their jobs. However, most teachers went along with the new mood in Germany and, in reality, there seems to have been little resistance. The membership of the Nazi Teachers' League leapt from 12,000 in January 1933 to 220,000 by the end of the year and 300,000 by 1936. This last figure represented about 97 per cent of the teaching profession.[19] The members of this professional body were expected to attend the indoctrination courses set up to mix educational training with military activities. By the start of the Second World War, 71 per cent of its members had attended these residential training camps. Within about a year of the Nazis coming to power, somewhere in the region of 25 per cent of teachers had joined the Nazi Party, compared with 10 per cent of the population as a whole by 1939.[20]

The way in which education was administered also changed under the Nazis. By 1935, the new Reich Ministry of Science and Education, with Rust at its head, took control of all education throughout Germany, and education ministries in the *länder* (states) were wound up. Education policy under the indecisive and depressive Rust soon became confused and academics joked that a new unit of measurement – 'the Rust' – now existed in order to express the amount of time between one initiative being set up and then countermanded by another one. By 1937, Rust's new Reich Education Ministry became responsible for all teaching appointments and in 1939 it became responsible for all examinations in Germany. It also reorganized the structure of schools to make them uniform across the whole of the country.

In addition to these schools, a new type of institution had been established in 1933. These were the so-called 'Napolas' (National Political Educational Institutions) and were intended to train the new ruling elite of the Third Reich. Its graduates ended up in the military, the SS and police. The running of these schools was in the hands of the SS and SA with predictably negative consequences for their academic performance. Eventually, the SS took over full responsibility for running the Napolas. The chaotic nature of Third Reich government – with its often contradictory infighting and duplication of roles – soon surfaced in the structure of education. The Nazi Party (as distinct from the SS and the SA) complicated educational structures by also setting up its own schools. The first type were the Adolf Hitler Schools, first set up in 1937, which were run by the Hitler Youth and overseen by regional party bosses. The aim of these institutions was similar to the Napolas but educational standards were low and the initiative ground to a halt during the Second World War. The next type of party school was the Order Castle, of which three were eventually established. They were designed to take the graduates from the Adolf Hitler Schools and to train them up for the highest administrative posts of the Third Reich. But academic standards in these schools – which were more concerned with physical and ideological fitness – also proved to be low. One successful graduate of the Adolf Hitler School system was the later Hollywood actor Hardy Krüger. After fighting in an SS unit in 1945, the seventeen-year-old Krüger was captured by the US army and after the war went on to act in such films as *The Wild Geese* (1978) and *A Bridge Too Far* (1977).[21]

The effects of the Nazi polices on education soon revealed themselves. First, there was an increase in the use of corporal punishment as a more brutal attitude towards discipline was enforced in schools. As one headteacher commented approvingly, it meant that 'a sharp Prussian wind' was blowing through those classrooms most in tune with the times.[22] Second, in a related trend, the führer-principle was emphasized in staffing relationships, with headteachers brought in from outside a school and teachers having little input into the decision making, since they were expected to obey their führer in all things. Third, there was an undermining of the teaching profession and the value of education. This may seem to contradict the importance that was placed on indoctrination within schools in the Third Reich. But in fact, Nazi policies actually undermined teachers and left them open to denunciation as we have seen; in addition there was a noticeable degree of contempt shown towards teachers from a government that subordinated all intellectual activity and endeavour to the crude demands of a militaristic state. As a result many teachers left the profession and entry numbers onto teacher training courses fell sharply. By the end of the 1930s the numbers of new teachers entering the profession reached only 31 per cent of the staffing needs of German schools. As a result class sizes went up. Fourth, educational standards declined. Students in the Hitler Youth were allowed to miss school in order to attend Nazi events and camps, with a predictable impact on their education. The presence of these Nazi young people further undermined teachers and threatened standards in the classroom. Confident of their role within the new Germany, they challenged teachers and teaching methods that did not meet with their ideological standards. They, like the Nazi ideology, regarded preparation for war as more important than sitting and passing examinations in a traditional school setting.

These effects spread across the German school system, which, thanks to the administrative changes of the 1930s, was more unified and centralized than it had been under the Weimar Republic. The same educational philosophy was also introduced to Austria after its incorporation into the Reich in March 1938. In Austria, in June 1940, the last legal remnant of an independent state ended when the Education Ministry was finally subsumed within the Reich government structure. By this time the main features of German schools were already apparent: race laws, Hitler's portrait in classrooms, the Hitler salute, Nazi content in the curriculum and lessons in 'German handwriting'.[23]

In contrast with the school system, the Nazi state had less control over the universities. Rust's Reich Education Ministry found it harder to impose itself on the more independent universities than it did on schools. In addition, the appointment of lecturers became something of a turf war between the Reich Education Ministry, the university administrators and the Nazi Students' League. By the start of the Second World War, 51 per cent of male and 71 per cent of female students had joined this last organization. In addition to these groups having an input into appointments, it was not unusual for local party bosses to intervene as well and in this complex in-fighting it was harder to impose a coherent policy overall. As late as 1938, the SD (the SS Security Service) reported on the confused situation regarding the administration of higher education and the frictions between different authorities. Between 1933 and 1934, the SA too took a leading role in attempting to 'bring into line' German universities. Many students joined the SA as a sign of allegiance to the new Germany. This strategy was thrown into disarray after the destruction of the SA leadership in 1934 and from this point onwards the SA were forced off campus and the central party organization took over the running of the Nazi Students' League. As part of this increasing interference from the party, new courses in race studies and German folklore were established at a large number of German universities during the 1930s. Jewish staff were dismissed and it was this anti-Semitism that caused Albert Einstein to renounce his German citizenship in 1933 and move to the USA. Prior to this the police had raided his country house and seized control of his bank account; members of the SA had several times raided his Berlin apartment.[24]

Under the Third Reich, German universities experienced problems similar to those caused to schools by government policy. In fact, student numbers dropped by some 60 per cent between 1931 and 1939. This collapse was particularly apparent in law and the humanities subjects. In many ways this was a direct result of Nazi activities. Attacks on the civil service as being lacking in radical zeal and on the teaching profession made these jobs far less appealing than under the Weimar

Republic. This impacted on the intake into those subjects that had traditionally provided most members of these professions. The general Nazi contempt for intellectuals, seen clearly in Hitler's public comments, depressed public regard for higher learning as a way of gaining advancement within the Third Reich. In contrast, the expansion of the armed forces during the 1930s made that a much more appealing career path both in terms of available jobs and social prestige. However, the intake for medicine increased, almost certainly as a result of the high regard of the Nazi administration for matters of 'racial hygiene' and eugenics. On the other hand, Nazi discouragement of women entering higher education led to a reduction in the number of female medical students, from just over 20 per cent in 1933, to just under 16 per cent in 1939. This decline was only reversed after the start of the Second World War when the drafting of young men caused a shortage of medical students.[25] This same discouragement of female students also affected the humanities. From 1934, the number of new female university students was fixed at no more than 10 per cent of that of men. From 1937, the female path to higher education was made even more difficult when female grammar schools were abolished. This was part of the Nazi aim of restricting women to domestic roles (see Chapter 12). Between Hitler coming to power in January 1933 and the outbreak of war in September 1939, the overall number of female students fell from about 16 to 11 per cent of those in higher education.

These factors aggravated relationships between the government and students. To this was added a demand for continued periods of labour service, including, in 1939, demands by the SS that students should assist in bringing in the harvest. This was so unpopular that the Gestapo was called in to deal with protests. These demands impinged enormously on study time[26] as well as on student freedoms.

Nevertheless, despite these factors there was still a high level of compliance with Nazi ideology amongst those at university in the 1930s. After the initial dismissal of about 15 per cent of university staff in 1932–4 (about a third of these on grounds of race), very few university lecturers were actually purged for anti-Nazi beliefs and the content of most courses continued as before, with perhaps a veneer of Nazi ideology. Few university staff members joined the professional body set up for them but much of the nationalist outlook of the Nazi state was shared by many at the German universities, both students and lecturers. At Freiburg University in 1933, the famous philosopher Martin Heidegger approvingly declared the Führer to be the new dominating force in German society and law. That same year, 700 university professors signed a declaration of support for the new government. The Nazi views on the need for German national revival and the right of Germany to dominate Eastern Europe were shared by many intellectuals. That they were not necessarily members of the Nazi Party did not mean that they disagreed with the world outlook of the party. In 1938, the German Central Institute of Education issued the following guidelines for the teaching of history in schools, but its tone would have been appreciated by many in higher education too: 'The German nation in its essence and greatness, in its fateful struggle for internal and external identity is the subject of the teaching of history.'[27]

In this then lies the crucial issue with regard to the Nazis and education. Despite all the reluctant students, teachers and lecturers, despite the resentment at Nazi demands and mismanagement – despite all these factors, there were in reality very few heroically protesting students or staff (such as the White Rose movement at Munich University, 1942–3). Most, as in German society as a whole in the 1930s, were broadly sympathetic with many aspects of the outlook of the new Germany, with its unifying themes and its expansionist aims. This made Nazi integration with education all the easier to achieve. This broad base of support, or acquiescence within education allowed many to look away from the brutality of Nazism and to focus instead on what was perceived as the process of national regeneration that the Nazis were bringing. In this, as in many aspects of life in the Third Reich, the willingness of ordinary people to compromise and come to terms with the new realities (though it might be denied later) was alarming.

12

THE NAZI IMPACT ON SOCIETY: WOMEN IN THE THIRD REICH

In 2006, a group of German citizens met at Wernigerode, south-east of Hannover, and the site of a *Lebensborn* ('well of life') birth clinic in the Third Reich. Together they shared experiences of being children of one of Nazi Germany's racial programmes. As one sixty-three–year-old discovered, his father had not been a member of the German military killed in Croatia but actually an SS major-general and his mother had given birth illegitimately since her SS lover was already married with three children. Another had discovered that her father had also been a married SS officer, who had got her secretary mother pregnant. Both babies had been born in an official Nazi maternity home and under the shadow of the Lebensborn programme.[1]

The SS organization Lebensborn was established in 1935 under the chairmanship of Himmler, head of the SS. Its aim was to increase the birth rate amongst those classified as racially acceptable. But how to increase the numbers of Aryan babies? A number of strategies were employed. The first was to persuade unmarried German women who found them-selves pregnant to give birth to their babies. Pregnant women could give birth in Lebensborn maternity homes, could register the birth in secret and the Lebensborn organization would arrange adoptions. In short, they provided mother- and child-care for racially selected people. It has sometimes been suggested that they acted as 'stud farms' to increase the numbers of Aryan children, but this was not the case. The first of these maternity homes opened in Bavaria in 1936. By December 1938, 653 mothers had used the Lebensborn mater- nity homes where the infant mortality rate – at 3 per cent – was half the German national average.[2] Himmler took a close interest in the health of these mothers and children, encouraging consumption of a healthy diet of porridge and wholemeal bread.[3] According to Lebensborn statistics, 71 per cent of those having their first baby were unmarried but only 26 per cent of those having their second child.[4] This suggests that the existence of the organization did not actually encour- age a lifestyle of promiscuity.

A mother was free to leave with her baby, or to keep it at the home for one year. After that time, if the baby was not removed by the mother, SS foster families were found. In most cases the full legal guardianship of the children lay with the Lebensborn organization. But adoption proved difficult. Many SS families were reluctant to adopt Lebensborn children since there was still a social stigma to their being born outside marriage. And there was a view held by some Nazi racial experts that amongst illegitimate children were found greater numbers of those clas- sified as 'hereditarily unfit'. Many unwanted children therefore ended up in foster homes, which were soon overcrowded.[5]

With the outbreak of war the organization also engaged in the kidnapping of children from occupied areas (for example, Poland) who were classified as being of 'Aryan appearance'. In Western Europe it also sought to have responsibility for so-called 'war children' resulting from relationships between local women (so long as they were racially acceptable) and occupying soldiers. Those nations deemed particularly accept- able were the Danish, Dutch and Norwegians. For reasons of competition over jurisdiction with other Nazi agencies (mostly in the Netherlands) and with local authorities (mostly in Denmark and Belgium), it was largely in Norway that the organization made most progress.[6]

The Nazi view of women

The Weimar Republic had a considerable impact on the rights of German women. Starting with the National Assembly election of January 1919, all women over the age of twenty had the right to vote. From this point onwards, women constituted the majority of German voters. As a result, 'German political culture was forever changed'.[7] German women could no longer be politically ignored and this was a situation inherited by the Nazis and engaged with as they sought to win the loyalty of women both before and after Hitler came to power in 1933. What is most striking is that the Nazi appeal to women voters went hand-in-hand with an intention to undo all of the moves towards gender equality that had been achieved under the Weimar Republic. Not all women voters may have realized the implications of Nazi policy, whilst others (facing a situation of collapsing public order and the difficulties of feeding their families in a time of social stress) may have felt that the priorities of national stability ranked higher. Support for conservative gender politics will have come more easily to those women from more traditional social backgrounds and, certainly, the Nazis gained significant numbers of votes from such areas of German society.

Whilst the Nazis had a very traditional idea of the role of women, they still saw them as extremely important. For the Nazis, the ideal woman should recognize 'matrimony and motherhood as the singular goal of fascist maidenhood'. Indeed, Alfred Rosenberg – one of the party's theoreticians – considered that eventually women would cease to have the right to vote or influence politics, since their primary role lay in the propagation of the Master Race.[8] Hitler commented that the German woman should recognize that her 'world is her husband, her family, her children, and her home'. All education should prepare them for this (see Chapter 11) and those who actively deviated from these norms attracted draconian punishment: prostitutes were imprisoned and forced sterilization was used to control others considered socially deviant. Nazi publications such as the SS journal *Das Schwarze Korps* (*The Black Units*) frowned on the use of jewellery, lipstick, powder, perfume and high-heeled shoes. It also disapproved of short hair and the wearing of trousers. In keeping with this view of women, Hitler kept Eva Braun out of sight. The same tendency was apparent in the Goebbels' marriage. In what was the unofficial 'First Family' of the Reich, Magda Goebbels played a dutifully discreet role although still one in the public eye, unlike the invisible Eva Braun. Clearly, even leading ladies should be seen and not heard.

And yet, as in so many areas, the Nazis were not consistent. One has only to recall Goebbels's affair with the glamorous Czech film actress Lída Baarová to recognize that the 'ideal woman' was often not centre stage in the 1930s. Similarly, film heroines of the Third Reich were as varied as Swedish-born Kristina Soderbaum (who did play the 'typical' modest and selfless maiden in Nazi propaganda films), British-born Lilian Harvey (glamorous star of escapist and at times sensual musicals, whose support for Jewish colleagues cost her a career in Germany) and Swedish Zarah Leander (playing parts of beautiful, independent-minded femmes fatales and whose refusal to closely associate with the regime earned her high-ranking enemies, such as Goebbels). Clearly, there was no single message emanating from the Nazi hierarchy about how a woman should appear. And even the ruthlessly sidelined and hidden Eva Braun continued with habits that Hitler disapproved of, from smoking and wearing make-up to nude sunbathing. Reading cheap novels and watching romantic films, she combined fanatical devotion to Hitler with adherence to personal habits far removed from the Nazi image of the 'ideal woman'; although her acceptance of her subservient public role was more in keeping with this image. When, in the dying days of the Third Reich, this woman – who would momentarily become Frau Hitler – entertained the other doomed inhabitants of the Führer Bunker as they drank, smoked and listened to 1940s pop songs, it was clear that the Nazi programme for women had not achieved all its goals.

The impact of the Third Reich on the lives of German women

Women's lives were affected in a wide variety of ways. Concern at the falling birth rate led to strategies designed to increase the size of German families. Loans were provided to assist married couples with children, which were subsidized by higher tax bills for single people and those married couples without children. This Law for the Encouragement of Marriage provided a loan of 1,000 Reichsmarks for newlyweds. At the birth of one child, 25 per cent of the loan was written off, rising to 50 per cent with two children, and the loan became a gift at the birth of the fourth child. The driving motive of this loan was to encourage women out of work, without them then appearing on the unemployment registers.[9] So great was the drive for children that, in 1938, childlessness was made a suitable ground for divorce, in an amendment to existing legislation.

In 1938, the Cross of Honour of the German Mother (usually called simply the Mother Cross medal) was established to reward those with large families. Its escalating metals reflected the achievements of those rewarded: bronze for four children, silver for six and gold for eight children. For really large families (twelve to fourteen children) there was the Gold Cross with Diamonds. Names for these awards were forwarded to the party by Nazi Blockwardens, who monitored the behaviour and attitudes of their neighbours. These nominations were then scrutinized by representatives of the party and the police. At this stage names of those regarded as unsuitable were sieved out. Those rejected included women who had children with several partners, any families categorized as 'genetically unfit' by 'racial hygiene' criteria (see Chapter 10) or who were in some other way classified as dysfunctional or 'asocial'. A drunken husband would also prove a liability for those hoping to gain the medal, as would a history of family debt and a female inclination towards smoking. The Propaganda Ministry expressed it clearly when it stated: 'The goal is not: "children at any cost", but: "racially worthy, physically and mentally unaffected children of German families".[10] In line with Nazi racial policy, all Jews and Gypsies were ineligible. The first holder of the Mother Cross was sixty-one-year-old Louise Weidenfeller, who was the mother of eight children and therefore was awarded the Mother Cross in gold. It should be noted that anxiety over a falling birth rate was not just a German phenomenon. France too, in this period, provided awards for large families and banned abortion and contraception.

These medals were awarded annually on 12 August (the birthday of Hitler's mother) and on 10 May, which was designated the Day of the German Mother. In fact, Mother's Day (or Mothers' Sunday) had first become a national holiday in the USA in 1914, when the second Sunday in May was so designated. During Weimar, the day became unofficially celebrated in Germany and the event was encouraged by German florists. In Britain, however, Mothering Sunday is a quite separate and much older event, which takes place on the fourth Sunday in Lent and is recorded as far back as the seventeenth century.

The Nazi attitude towards families was, though, ambiguous. On one hand, the banning of abortion and contraception (though the latter was impossible to enforce) was accompanied by support for the traditional family. On the other hand, the drive for an increased birth rate meant that this aim was higher than the protection of legitimacy. Hence the Lebensborn programme to deter abortion amongst those women who became pregnant outside marriage. Indeed, from 1938, the relaxation of divorce laws sought to encourage remarriage with the possibility of children. And the SS was particularly notable for its pursuit of children over legitimacy. In this they were encouraged by their own self-perception as radicals at odds with Christian principles and the teaching of the Church. There was even talk, in 1943, of a future law in which fathers of four children would be instructed to father more children by other women. This never went beyond an SS fantasy but it reveals the bizarre thinking that circulated amongst senior members of that organization. However, under the pressures of the Second World War, family policy did become more radical in other areas. With the massive loss of life on the Eastern Front after 1941, the incentive to increase the birth rate was even greater than in the 1930s. And so, from 1943, abortion became a capital crime in Germany. However, the Nazi obsession with racial purity meant that, even while this drive against abortion was going on, somewhere in the region of 30,000 women underwent abortions (accompanied by forced sterilization) on grounds of so-called racial hygiene, because they were considered unfit to have children.

Since a woman's proper place was in the home there was no sympathy for the working woman, unless she was the peasant wife assisting her husband on the land. As a result, government policy was set against women's employment opportunities. In 1932, Hitler declared his intention of removing 800,000 women from the labour force. To a male audience suffering from the unemployment caused by the depression there were, no doubt, attractions to the promise. In 1934, all married women doctors and civil servants were dismissed from their posts and, from June 1936, no woman could act as a judge. Women were also barred from jury service, since they were considered to lack a sufficiently logical and objective outlook.

From 1933, Hitler appointed Gertrud Scholtz-Klink as the Reich Women's Leader and the head of the Nazi Women's League. Her role was to promote the Nazi view of women. From 1934, she was also given responsibility for policy towards women as it affected the activities of the Labour Front (see Chapter 7). As a result, older members of the Nazi organization for girls – the League of German Girls – were expected to devote a year to farm work or domestic service.

The aim was to encourage these eighteen–year-olds away from professional ambitions and towards marriage or a 'female role' in the job market. During the 1930s, the number of female university graduates fell dramatically and only began to rise again during the Second World War, as young men were called up for military service.

Yet Nazi rhetoric was greater than the ability of the government to drive women out of the workplace. Under the Third Reich, the number of women in the labour force *actually rose* in real terms, from 11.5 million in 1933 (or 36 per cent of the total work force) to 12.8 million in early 1939 (37 per cent of the total work force). If the annexed territories are added, the figure rises to 14.6 million (or a surprising 50 per cent of the total work force). By 1944 – with the demands of war – the figure reached 14.9 million German women (including Austria) working (or 53 per cent of the total civilian labour force and over half of all German women aged between 15 and 60).

Much of this growth in female employment was driven by the expansion of the armaments industries. This is demonstrated by the fact that the number of women industrial workers rose by 28.5 per cent between 1933 and 1936. And it went up by a further 19.2 per cent over the next two years. What is particularly surprising – given Nazi attitudes towards marriage and families – is the fact that many of these new industrial workers were married women and mothers. In 1939, almost a quarter of employed women had children.[11] That this had happened *despite* what the regime wanted to occur, is clear. Although the economy by the late 1930s was facing serious manpower shortages it was with reluctance that the government, in October 1937, finally ended the demand that a woman leave her job in order to benefit from the marriage loan. In the face of this need for workers, the Nazi government 'responded passively'[12] and let the matter drift. As in so many areas of the Third Reich, one policy (the drive to expand armament production) contradicted another (the wish to restrict women to childbearing domesticity). And the end product was that more women went out to work at the end of the Third Reich than at the beginning, despite the intentions of the regime.

There were positive aspects of policy regarding women, which clearly increased their support for the regime. The marriage loan has already been referred to. Then there were generous tax reliefs and family allowances for those with children. Furthermore, pregnant women workers were given six weeks off work, on full pay, before and after a birth – a right found nowhere else in the world in the 1930s. Medical services were also improved for women and, by 1944, five million German women had visited the new Maternity Schools. And double this number had used the services of other advice centres.[13]

Women's fashion in the Third Reich

Nazi propaganda posters presented the 'ideal German woman' in modest peasant clothing and rejecting cosmetics. In reality, the wives of concentration-camp commanders often wore fashionable dresses, sewn by Jewish prisoner seamstresses, and bought American make-up. During the Second World War in Auschwitz there was a sizeable group of prisoners making clothes for the wives of SS officers. Many of the raw materials for this came from the clothes of wealthy Jewish women seized on arrival at the camp and sorted in the section of the camp known as 'Canada'. This tailoring studio was set up as a result of a direct request by the wife of the commandant, Rudolf Höss. Already, an attic in the villa of the Höss family had been converted into a studio where two female prisoners designed and made clothes for them. In the new and larger tailoring studio when work particularly pleased a female guard they might respond with an extra piece of bread for the undernourished woman prisoner responsible. Few workers survived the war. But Frau Höss did and, when she was apprehended by British troops, was found to be in possession of large quantities of hand-tailored clothes, looted from those murdered at Auschwitz.[14]

Even German women who didn't have such connections sewed their clothes using patterns by *Vogue* or chose styles that imitated those of Britain, France and the USA. As Dr Irene Guenther has commented: 'Most women wouldn't have been caught dead in a dirndl dress. It's really clear that they weren't buying into their government's unrelenting propaganda.'[15]

The German fashion industry in Berlin in the 1920s had made more money than the more recognized Paris fashion industry. However, in 1933, the Nazis set up the German Fashion Institute, with the aim of challenging French dominance even more dramatically. Despite this, most German female consumers preferred the French labels. Overall, the Nazis never really systematically followed through from their image of healthy peasant women to a real attempt to organize how women looked. There were efforts in some areas to ban use of lipstick and trousers but these never became accepted policy. Overall, that policy was ambivalent and conflicts arose between those wishing to see the German fashion industry dominate Europe and those wishing to impose a peasant image of Blood and Soil.

It was other policies that eventually impacted on what women wore. The drive for autarky limited supplies from abroad and wartime shortages imposed even tighter restraints. Despite this, women continued to express themselves in ways far removed from the peasant poster girls. And in this they were at least partly assisted by the lack of resolution of the Nazi administration and its inbuilt contradictions. Ursula Schewe – owner of a wartime fashion salon in Berlin, then, after May 1945, providing tailoring services to Soviet officers and then for their wives – would later insist that: 'Fashion is neutral. In fact, fashion has *absolutely nothing* to do with politics.'[16] The peasant poster girls of the Third Reich might have begged to differ, but most German women would probably have agreed with Ursula.

The role of women in the Third Reich
Women opposed aspects of the Third Reich in sufficient numbers to cause the Nazis to open a concentration camp for women at Moringen in October 1933. A second camp was

built at Lichtenburg in 1939 with a third and more famous one being opened in 1940 at Ravensbrück.

Yet, despite these women prisoners, and despite the over-whelmingly masculine nature of the Nazi leadership and machinery of oppression, it must be recognized that huge numbers of German women contributed to the Third Reich at various levels.[17] The female contribution to industrial production, for example, was highly significant. They managed to find wartime advancement despite the earlier push towards hearth and home of the 1930s. And this had happened even before the outbreak of war. In fact, the 52 per cent of German women aged between 15 and 60 in work in 1939 can be contrasted with comparable figures of 45 per cent for Britain and 36 per cent for the USA at this time.[18]

However, the part played by women in Nazi *crimes* has often faded from the German collective memory. Yet women acted in large numbers as nurses under the T4 euthanasia programme; they staffed the Lebensborn maternity homes; they operated as secretaries in the clerical services of the SS and Gestapo; in the 1940s, they bought the possessions of Jews that were sold at government warehouses; women made up a majority of wartime Block Wardens who reported neighbours to the authorities; Dusseldorf Gestapo records refer to female denunciators trying 'to change the power balance of the household by denouncing their husbands as spies or Communists or anti-Nazis'; and 3,200 served as SS concentration-camp guards. In short: 'The cliche of Gold Mother Cross-wearing women having 10 babies and baking bread was a myth. Women could and did advance themselves massively through the Third Reich.'[19] As Dr Herta Oberheuser – who killed children at Ravensbrück concentration camp in order to experiment on their corpses and also conducted medical experiments on other prisoners – later commented: 'Being a woman didn't stop me being a good National Socialist. I think female National Socialists were every bit as valuable as men in keeping what we believed in alive.'[20]

Yet women featured in small numbers in the post-war War Crimes Trials; for example, Dr Oberheuser was the only female defendant in the Nuremberg 'Medical Trial'. This may partly reflect the much greater proportion of men involved in such atrocities but may also have involved something deeper. This is almost certainly an unwillingness to accept that women too played a significant part in the history and horror of the Third Reich. The traditional role of women as carers made this involvement all the more shocking in the aftermath of the Second World War. This coincided with the fact that, in the ultimate collapse of Germany, women had suffered acutely in the final month of disintegration (for example, as victims of mass rapes committed by invading Soviet forces) and, following defeat, there was a collective desire to re-establish some kind of normality based on families and homes after years of social destruction. In this process many German women had clearly become victims and, in the absence of many men, it was women who provided a stable point around which homes and families could once again be built out of the chaos of 1945. Neither of these latter factors seemed to be compatible with charges of active complicity in the criminal workings of the Third Reich. The fact that this involvement also did not square with the 1930s image of the ideal German woman as being focused on hearth and home made it possible for many to hide behind this, as part of a collective process of denial.

In this, of course, they were not alone. Huge numbers of Germans and other nationalities – regardless of gender – sought to distance themselves from Nazi crimes after 1945 and this became part of a process by which responsibility for these crimes became associated mostly with a small group of influential and powerful individuals and ultimately with Hitler. This was a process that allowed many other implicated people to reinvent themselves, post 1945, as uninvolved in the criminality of the Third Reich, or even as its victims. A national example of this could be cited as Austria. In many ways women were the most successful example of this process, in their denial of involvement and in their re-writing of their gender-past. Yet the evidence suggests otherwise. Huge numbers of women voted Nazi (see Chapter 3); many welcomed a new-found sense of order and stability even while chafing at the restrictions placed on them after 1933; others learned to work within the new social order though at times subverting it; a significant number provided enthusiastic support for the regime through women's organizations, and finally played a significant part in the wartime efforts. The reality is that neither gender stood apart from complicity in, or adjusting to, the actions of the Third Reich.

13

THE NAZI IMPACT ON SOCIETY: THE CHRISTIAN CHURCH

First they came for the communists, and I did not speak out –
because I was not a communist;
Then they came for the trade unionists, and I did not speak out
– because I was not a trade unionist;
Then they came for the Jews, and I did not speak out – because
I was not a Jew;
Then they came for me – and there was no one left to speak out.

In this way, on 6 January 1946, Pastor Martin Niemöller (1892–1984) looked back on his experience of the Third Reich. There are several versions of this famous statement but this is perhaps the best known and, evidence suggests, the original version.

Niemöller served in the German navy during the First World War and eventually rose to be the commander of the submarine U-67. In this position he won the coveted Iron Cross First Class and, at the end of the war, resigned his commission since he refused to serve under the republican government of Weimar. After studying theology he was ordained in 1924 and became a pastor in the Protestant Lutheran Church. As a keen nationalist, Niemöller was a member of the Freikorps units (see Chapter 1) even while he was studying theology. By 1931, Niemöller had become the pastor of a large church in Dahlem, which was a well-to-do suburb of Berlin.

Along with many other Germans, he looked back with nostalgia to the Germany of the Kaiser, opposed the Weimar Republic and was sympathetic to the rising Nazi movement. As an anti-communist he hoped that the Nazis, under Hitler, would promote unity and a national revival. However, this support rapidly turned to disillusionment. He opposed the so-called 'Aryan paragraph', which the Nazis introduced into numerous laws, because he asserted that banning Jews from membership of groups, or employment, clashed with Christian principles. However, Niemöller's defence of Jewish converts to Christianity did not at first lead him to a thorough defence of Jews. In 1935, he repeated the belief – current amongst many Church writers since the Middle Ages – that the Jews were under the punishment of God for the crucifixion of Jesus. That (in effect) this medieval charge of 'Christ-killers' should be voiced by as prominent an opponent of Hitler as Niemöller is an indication of how deeply this antipathy towards Jews ran in many mainstream European churches and reminds us why many regard Niemöller as representing the flawed nature of much of the German opposition to Nazism. In short – whilst protesting at Nazi brutality – many in opposition had an alarming degree of sympathy towards some features of the Nazi worldview. This is not surprising since it was rooted in many attitudes and values of traditional German society (and these strands of thought were not limited to Germany). Revealingly, when Niemöller met Hitler, in 1932, he had been consoled by the promise that there would be no anti-Semitic pogroms, or ghettos, in Germany – only legal restrictions regarding the Jews. That the promise of restrictions caused him few concerns reveals how deeply ingrained anti-Semitic preju-dices were in many Germans.[1]

However, in protest at the attempted Nazification of the Protestant Church, Niemöller, along with other leading theologians such as Karl Barth and Dietrich Bonhoeffer, founded the 'Confessing Church'. Within this new grouping there were those – such as Pastor Hermann Maas – whose opposition to all forms of anti-Semitism contrasted with the less clear-cut opposition voiced by Niemöller.

Despite this, Niemöller increasingly attracted the anger of the Nazi leadership as he opposed Nazi attempts to control the churches and to subvert Christian beliefs. His sermons became increasingly pointed in their attacks on the values of the Third Reich.[2] In 1937, he was arrested and he was brought to court in 1938. As a result, he was fined and imprisoned for seven months. In fact, his time in prison awaiting trial had lasted longer than the actual sentence. Consequently, the court released him. This in itself is an insight into how even a dictatorship as ruthless as the Third Reich could not always predictably choreograph the courts as late as 1938. However, this was no consolation for Niemöller. His arrest by the Gestapo on leaving the court made it clear that, however disorganized Nazi repression might some- times be, it was always vindictive and rarely evaded for long. From 1938, until his liberation by US forces in May 1945, Niemöller would remain in prison: first at Sachsenhausen, then at Dachau concentration camps. In his last month of imprison- ment he was moved to the Tyrol along with a number of other high-ranking prisoners. However, others in the Confessing Church did not survive the war. On 9 April 1945 (just under a month before Niemöller was liberated), Bonhoeffer was hanged at Flossenbürg concentration camp. In Niemöller's suffering and in Bonhoeffer's matryrdom, the German churches had gone some way towards making atonement for their failure to comprehensively confront Nazism for what it was: the enemy of Christian beliefs and values.[3]

The Nazis and the Christian Church

Nazism was in its nature utterly incompatible with New Testament Christianity. In addition to core beliefs in love and forgiveness – which the Nazis found weak – was its Jewish heritage. Rooted in the Old Testament and in Judaism, the Church puts its faith in a Jewish Messiah, Jesus, and reveres the gospels and letters written by the Jewish followers of Christ. Furthermore, it holds that faith in Christ transcends all barriers of ethnicity and class: ideas that were utterly alien to the ideology of the Nazis. Given this, the obvious questions immediately present themselves: why were so many German Christians supportive of the Nazis in their rise to power?; and why were so few involved in active opposition once the realities of the Third Reich became apparent?[4]

The answers are complex but can perhaps be reduced to three key factors: the particular history of the German churches; the medieval legacy of antagonism towards Judaism; and the European context of the 1920s and 1930s.

One of the features of the German churches was a close alliance between Church and state. This had emerged out of the German Reformation of the sixteenth century and had been strengthened in the Prussian takeover of Germany in the late nineteenth century. As a result, German Protestantism lacked political radicalism and its support for government had become subservience. This was, of course, not a situation unique to Germany. But it did leave the Church peculiarly open to being influenced by Prussian-style nationalism, German-centredness and an unwillingness to challenge the state.

For Catholics, fairly recent history had been different but had also played a part in forming attitudes, which affected strategies in the 1930s. From 1871 to 1877, the Catholic Church in the newly formed German Empire (united under Prussian leadership in 1871) had found itself engaged in the so-called *Kulturkampf* (culture struggle) with the government, under Chancellor Bismarck. This involved an apparently unlikely coalition of the government, liberals and conservatives pursuing a series of policies that included: a desire to see Protestantism dominant in Germany (popular amongst Prussian conservatives), efforts to ensure that intellectual life was free from Catholic clerical influence (popular amongst liberals) and the establishment of a German community that was free from the external influence of the Pope (popular amongst members of the Prussian-dominated government). Whilst this conflict had calmed down by the 1880s, it left a legacy that would influence the 1930s. Realizing the damage that could occur through a reopening of conflict with the state, German Catholics were keen to reach an understanding with the Nazi regime that would safeguard the Catholic Church and prevent an open clash. However, there were many areas of Catholic culture in Germany that were likely to become areas of friction with the Nazis. For a start, the Catholic Church had supported and been represented through the Centre Party. This was dissolved in 1933 but the Nazis realized that there was a heritage of Catholic political activity that they were determined would not reappear. In addition, there were a whole series of Catholic community and youth organizations; many of these had been developed since the Kulturkampf in order to defend Catholic values. The Nazis regarded these as competitors, since it had its own agenda for dominating Germany. As a result, the Catholic Church in the 1930s was both keen to avoid conflict and almost inevitably on a collision course with the Third Reich whatever concessions it offered.

With regard to the Jewish community, the German churches suffered from the almost casual racism that had infiltrated much of the intellectual thought-life of Europe from the Middle Ages onwards. This dark heritage of scapegoating Jews for social problems and treating them as 'alien others' (no matter the reality of their integration into German society) meant that Jews were not regarded by many European Christians as a closely related religious group. Indeed, they had been condemned as 'Christ-killers' throughout the Middle Ages and the Jewish heritage of Christianity had largely been erased from the understanding of many members of the Church. When Goebbels sniped at the Swedish actress Zarah Leander that she had a Jewish name (Zarah/Sarah), she replied that it had clearly escaped the Propaganda Minister's attention that the name 'Joseph' was first recorded in the Old Testament. Clearly, it had not occurred to the fanatical Nazi that he carried a Jewish name.

Finally, the perceived threat from communism, in the period after 1917, led many Church members to fear it (and secularism) more than any other political ideology. Given the persecution of Christians in the newly formed USSR and the blatantly atheistic ideology of the Soviet government, it seemed that the main threat to Christianity came from this direction, rather than from Nazism. This assessment was encouraged by the way in which the Nazis (who in reality had no adherence to Christian principles whatsoever) referred to themselves as defending Christian civilization and to the Führer as being sent by God. For those Church members eager to overlook the unpleasant features of Nazism, these words gave them assurances that Christianity would not be threatened. Some Church members went even further and genuinely believed that the 'revival' in German national life promised by the Nazis would include Christian values and the safeguarding of the life of the Church. This would prove to be wishful thinking, which ignored the evidence so clearly visible in the Nazi Party and its leadership.

Conflict

The German Protestant community – numbering 40 million and making up two thirds of the German population – had provided a great many of those who had voted Nazi in the years leading to Hitler's appointment as Chancellor.

In the early days of Nazi rule, the new government harnessed support by actions that seemed to signal its alliance with this section of the population. The 450th anniversary of Martin Luther's birthday in 1933 was accompanied by massive celebrations. In addition, the new regime sought to reassure Protestants and the old Prussian traditionalists by the so-called 'Day of Potsdam' in March 1933. Since the Reichstag Fire of February 1933 (see Chapter 4) had deprived the German parliament of a place in which to hold its inaugural meeting, an alternative venue was chosen in the Garrison Church at Potsdam. Here were buried the Prussian kings Frederick William I and Frederick II and it was to this traditional centre of Prussian royalty that Chancellor Hitler and President Hindenburg came. Hitler was in civilian clothes, the black, white, red of pre-Weimar flags were much in view and the day started with traditional religious ceremonies. The Protestant service took place in the Church of Saint Nicholas and a Catholic Mass took place in the parish church. It was choreographed to reassure.

But already cracks were beginning to appear in this facade. Hitler and Goebbels, both nominally Catholic, did not attend the Mass because Catholic bishops were still maintaining a ban on Nazi Party membership.

Within the Protestant churches though, things looked more hopeful for the Nazis. Since 1932, a group of Nazi sympathisers amongst the clergy – calling themselves the 'German Christians' – sought to bring the Church into line with Nazi ideology. In the early summer of 1933, this led to the establishment of a 'Reich Church' to replace the regional churches that had made up the old Evangelical Church of the old-Prussian Union (as the German Protestant Church was called). Supported by Hitler and given massive propaganda support by Goebbels, its leader as Reich Bishop was Ludwig Müller, a Nazi. Under his leadership crude anti-Semitic strategies were imposed on the Protestant Church. Whilst he had achieved his dominant position through behind-the-scenes politicking and threats, there was an alarming level of support for this Nazification of the Church from those living on the borders of the Reich (where ethnic tensions over disputed frontiers were high) and amongst less well-educated pastors. Pastors who were members of the 'German Christians' were known to preach in SA and SS uniforms. Some called for the abandonment of the Jewish Old Testament and the writings of 'the Rabbi Paul'. There was talk of substituting the swastika for the Cross and Jesus was spoken of as an 'Aryan hero' and his Jewish origins ignored.[5]

By September 1933, opposition to these activities was growing. In that month, Niemöller and Bonhoeffer led a group that set up the 'Pastors' Emergency League', as a rallying point for those clergy who opposed the racially motivated ideas of the 'German Christians'. Unlike the latter, the former group, which would, from 1934, be called the 'Confessing Church', drew a greater proportion of its membership from better-educated pastors and it had a much larger number of women in its ranks. The Confessing Church refused to expel Jewish converts and insisted that its basis for faith lay solely in the Bible, which the Nazis had attempted to edit, attack and undermine. By the end of 1934, the Nazi hopes of creating one unified – and Nazified – Reich Church were in ruins. Müller, who had failed in this attempt to bring the Protestant Church into line, eventually committed suicide in July 1945 in the wreckage of the Third Reich that he had helped to build.

University theology departments soon mirrored the splits within the Church. At the University of Bonn, the leading theologian, Karl Barth, was a supporter of the Confessing Church and was opposed by the dean, who was a 'German Christian'. Soon, over two thirds of the lecturers had been dismissed or transferred. At Munich University, the Nazi authorities closed down the theology faculty entirely.

In the face of this opposition, the Nazi authorities cracked down on dissent. Pastors who criticized the regime were banned from preaching or had their pay stopped. Others were arrested and, by 1937, some 700 were in prison, including Niemöller. In prison, he finally rejected his earlier anti-Semitic opinions. Frequently beaten by his guards, he would remain in prison until the end of the Second World War. The Protestant Church he left behind remained divided. A minority continued to back the discredited Reich Church with its enthusiastic Nazis; a minority supported the increasingly beleaguered Confessing Church; most kept silent. All too often Church leaders were led by German public opinion rather than leading it. In the late 1930s, Bishop Meiser, head of the Bavarian

Protestant Church, still offered public prayers thanking God for Hitler.

The 20 million Germans in the Catholic Church found that they, too, were under increasing pressure in the 1930s. The Nazis faced this Church with particular ambiguity. On one hand they opposed its allegiance to an internationally organized community that looked outside Germany for leadership; on the other hand they admired its organization, influence and discipline. A number of leading Nazis came from a Catholic background. These included Hitler, Goebbels and Heydrich – the head of the SS Security Service (the SD). All had become determinedly anti-Christian. The Nazis particularly resented the fact that – unlike the Protestants – German Catholics had actively opposed the Nazis in their rise to power. The Catholic community had solidly voted for the Centre Party until its dissolution in 1933, had sat through sermons condemning the Nazis and in many areas had been openly told that no Catholic could join the Nazi Party. But once the Nazi Party was in power, what would be the stance of the Catholic Church?

To start with, it made concessions clearly intended to defend the integrity of the Catholic Church by surrendering certain areas of activity. So, in 1933, the Centre Party was wound up and Catholic trade unions were dissolved. In July 1933, Pope Pius XI concluded a Concordat with the Nazi state. In return for the Catholic Church's agreement to keep out of political activity, the Nazi government agreed to respect the various Catholic organizations in Germany. Like every other institution that sought to reach an understanding with Hitler, the leadership of the Catholic Church soon discovered the worthlessness of these assurances.

Even before the summer of 1933 was over, Catholic newspapers were being shut down and the activities of Catholic organizations were being restricted. Although alarmed, the Church hierarchy did not protest, in the hope that statements of obedience would serve to deflect the Nazis from these attacks. It was a vain hope. There were, though, public criticisms voiced of the regime's persecution of non-Aryan Catholics. However – as with many in the Protestant community – this did not extend to a defence of Jews unless they had converted to Christianity. During 1934, increasing pressure was put on Catholic young people to join the Hitler Youth and violent attacks were mounted on them by Hitler Youth members.

All of this was starting to resemble the 'Culture Struggle' under Bismarck. Increasingly, radical Nazis began to speak of a 'Church Struggle' in both their conflicts with sections of the Protestant Church and particularly with regard to the Catholic Church. On the Nazi side these radicals looked to the writings of the anti-Christian Alfred Rosenberg. In his *The Myth of the Twentieth Century* and in a number of other books, he rejected central beliefs of Christianity such as the immortality of the soul and Christ's power to save human beings from their sins and he accused Catholicism of being a Jewish invention. Given the long, sad history of anti-Semitism within European Catholicism, this was a typical piece of Nazi fiction. By 1935, this had turned into a public dispute between Rosenberg on one side and Clemens von Galen, Bishop of Münster, on the other. At the same time as condemning Rosenberg, Galen defended the rights of Catholic schools to carry out religious instruction. Galen was too high profile to arrest and he was to continue his protests against Nazi activities. In 1941, he condemned the euthanasia of the T4 Programme, forced sterilization, Gestapo terror and the concentration camps. He also protested at the closure of Catholic churches and monasteries. He survived because the Nazi leadership considered that arresting him would have a seriously negative effect on support for the regime in Catholic areas; action was postponed until the end of the war. But Galen outlived the Third Reich and eventually died in 1946, from an infected appendix. In October 2005, his official beatification – a stage on the possible route to canonization – was declared by a German pope, Benedict XVI, who in 1941 had himself been forced to join the Hitler Youth and whose cousin (a teenager with Down's syndrome) had been murdered under the T4 Programme.

The activities of Bishop Galen reveal just how sharp the conflict between the Catholic Church and the Third Reich could be and how Nazi atrocities could be confronted. And yet Galen never publicly condemned the deportation and murder of the Jews.[6]

By late 1936, the so-called 'Church Struggle' in Catholic areas, with its attacks on Church schools and harassment of priests, combined with discontent at low wages, shortages and rising costs of consumer goods to make for a noticeably cool relationship with the government. But none of this was sufficient to cause any significant problems to the regime and none developed into anything that could be described as political opposition.[7] Indeed, after a long meeting with Hitler in November 1936, the Catholic Archbishop of Munich-Freising, Cardinal Faulhaber, left convinced that Hitler 'undoubtedly lives in belief in God' and 'recognizes Christianity as the builder of Western culture'. And this was at a time when conflict with the church was escalating.

In February 1937, Hitler instructed senior Nazis to tone down their anti-Christian rhetoric; it was not convenient with the looming possibility of a major war. But despite this, the conflict increased because ordinary Nazis and local leaders could not be controlled. Even senior Nazis such as Gauleiter of Upper Bavaria Adolf Wagner wanted to keep the conflict going. Nationally, the Nazi-dominated media in 1937 carried lurid accounts of sexual crimes supposedly carried out by members of Catholic religious orders. And this was organized by no less important a Nazi leader than Goebbels. Such anti-Christian Nazis were encouraged by the attitude expressed by Hitler. At the same time as urging a more discreet handling of the Church issue – for short-term political reasons – he was also telling leading party leaders that the Christian faith was 'ripe for destruction' and that his long-term aim was the destruction of the German clergy. To Nazis – imbued with the strategy of working towards the Führer – this was more than sufficient to be interpreted as a 'green light'. As he gave this encouragement, Hitler made it clear how this would fit into his overall grand strategy: by 1943 at the latest he expected a 'great world showdown' and by 1952 he expected to have brought an end to the religious arrangements that had characterized Germany since the Peace of Westphalia had ended the Thirty Years War in 1648.[8] Goebbels, though, was careful to distance Hitler from the potentially explosive sexual scandals being aimed at the Franciscans. As with many areas of Nazi policy, Hitler kept (or was kept by others) at a discreet distance from strategies that ran the risk of embarrassment, failure or that were controversially radical even within the context of the Third Reich.

The conflict was very real. In 1937, the last non-Nazi member of the cabinet resigned after demanding that Hitler stop attacking the Church and refusing the gold party badge the Führer was awarding him. Catholic priests in some areas refused absolution to those who joined the Hitler Youth. In Oldenburg, faced with huge opposition, the party authorities were forced to back down on a policy of removing crucifixes from public buildings. In March 1937, the Papal Encyclical – entitled 'With burning sorrow' – was read in Catholic churches, condemning the Nazi breaking of the Concordat. Despite this protest, about 33 per cent of Catholic priests experienced some form of state harassment by 1945 and, by 1939, all Church schools had been either taken over by the state or shut. But with the outbreak of war the campaign against Christianity became muted by the need to promote national unity.

The struggle with one religious group, though, did not end with the start of the war. Although not part of the historic Christian Church in Germany and with doctrinal differences that further distanced it from orthodox Christianity, the Jehovah's Witnesses suffered a level of persecution out of proportion to their size. This was because they refused oaths of loyalty to the state, would not give the 'Heil Hitler' salute and refused to serve in the armed forces. They were unique amongst the German religious groups in their total opposition to the

Third Reich. By 1945, somewhere in the region of 10,000 (of the total membership in Germany of about 30,000) had been imprisoned and 950 died in the concentration camps.[9]

Had the Nazis won the war, the struggle with the Church would undoubtedly have been renewed. Their concept of what was intended to replace it was unclear. For some Nazi leaders there would remain a form of Christianity, but unrecognizable as it would be moulded in line with Nazi ideology.[10] For others, the party itself had already become a semi-religious faith.[11] The most dedicated Nazis wished for a return to a semi-pagan set of rituals and beliefs picked out of the Germanic pagan past. The SS provided a black-uniformed 'religious order', who regarded themselves as Nazi crusaders and members of a 'Military Order of Nordic Men', engaged in holy war against enemies of Nazism.[12] In fact, it was the Nazis who coined the term 'neo-paganism', although Himmler was always more of an enthusiast than Hitler.[13] Whilst this neo-paganism had a following within the party it did not receive official encouragement from the state.[14] However, it is likely that it would have been more actively pursued in the aftermath of a failure to successfully dominate the German Church. Clearly, those members of the Church who, in 1933, had hoped for some kind of working relationship with the Third Reich had been in a state of denial regarding the nature of the new regime.

THE NAZI IMPACT ON SOCIETY: THE CONTROL OF IDEAS

The fate of Mickey Mouse under the Third Reich offers a bizarre insight into the impact of Nazi policies relating to the media and the control of ideas. It is often stated that Hitler hated the most famous mouse in the world and ordered the Disney films featuring him and other cartoon characters to be banned. The Nazis accused Walt Disney himself of having Jewish ancestry and feared that his innocent-seeming cartoons threatened Germans with being 'infected by undesirable cultural influences'.[1] Even more striking is the interpretation that Mickey Mouse, in a number of ways, could be seen as positively symbolizing the Jewish 'outsider' overcoming adversity and that, consequently, Hitler loathed the portrayal of the mouse as clean and harmless since his propaganda machine was focused on representing Jews as dirty vermin. As such, this positive image seemed designed to undermine Nazi racial stereotypes that were being employed in Germany to attack Jews. As a consequence: 'In Hitler's twisted mind, Disney employed Mickey as a means of countering all the anti-Semitic prejudices he – Hitler – had set out to further entrench.'[2] As such, Mickey Mouse, it has been claimed, was declared 'an enemy of the state' in 1936[3] and further, it has been stated, was banned as 'a decadent rat'.[4]

When, between 1980 and 1991, Art Spiegelman used the graphic novel form to recount how his own father had survived the Nazi genocide as a Polish Jew, he represented the Jewish victims of Nazism very positively as innocent mice assaulted by Nazis represented as cats. Its title *Maus: A Survivor's Tale* encapsulated this image (the German for 'mouse' being *'maus'*). In 1992, *Maus* won a Pulitzer Prize Special Award. Art Spiegelman himself has explained that his depiction of Jews as mice was a deliberate reaction to the Nazi portrayal of them as vermin. It was also influenced by Hitler's reported hatred of Mickey Mouse as being part of 'a Jewish art-form'.[5]

However, as recent study has revealed, Disney characters were actually extremely popular in Nazi Germany, as across the world.[6] In 1937 (a year after the alleged banning of Mickey Mouse in Germany), Goebbels gave Hitler a Christmas present of no less than 18 Mickey Mouse films[7] and Hitler was reportedly 'delighted'.[8] Despite the disapproval of some Nazis, neither Mickey Mouse nor any other Disney character faced being banned by the censors in Germany in the 1930s. This was because the films were so massively popular. The only exception to this was the banning of the film *The Mad Doctor* (released in 1933), which featured an attempt to cross the dog Pluto with a chicken and may have been considered a sideswipe at Nazi eugenics. In fact, *The Three Little Pigs* (not, of course, a Mickey Mouse film) was well received by Nazi censors because they interpreted the wolf – when in the guise of a travelling brush salesman, wearing a false nose – as representing a Jewish character, of the type frequently seen threatening Aryans in German films and picture books. The scene was later removed by Disney.[9]

The banning of *The Mad Doctor*, which featured Mickey, may have given rise to the oft-quoted statement that the Nazis banned him. British censors also briefly banned this short film, thinking it would frighten young children. In fact, it was Nazi financial policies applied to the film industry that caused the most problems for Disney. From 1934 onwards, import duties on films were quadrupled and strict controls on exporting currency from Germany made it almost impossible for US companies to make money out of films shown there. As a consequence, Universal and Warner Brothers ended their operations in Germany and, by 1937, the end of Disney's contract with UFA (the principal German film studio), plus the collapse of one of their German distributors, caused massive problems for the distribution of Disney films. Hitler was one of the few Germans able to enjoy Mickey Mouse that Christmas. By 1939, few Disney cartoons were being shown in the Third Reich.[10]

The fate of Mickey Mouse raises a number of questions about the Nazi control of ideas. What was an acceptable way to express art in the Third Reich? What would be encouraged, what tolerated and what obliterated? How would a dictatorship strike a balance between its own propaganda aims and the wishes of audiences and readers? What foreign influences would be banned, and which allowed? And what was the best way to manipulate art and culture: direct propaganda, or more subliminal methods?

What is clear is that the Nazi control of ideas was successful in many areas. After all, a monopoly on the transmission of information could not fail to have an impact. A claim by a captured German soldier in Normandy to the American R. R. Hughart (of the 82nd Airborne Division), revealed how a culture of relentless propaganda could have its effect:

'There isn't much left of New York any more, is there?'
'What do you mean?'
'Well,' he said, 'you know it's been bombed by the Luftwaffe.'[11]

The early impact of the Nazis on the arts and media
The intention of 'bringing Germany into line' and 'coordinating' German society so it resembled the Nazi view of life extended into all areas of the arts and the media. All ideas and

methods of communication had to be brought into line with Nazi values, or be destroyed. Jewish musical conductors and non-Jewish ones associated with music of which the Nazis disapproved found their concerts disrupted by the SA and pressure brought to bear on their employers to dismiss them. In this way, Bruno Walter, the Jewish conductor of the Leipzig Gewandhaus Orchestra, and Hanns Eisler, identified as a left-wing composer, were driven from their jobs. They were only two of hundreds who found that the Nazi accession to power in 1933 meant the end of their careers in Germany.

The 'coordination' of the arts and media was overseen by Joseph Goebbels. On 13 March 1933, a special decree set up the Reich Ministry for Popular Enlightenment and Propaganda, with Goebbels as its head. He had earlier impressed Hitler with his propaganda work as Gauleiter of Berlin. Goebbels's new ministry would be responsible for making sure that theatre, film, literature, the arts, the press and broadcasting reflected the Nazi view of the world and Nazi values. It would also influence education, although this was run by a separate ministry with its own agenda for forcing education into the appropriate mould. Goebbels was also responsible for the government's public relations generally and this included the relationship with the foreign press.[12]

Goebbels's ministry was staffed by young, well-educated Nazis who were committed to the transformation of Germany. Together they mounted a ferocious attack on what they called 'cultural Bolshevism'. This included the removal of Jews from all areas of cultural life and the destruction of modern experimental forms of artistic work such as abstract art and atonal music, which the Nazis regarded as 'un-German'. In time it extended into all areas of artistic life. Those designated as 'un-German' composers, such as Mendelssohn, were banned and attempts were made to ban jazz, which was condemned as 'nigger music' by the Nazis. Whilst attempts to outlaw the saxophone (because it was associated with jazz) failed, and attempts to ban jazz itself failed to eliminate it, the Nazi persecution was more successful in many other areas.

It resulted in a situation where there was no longer an independent press and only officially approved German forms of culture were free from brutal attacks. Writers and artists condemned by the Nazis found their plays, pictures and books banned and burnt and, those who could, left Germany. These included such famous names as the playwright Bertolt Brecht, the novelists Erich Maria Remarque (author of *All Quiet on the Western Front*) and Thomas Mann (a winner of the Nobel Prize in Literature) and painters such as Paul Klee. Around 2,000 people working in the arts left the country after 1933, including some of the most internationally famous German artists and writers of the time. The government's removal of their German citizenship caused them considerable hardship and problems abroad.

Interestingly, Goebbels had rather more open views on art than Hitler and favoured some modern painters, such as the work of Emil Nolde. But it was Hitler's view on art that prevailed and he ordered Nolde's paintings to be removed from Goebbels's new house in the summer of 1933 and Nolde himself was expelled from the Prussian Academy of Art, despite having been a member of the Nazi Party since 1920. All over Germany 'unacceptable' curators of art galleries and museums were sacked and others quickly fell into line with expectations. Modernist art pieces were removed from display and some keen Nazi curators set up special exhibits of it under titles such as 'Degenerate Art' and 'Art Horrors'. What was left as German official art-culture can be characterized as rigid, stereotypical images and ideas that repetitively communicated the Nazi obsessions with race, war and control.

Newspapers were banned if they did not follow the Nazi line. The Communist Party and Social Democrat newspapers were shut as soon as their parties were banned. Other newspapers responded to government demands and arrests by 'voluntarily' acting to coordinate themselves. In April 1933, the journalists' union, the Reich Association of the German Press, elected a Nazi as its chairman and promised to ensure that only journalists acceptable to the Nazis would be allowed to join it and so be employed on newspapers. In June 1933, the same policy was adopted by the German Newspaper Publishers' Association. The press was now firmly muzzled.

Also in June of that first year in power, Goebbels brought all radio broadcasting under his control and rapidly sacked 13 per cent of employees because they were Jewish, or because they held liberal or left-wing views. One month later, Goebbels went further and set up the Reich Film Chamber, which over-saw the whole German film industry and controlled its output. Film makers and actors who were Jewish, or whose views and work the Nazis disapproved of, lost their jobs. Those who remained fell into line with the new expectations; many secured their jobs by joining the Nazi Party.

Taking the control of ideas further

Victor Klemperer, in his diary entry for September 1934, noted down features of propaganda as outlined by Goebbels at that autumn's Nazi Party Rally at Nuremberg. It should not lie; it should be creative; it must 'educate' the people; it must prepare people for unpopular policies; it must listen to the people and speak the language of the people.[13] The first characteristic would be strained to breaking point by Goebbels's under-standing of what was 'true' but even that revealed a subtlety in his grasp of how the control of ideas should be achieved. It was more effective to manipulate than to simply invent, as this would resonate more with the experiences of the listener and was therefore more likely to be accepted.

The other characteristics, though, were also revealing. They help explain why – for all his fanaticism and moral crudity – Goebbels was a more complex manipulator of messages and their media than many others in the Nazi hierarchy. He had to battle in order that his strategy would prevail over competitors within the party. The methods used in the propaganda would be remarkably modern and would extend well beyond Goebbels's own area of responsibility. This modern style would be seen in cinema, radio, set-piece dramatic public events and innovative use of print techniques. Paradoxically, these modern methods would be used to convey a message of what has been described as 'pseudo-archaic certainties' such as 'Blood and Soil', classical and traditional forms of art and music, buildings of classical style but mammoth proportions.[14] In this way the Nazi control of ideas appeared, at the same time, both modern and backward looking.

By 1935, Goebbels had succeeded in fighting off the ambitions of others in the Nazi Party who had contested his right to control culture. The most high profile of these rivals was the party's racial ideology theorist, Alfred Rosenberg. In the film industry, though, Goebbels was allowed a fairly free hand and, from 1935, the two largest film studios – UFA and Tobis – were in effect nationalized. He had the same freedom with regard to radio and literature as well. The one exception was Hitler's personal intervention, which led to Leni Riefenstahl being commissioned to shoot the film *Triumph of the Will* in 1934.

The exception of *Triumph of the Will* is very revealing. It would be the only film made about Hitler in the entire period of the Third Reich. Commissioned to film the Nazi Party Rally at Nuremberg, Riefenstahl used innovative techniques (moving cameras, telephoto lenses, aerial photography, dramatic and varied music) to produce a film unlike any earlier documentary. It would influence film making long after its first screening in March 1935. Lasting 114 minutes, it received widespread acclaim. It won the Gold Medal at the Venice Film Festival in 1935, and the Grand Prize at the Paris Film Festival in 1937. Earlier it had won the National Film Prize in Germany and the award was presented by Goebbels himself. This must have been particularly difficult, since he had opposed the concept and methods of this propaganda film from the start. He also clearly resented the fact that the commissioning had been done outside the usual channels of his Propaganda Ministry. But it was more than a matter of personal pride. Goebbels had a different concept of how film should be used. For him the style should avoid parades and spotlights and should, instead, be more subtle, even at times escapist. For this reason – despite its massive success – *Triumph of the Will* did not set the tone for the film industry of the Third Reich.

The films produced by the UFA (Germany's principle film studio) were not of the Riefenstahl type. Its stars, such as the Swede Zarah Leander and the immensely popular Hans Albers, appeared in films that offered adventure and escapism. Leander was so popular that she could even survive the antagonism of Goebbels, who clearly resented her distancing herself from the Nazi Party. And Albers could even maintain his massive screen presence while having a Jewish girlfriend – Hansi Burg – although for her own safety she left Germany for Switzerland and then Britain. They were reunited after the war.

By 1938, the categorization of German films might cause some surprise: 10 per cent political, 41 per cent dramas, 49 per cent comedies.[15] During the war, Goebbels encouraged escapist films such as the fantasy comedy *Münchhausen* (1943) and historical dramas – designed to inspire Germans through heroic events from German history – such as thinly veiled 'parallels' between Hitler and Frederick the Great in *The Great King* (1942) and the Napoleonic era film *Kolberg* (1945). However, it should be remembered that many of the characters in the 'non-political films' had to conform to Nazi stereotypes. And so-called historical dramas such as *Jew Süss* (1940) simply transferred Nazi anti-Semitism into an eighteenth-century setting. The infamous *The Eternal Jew* (1940)[16] – which included scenes filmed in the Lodz ghetto in Poland – was racism of the starkest kind, with its 'parallels' drawn between East European Jews and disease-carrying rats.[17]

With the decline in exports of German films abroad (partly due to the hostility of foreign film distributors towards the repressive policies of the Nazis) and the reduction of foreign imports (due to Nazi tax and currency laws), most Germans by 1939 could only see films produced within Germany. Of these, about 65 per cent were being made by state-financed companies and the remainder were subject to the strict controls of the Propaganda Ministry.

The Nazi control of radio broadcasting was advanced by the rapid expansion of radio ownership in the 1930s. Government subsidies enabled manufacturers to produce cheap 'People's Receivers'. By the outbreak of the Second World War, the proportion of German households owning a wireless – about 70 per cent – was one of the highest in the world, comparable with US wireless ownership of 82.8 per cent in 1940.[18] These 'People's Receivers' had a limited range, which meant that most Germans using them could not listen to foreign broadcasts. Public loudspeakers allowed for special speeches to be heard in public spaces and those around were to stop and listen. However, by 1939, two thirds of the broadcast material was music and fulfilled Goebbels's instruction that radio should not be boring. This music was almost entirely popular music, despite Hitler's passion for Wagner.

During the 1930s, the Nazi control over newspapers meant that, with minor exceptions, only regime-approved news was available. The Nazi Party's own daily newspaper – the *Völkischer Beobachter* – became the first German newspaper to sell more than one million copies a day. Mass orders by Nazi organizations boosted the sales of the sensationalist and semi-pornographic *Der Stürmer* and *Der SA Mann* (*The SA Man*) This control of the press did have its downside for the regime, as Gestapo reports indicated popular irritation at the uniformity of press coverage and the way in which news was suppressed even when it was common knowledge. This also led to some seeking information from foreign sources.[19]

The banning of Jewish writers and others who offended the regime meant that the same uniformity extended to books. Novels about heroic SA men and German peasants became commonplace. The Reich Chamber of Literature ensured that themes fitted the prevailing ideology. Since 1933, the police had been granted the right to seize offending books and, by the end of that year, more than 1,000 titles had been banned. The list of banned titles continued to escalate after this. In May 1933, there had been the infamous book-burning in university towns. It was an action instigated by Nazi students as part of their contribution to 'coordinating' Germany.[20] Just under a century earlier, in 1821, the German writer Heinrich Heine had commented that: 'Where they burn books, so too will they in the end burn human beings.' His words proved tragically accurate and his own work went into the flames during the Third Reich. In addition to the banning of the works of Jewish and left-wing authors, the Nazi censors also outlawed foreign books that offended them in some way. Dickens's *Oliver Twist* and Scott's *Ivanhoe* were deemed unacceptable. From 1936, no German could receive a Nobel Prize, after one was awarded to the journalist and essayist Carl von Ossietzky. He himself was banned from accepting the prize and died in 1938 following brutal treatment in concentration camps.

In the field of sculpture the style that had emerged by the mid-1930s was Aryan supermen produced in stone: larger than life, muscular, heroic, aggressive . . . and lacking in individuality and expression. Alongside these images of the 'new man' with his steely masculinity were sculptures 'celebrating the peasant, the heroic worker and German womanhood – generally in the form of the fertile female'.[21] This was the style that was to replace 'degenerate art'. A sculptor who was admired in this period was Arno Breker, who from 1934 to 1942 was commissioned to sculpt a great many pieces including two pieces to celebrate the Olympics of 1936; in 1937, he was made 'Official State Sculptor'. Over 90 per cent of his sculptures were destroyed by the Allies at the end of the war, although he himself continued to work in this artistic field until his death in 1991. Like many who gained commissions under the Nazis there was later controversy over his role. Whilst some accused him of working for the Nazis, his supporters argued that he had never supported Nazi ideology but had simply accepted commissions. After the war he produced sculpted portraits for famous figures as varied as

Jean Cocteau (1963), the king of Morocco (1970), Salvador Dalí (1975) and Anwar Sadat (1980).[22]

The same larger-than-life approach dictated new styles of architecture too, which mixed pre-modern effects with modern technologies.[23] The huge new airport terminal at Tempelhof was one example. The Reich Chancellery was another. The man commissioned to build the new Reich Chancellery between 1938 and 1939 was Albert Speer, the new Building Inspector for the National Capital. This was only part of a vast building plan, which aimed to see Berlin transformed into the world capital – Germania – by the early 1950s.

The many early attacks on art designated as 'degenerate' culminated in the 1937 exhibition of Degenerate Art in Munich. The pieces were deliberately hung at odd angles and poorly lit in order to make their appearance more jarring and literally out of line with the new German style. This was particularly interesting because Goebbels was secretly sympathetic to aspects of such art; but he mounted the exhibition in a deliberate attempt to gain favour with Hitler, who hated it. The actual selection of the pieces to display was largely left to the President of the Reich Chamber for the Visual Arts, Adolf Ziegler. Ziegler's anatomically detailed paintings of classical-style nudes had earned him the nick-name 'Reich Master of Pubic Hair'. Despite the acceptability of his style he fell foul of the regime during the Second World War and spent six weeks in Dachau concentration camp for 'defeatism'. On release he retired, survived the war, but could not revive his artistic career that had been so closely associated with the Third Reich and he died in 1959. In 1937, though, the exhibition he organized attracted over two million visitors. The art exhibited included work by, among others, Picasso, Matisse, Klee, Kandinsky, Beckmann and Kirchner. Depressed at the rejection of his art, Kirchner committed suicide in 1938. In 1939, the similarly rejected artist Oskar Schlemmer was painting camouflage on military structures because no one would buy his pictures. The Degenerate Art exhibition later went on tour to Berlin, Düsseldorf and Frankfurt.

By 1938, Nazi control of the media was fairly complete. This meant that wherever the public looked – cinema screens, newspapers and magazines, novels, art galleries – the message they received was one of which the Propaganda Ministry approved. This was further refined by the monitoring of public opinion by Block Wardens, Gestapo agents and the SS Security Service (the SD). This assisted the regime in responding to areas of concern and discontent with campaigns designed to reduce tensions in these areas. In many ways the biggest challenge the regime faced was that people tended to be bored by the lack of variety and the constant reiteration of party-approved themes. However, despite this, the relentless Nazification of ideas had its effect. Anti-Semitism clearly increased even if, for most Germans, it was a passive lack of concern for the rapidly reducing rights of others, rather than murderous intent. The inevitability of Nazi rule became accepted, with no likelihood of any alternative form of government. The creation of a sense of unity and purpose helped reduce antagonisms towards the day-to-day failings of the state. And the enforced pageantry might be wooden and knee-jerk as loyal Germans automatically put out flags on the new national holiday to celebrate Hitler's birthday (April 20th) and gave the Hitler salute, but the effect was to create a greater sense of uniformity. This, for all its artificiality, was boosted by the presentation of the Führer as above all criticism. Posters carefully presented him as a man of destiny raised from the trenches of the First World War, in tune with all levels of society, self-sacrificing, loving animals and children. This propaganda-generated personal popularity was enhanced by the mounting foreign policy successes of the 1930s.

The overall impact of the Nazis on the communication of ideas

Overall then, the Nazi policy on the control of ideas was a mixture of outright repression and, in certain areas, flexibility. Jewish artists and writers were gone, victims of the 'Aryan paragraph' inserted into laws and forced on all organizations.

By 1937, modernism in art was suppressed. Hitler's uncompromising attitude on this had won out over Goebbels's more relaxed view. But other areas remained intact. Classic German literature and music (so long as it was not written or composed by a Jew) was still enjoyed. And on the fringes of acceptability there still existed clandestine jazz clubs and dance halls where swing music could be enjoyed. The latter were condemned but not hunted down. Goebbels had realized that they did not, in reality, pose any real threat to the state, even if they offended the purists in the party. The Security Service of the SS (the SD) even reported, in 1938, that 'degenerate art' was still being viewed in private galleries. For all the strident propaganda of *Triumph of the Will* and *The Eternal Jew*, German cinema also included historical dramas with clear Nazi racial messages such as *Jew Suss* and period pieces such as *Kolberg*, along with escapist films such as *Münchhausen*. It was this mixture of crude repression and manipulative creativity that made the propaganda of the Third Reich so distinctive.

15

GERMANY AND THE WORLD, 1933–9

Hitler conducted foreign policy in a different fashion from other leaders. In March 1939, the Germans occupied what was left of the Czech state after they had already taken its western regions in October 1938. The prelude to the invasion was a bullying meeting between Hitler and the sixty-seven-year-old Czech President Emil Hácha. The President had flown to Berlin to try to save his country from German attack. During the stressful meeting with Hitler, Hácha collapsed with a heart attack as Prague was threatened with destruction. He had to be revived with an injection by Hitler's doctor.[1] Finally, he agreed to 'invite' the Germans in, to spare his people from violent assault. Thus, the Germans could maintain the fiction that they had not invaded. Just how it had come to this state of affairs is the subject of this chapter.

Germany and its European neighbours . . . unfinished business

When Hitler came to power in 1933, the relationship of Germany with its European neighbours was overshadowed by the effects of the Treaty of Versailles (1919). German politicians of all persuasions were committed to revising this treaty in order to regain land lost by Germany at the end of the First World War. Even as respectable a Weimar statesman as Gustav Stresemann – whilst agreeing to accept the western borders of Germany in the Locarno Treaties (or Locarno Pact) of 1925 – left those on the eastern border open to revision. Here there was unfinished business with the Poles and also the Czechs. In this respect, much of Hitler's foreign policy in the 1930s was not that dissimilar from what might have been pursued by any other German regime at the time, especially a nationalist one. And he was also part of a much longer tradition of German politicians who aimed to dominate central Europe (in German, *Mitteleuropa*, literally 'middle Europe') and expand German territory and influence eastward. In fact, this *Drang nach Osten* (drive to the east) can be dated back to the twelfth and thirteenth centuries when it targeted the territory between the rivers Elbe and Oder for conquest and colonization. Later, in the eighteenth century, Prussia had joined Russia and Austria in the dismemberment of Poland.[2] More recently, in 1918, the Treaty of Brest Litovsk had exacted a high price for allowing the new Bolshevik government of Russia to exit the disastrous First World War. By it, 25 per cent of Russia's population and industry was stripped from it by the Germans; the Baltic States (Estonia, Latvia, Lithuania), Russian-administered Poland, Belorussia and the Ukraine passed into German domination and economic exploitation. This situation was rapidly reversed by the German collapse, in the summer of 1918, and eventually defeat. However, it gives a flavour of German plans for Eastern Europe and its savage terms should be borne in mind when recalling German protests at how they were treated by the Treaty of Versailles.[3]

All of this is important to remember because it helps explain the popularity of much of the foreign policy of the Third Reich within Germany in the 1930s. And it explains why many civil servants in the German foreign office found they could accommodate themselves within the objectives of the Nazi government in its relationship with its neighbours.

In the same way, wars of conquest were quite acceptable to the military elite, especially as such wars would accompany a massive expansion of the size and influence of the German military.

Nevertheless, despite the continuity between traditional German foreign relations and the Nazi actions of the 1930s, Hitler added a distinct radicalism and aggressiveness to it, which grew out of the racial ideology of the Nazi Party.[4] This was not a new element in German outlook (especially with regard to Poles and other Slavic peoples of the East) but under the Nazis its intensity increased. This was driven by the Nazi obsession with gaining Lebensraum for the German people in the East.[5] In *Mein Kampf*, Hitler had written:

> If one wanted land and soil in Europe, then, by and large, this could only have been done at Russia's expense, and then the new Reich would again have to start marching along the road of the knights of the orders of former times to provide, with the help of the German sword, the soil for the plough and the daily bread for the nation.[6]

As a result, we must avoid interpreting the foreign policy of the Third Reich as traditional German aims that escalated accidentally into a general European war. Wars of conquest were hard-wired into the Nazi outlook. And these always had the potential to develop a brutality whose scale would be shocking. But even these aspects of Nazi planning and outlook were, at the same time, related to long-established German attitudes towards neighbouring states. For, whilst Hitler had no blueprint for his actions and could not predict the course of events in the 1930s, his cynical and cunning manipulation of the weakness of others was always aimed in a general direction: the destruction of the Treaty of Versailles, the domination of Europe by Germany and wars of racial conquest in the East.[7] But as the 1930s unfolded, this was far from clear to many observers of Europe, because, in many ways, Hitler appeared to have a limited set of goals, focused on revising the most objectionable aspects of the Treaty of Versailles. And to many, these objectives might even appear reasonable. It was a misapprehension that Hitler would ruthlessly manipulate.

As Göring commented, 'Foreign policy above all was the Führer's very own realm', along with military matters. Hitler, 'busied himself exceptionally with the details in both these spheres'.[8] Given the issues we have just explored, this should come as no surprise.

Hitler: the affronted 'peacemaker'

Hitler was skilful at anticipating the actions of others and trapping them in their own self-interest. In May 1933, he called for other European nations to follow Germany in being disarmed. This was disingenuous of course because Hitler was committed *to re-armament*. But when the French rejected a British proposal for the reduction in the size of the large French army accompanied by an increase in the size of the small German one, it gave Hitler the excuse to leave both the Disarmament Conference and the League of Nations. The insincerity of Hitler's position was immediately obvious in that he pressed on with German rearmament while at the same time (1934) signing a non-aggression pact with Poland. This clearly meant nothing since, by September 1939, he was conducting a murderous war in Poland, but it gave the impression that Germany had no aggressive plans for Eastern Europe and it weakened French influence since it reduced Polish anxieties.

The fact that Germany was not yet ready for any openly aggressive moves was revealed in reactions to the murder of the Austrian Chancellor, Dollfuss, by Austrian Nazis in July 1934. So concerned was the Italian dictator, Mussolini, at the possibility of German control of Austria that he moved troops to the Austrian border and promised assistance to Austria to safeguard its independence. As a result, the German government made no attempt to exploit Austria's crisis.

The reoccupation of the Rhineland, 1936

In 1936, Hitler took his first major risk. Under the Treaty of Versailles, Germany was forbidden to station troops in the Rhineland, on the border with France. But Hitler felt ready for his first foreign policy gamble for a number of reasons. First, in March 1935, he had announced the existence of a German air force (the *Luftwaffe*) and the reintroduction of conscription. Both broke the Treaty of Versailles but no retribution followed. Second, no sooner had Britain, France and Italy condemned Germany's actions in a meeting at Stresa, Italy, in April 1935 (the Stresa Front), than Britain had undermined it by agreeing to an increase in the size of the German navy. This lack of a united front against the challenges offered by Hitler would be a characteristic of the 1930s. Third, the Italian invasion of Abyssinia, in October 1935, split the potential opponents of Germany. When even the weak response of the British and French to this blatant act of Italian aggression proved too much for Mussolini, he drifted into the German orbit.

As a result, on 7 March 1936, Hitler ordered German troops into the Rhineland. Had Britain and France opposed this, the German troops had orders to withdraw and Hitler would have been humiliated. Indeed, so nervous was Hitler that he only moved in twelve infantry battalions and eight groups of artillery and most of these were ordered to stay on the Rhine's eastern bank. But the British and French did nothing. As a result, the Locarno Pact was a dead letter, the League of Nations (whose job it was to uphold the Treaty of Versailles) was seen to have no authority and the resolve of the British and French to control Hitler was seen to be non-existent. A number of historians have argued that, in retrospect, this was the last opportunity to prevent the Second World War and it has been claimed that within France a sense of inferiority in the face of a resurgent Germany led to a failure to maintain the advantages France had gained from the legacy of the First World War: Germany disarmed and the Rhineland demilitarized.[9]

Making friends and influencing people

Pablo Picasso's famous painting of the destruction of the
Basque town of Guernica illustrates the horrors of the Spanish
Civil War (1936–9). Its monochrome starkness and its central
image of a grieving woman and a wounded, screaming horse
impress themselves on the memory. The whole design
communicates grief and anger.[10] But what the painting does
not show is the nationality of the planes that dropped the
bombs. For the aircraft that devastated Guernica were
German.

Both Germany and Italy actively supported General
Franco and the Spanish Nationalists in the Spanish Civil War
and drew closer together as they did so.[11] In October 1936,
the Rome–Berlin axis was signed, which showed how far
Mussolini had shifted since the Stresa Front.[12] In November
of that same year, Germany signed the Anti-Comintern Pact
with Japan, which committed both countries to opposing the
spread of communism. Hitler was no longer isolated and his
successes so far had won him widespread support within
Germany.

It was about this time that Hitler abandoned hopes of some
kind of alliance with Britain. The failure of von Ribbentrop
(the new German ambassador in London) to gain British
acceptance of German ambitions in Eastern Europe in return
for a promise of non-interference in the British Empire indicated that Britain remained a potential adversary in any future
war. However, the arrogant and awkward von Ribbentrop
was unlikely to win over the British.[13] His social gaffes –
including greeting George VI with the Nazi salute – soon
won him the nickname 'Herr Brickendrop'. During a dinner
with Winston Churchill, Ribbentrop is reputed to have
boasted: 'The next war will be different, for we will have the
Italians on our side.' To which Churchill replied: 'That's only
fair; we had 'em last time!'

The Hossbach Memorandum and the reality of Hitler's ambitions

Exactly what was going through Hitler's mind at this time is revealed by a document known as the 'Hossbach Memorandum'. This was the minutes of a meeting that took place in the Reich Chancellery, Berlin, on 5 November 1937, between 4.15 and 8.30 p.m. In just over four hours, Hitler outlined to the five senior officers present, along with von Neurath, the Foreign Minister, his long-term ambitions. The name of the document recording the gist of the meeting is derived from Colonel Hossbach, who made notes. This document is not without its difficulties. Hossbach only made notes at the time and it was five days later – on his own initiative – that he filled in the gaps from memory. The original document has not survived. Modern versions are based on a typed copy, which, by the time it appeared as evidence at the Nuremberg Trials in 1946 (as evidence PS-386), could not be definitely identified by Hossbach as an exact copy of his original minutes. Nevertheless, the message of the original meeting is clear enough.[14]

The policy of German autarky was, Hitler explained, only partly achievable. Britain and France would oppose German domination of Europe. Consequently, in the long term, the problems Germany faced could 'only be solved by means of force'. Hossbach noted that it was Hitler's 'unalterable resolve to solve Germany's problem of space at the latest by 1943–5'. However, earlier opportunities might arise if France was seriously distracted by internal problems. In such a scenario: 'Time for action against the Czechs had come'. The situation would be similar if France was distracted by war. Either way, the objective 'must be to overthrow Czechoslovakia and Austria simultaneously'. This would be prior to action against the French.[15] Whilst long-term plans for war against Poland and the USSR – clearly objectives from the contents of *Mein Kampf* and other evidence – were not included on the agenda of this meeting, the Hossbach Memorandum shows clearly that Hitler's tactical opportunism should not be used to obscure the clear evidence of long-term planning for domination of Europe by military means.

1938: a step-change year?

It is surely no coincidence that the year following the meeting in the Reich Chancellery has been identified by a number of historians as one that saw a ratcheting up of Nazi radicalism. Abroad it was a year that ended with the rule of the Third Reich extended to include Austria and the Sudeten area of Czechoslovakia. In Austria, this was accompanied by vicious assaults on the Jewish community. At home the events were similarly seismic. The more cautious nationalist Schacht had recently been replaced by Göring as driver of the German economy, and, in early 1938, the Foreign Minister, Neurath, lost his job to the Nazi Ribbentrop. Within the army, General von Blomberg, Minister for War, was forced to resign when police records revealed that his wife, Erna, had once posed for pornographic photographs. The fact that Hitler had acted as best man at their wedding added a further twist of embarrassment to the scandal. Shortly afterwards, Göring and Himmler presented evidence implicating army Commander-in-Chief Colonel-General von Fritsch in involvement with a rent boy. The fact that he was innocent emerged too late. By that time, Hitler was free of two leading generals who had expressed opposition to war with Britain and France. Hitler took this opportunity to abolish the post of Minister for War and took on the role of supreme commander of the armed forces himself. In October, Jews of Polish origin were expelled from Germany. Then, in November, came the brutal outpouring of violent anti-Semitism in Kristallnacht. No wonder that Giles MacDonogh described the year 1938 as 'one of cataclysmal change for Germany'.[16]

The Anschluss with Austria, March 1938

Q: Which part of the world has the hottest climate?
A: Austria, of course; lots of people turned brown there overnight.[17]

So ran a joke popular in Germany in 1938, brown being the colour of the uniforms of Nazi paramilitaries. For in March of that year, Austria had been brought into the Reich and the event had been accompanied by widespread displays of loyalty to the new Nazi order.

Even before the Nazi takeover, Austria in 1938 was a semi-fascist one-party state. The Socialist Party and the Communist Party were banned and freedom of the press had been abolished. But it was independent of Germany and its leader, Schuschnigg, was determined to keep it that way. But Austrian Nazis were increasingly causing his government problems and were being encouraged from Berlin. A meeting with Hitler bullied Schuschnigg into including Nazis in his cabinet, but, on returning to Vienna, Schuschnigg decided to put Austrian independence to a referendum. Hitler was furious and as the level of threat from Germany increased, Schuschnigg resigned and was replaced by the Austrian Nazi Seyss-Inquart, who invited in the Germans. On 12 March 1938, German army units crossed the border to put into effect the Anschluss with Germany.

The final decision to fully absorb Austria into the Reich was confirmed by a referendum in which 99.73 per cent of the votes were cast in favour of union with Germany. Another joke at the time cynically commented on the fate of Austria:

Q: Why was the YES column on the voting form printed in capital letters and the NO column in small ones?
A: The YES was meant for the short-sighted and the NO for the far-sighted.[18]

However, despite the evidence of widespread support for the Anschluss in Austria, the later defeat of the Third Reich gave Austrians an opportunity to reinvent their recent past. In April 1945 – while many Austrians were still fighting for the Third Reich – the 'Proclamation of 27 April' by the provisional Austrian government embraced the concept of Austria as victim. That summer the new Austrian Foreign Ministry put forward the new orthodoxy that Austria had not been a willing ally of Germany; instead, Austria had been 'occupied and liberated'. This presented the Anschluss as the forcible occupation of a helpless people and Austria's first post-war government encapsulated this view in a famous publication in 1946: *Justice for Austria! Red-White-Red-Book*.[19] It was (as the historian Günter Bischof put it) a '"Rip van Winkle myth" of dormant Austrian statehood.'[20] It is the same myth that is perpetuated in the charming musical *The Sound of Music*, where a concert audience sings *Edelweiss* as a sign of Austrian independence and defiance, to the annoyance of Nazi officials.

The turn of Czechoslovakia, 1938

With Austria absorbed, western Czechoslovakia was surrounded on three sides by German territory. The next crisis centred on the area of the Czech state called the Sudetenland, which bordered Germany and contained a minority of 3.5 million Germans. For years the Nazis had funded the Sudeten German Party, whose leader, Henlein, demanded self-determination. As tension mounted between Berlin and Prague, a short-lived united front by the Czechs, France, the USSR and Britain forced Hitler to back down in May. But this prompted him to set 1 October as the date by which he would deal with the Czechs. As the threat of war increased, the British Prime Minister, Chamberlain, flew on his own initiative to negotiate with Hitler at Berchtesgaden. Returning home he persuaded the French and coerced the Czechs into falling in line with Hitler's demands. But on returning to Germany for a second meeting at Bad Godesberg, Chamberlain found Hitler had upped his demands. An immediate German occupation of the Sudetenland was now the only solution he would accept.

War seemed inevitable. But Mussolini suggested a conference, which met at Munich in September. Here Germany, Britain, France and Italy agreed that Germany could take the Sudetenland. There was a vague promise – never ratified – to guarantee the security of the rest of Czechoslovakia. This was 'appeasement' in action. As such it built on the earlier inaction in the face of treaty-breaking and aggression by both Hitler and Mussolini.[21] The Czechs were not invited to the conference talks. Neither were the Russians. At the same time as Germany carved off the Sudetenland, the Poles and Hungarians took the opportunity to seize disputed parts of the borderland of the Czech state. With Germany triumphant and Britain and France clearly impotent, the countries of central Europe came to terms with the new realities. Romania guaranteed oil supplies to Germany; Yugoslavia signed a trade agreement; Hungary joined the Anti-Comintern Pact.

Despite gaining all he had demanded, Hitler was angered at the outcome. The evidence suggests that he had wanted the crisis to result in a localized war and felt cheated of his 'entry into Prague'. For now the Czechs had been reprieved. But it was a stay of execution that would last for only six months.

March 1939: the opening of eyes

In all Hitler's moves so far, those who hoped for the best could delude themselves that he was simply righting the wrongs of the peace treaties that followed the end of the First World War. Furthermore, his actions had brought Germans under one common government and could be described as within the principle of self-determination. However, in March 1939, Hitler dismembered Czechoslovakia. 'For the first time, Germany lacked even the pretence of a respectable ethnic rationale for its action.'[22] The expansionist ambitions of Hitler were clear for all to see.

On 15 March, German troops occupied the remainder of the

Czech state. Technically, since November 1938, it had been titled Czecho-Slovakia, since the weakened government in Prague had been forced to accede to demands for autonomy in Slovakia and Ruthenia. The Hungarians took the opportunity afforded by the German invasion to annex parts of Ruthenia and parts of Slovakia. Slovakia itself became a German puppet state.

In the same month, Hitler seized Memel from Lithuania, which was now dominated by Nazi Germany. The betrayal of the Czechs by the British and French at Munich had created a landslide of change in central Europe.

The Nazi-Soviet Pact, the invasion of Poland and the start of the Second World War

Now it was the turn of the Poles. Germany demanded the German-speaking city of Danzig (loosely administered by the League of Nations) and the 'Polish Corridor' (which divided East Prussia from the Reich and gave Poland access to the Baltic). Faced with the disaster that had occurred in central Europe the British offered a guarantee of support for Poland if it was attacked by Germany. But even now the British were slow in their pursuit of an alliance with the USSR. The matter was further complicated by Poland's refusal to allow Soviet troops onto Polish soil. Consequently, the world was shocked when, on 23 August, Germany and the USSR signed a non-aggression treaty. It was a meeting of enemies that satisfied both – temporarily. Hitler now knew that he could attack Poland without the USSR becoming involved. Stalin knew he had bought time. And Hitler was confident that the French and British would not intervene. In a meeting with his generals on 22 August, he concluded, 'Our enemies are little worms; I saw them at Munich.' This was the legacy of appeasement.

In the run up to war the usual atrocity stories were manufactured in the German press. This time though they were accompanied by macabre 'evidence' when prisoners from concentration camps were dressed in Polish uniforms and gunned down beside the German border radio station they had allegedly been attacking.

At 0445 hours on the morning of 1 September 1939, Germany attacked Poland. On 3 September, Britain and France declared war. Hitler, as always personally incapable of taking responsibility for any problem he had wilfully caused, bitterly blamed von Ribbentrop for the fact that Britain had defied his wishes and gone to war with the Third Reich. It was a strange start to Hitler's war. The British, whom he had long hoped would be neutral or an ally, were at war with him, and the USSR, whom he loathed, was his ally. Clearly, not everything had gone according to Hitler's long-term planning.

Was Germany to blame for the Second World War?

By the 1970s there was a hotly contested school of thought, particularly associated with the British historian A. J. P. Taylor, which argued that the Second World War was preventable but the events leading to it had been badly handled by the West. In this interpretation, Hitler did not have a clear plan for a general European war. Instead, his plans were largely pragmatic and developed with time and success. In his foreign policy plans, Hitler was not greatly different from many earlier German politicians of the Second Reich and the Weimar Republic.[23] Indeed, his ambitions were not greatly different from those of other – Western – leaders who similarly wanted their nations to be the leading state within Europe. When war occurred in 1939 it was more a case of accident than design and resulted from errors made by many of the leading players. Hitler, in Taylor's view, was largely an opportunist whose only distinguishing features were his pursuit of power and anti-Semitism. He had little by way of a programme and his foreign policy drifted from one opportunistic action to another. More central to any explanation of the outbreak of the Second World War was the flawed nature of the Treaty of Versailles.[24]

By the early twenty-first century this way of explaining the foreign policy of the Third Reich has been largely abandoned.

In conversation with the film-maker, author and former head of history at the BBC, Laurence Rees, in September 2009, a number of leading historians outlined their understanding of how the Second World War came about. And their comments reveal how far the views of historians have developed since the 1970s. Richard Evans identified the crucial part played by Nazi ideology in that, in his opinion, 'Hitler's beliefs are absolutely paramount as a causal factor in the Second World War . . . he intended there to be a general European war really absolutely from the outset.' This is a point corroborated by Evans's fellow historian of the Third Reich, Ian Kershaw: 'The German expansion, as Hitler repeatedly said, could only come about through the sword.' And this was an area in which the military ambitions of the Third Reich were deeply entangled with Nazi economics. Adam Tooze has focused on the economic aspects of Nazi policy and the way in which it was geared to expansionist aggression. As he reminds us, 'The idea that the Nazis could have somehow just extended the prosperity of the 1930s into some sort of peaceful VW future of modernity and satisfaction – well, it's just not on the cards for Hitler's regime.' Furthermore, the kind of political persona that Hitler had developed meant that such a conventional set of aims was never remotely on his agenda. As Tooze reminds us: 'This is a man for whom politics is drama, a tragic drama that may not have a happy ending'. This is an interpretation strongly supported by the hard facts of Nazi economic activity. By 1939, Nazi spending on rearmament was running at about 33 per cent of German GDP, compared with a normal state's spending of up to 4 per cent of GDP. In fact, military expenditure in the Third Reich by the end of the 1930s was ten times what NATO expected of its members at the height of the Cold War in the 1970s and 1980s. The conclusion is clear: Nazi Germany was driving relentlessly towards a war of conquest.

But while this programme was fundamental to the implementation of Nazi race-based foreign policy (and indeed was inspired by this ideology) it was also one that struck a chord with large sections of German society because it drew together many strands of dissatisfaction with the outcome of the Treaty of Versailles. As the historian Richard Overy reminds us, while Hitler was the prime factor, his ideology had combined with the consequences of the Versailles settlement and consequently had fused his racial radicalism with a widespread German desire to destroy that settlement, along with a long-standing German foreign policy aim of dominating Central Europe alongside a drive to the East. It was this combination of the traditional aims of the Second Reich and nationalist anger at the 1919 settlement with Hitler's racial worldview that so 'distorted the international order' and made the circumstances of September 1939 possible.

And by September 1939, the invasion of Poland left even the architects of appeasement in Paris and London with little choice, if they were to maintain any credibility and influence in the world. Anita Prazmowska identifies how an attack by Germany on Poland in 1939 dangerously tipped the balance of power in Europe in Germany's favour. As a result, the Western Allies had little alternative but to act, despite the fact that their failure to bring the USSR on board meant that there was little they could actually do to save the Poles. She sums up the significance of the declaration of war in September 1939: 'It is not a fight for Poland, it is actually an attempt to indicate to Germany the unacceptability of her behaviour.' Little wonder that Laurence Rees concluded that, 'Hitler emerges, surely without question now, as the person most responsible for the war.'[25]

As a result, we can conclude that Hitler was not a politician like any other. Rather, he was committed to a Europe-wide war and was obsessed with a racially distorted version of geo-politics.[26] Unlike the traditional nationalist consensus, which even Stresemann had subscribed to, Hitler was determined to move beyond dismantling the restrictions imposed by the Treaty of Versailles; instead, his aim was the conquest of a massive slave empire in the east of Europe as far as the Urals.

As a consequence, throughout the 1930s, he was committed to a desperate rearmament programme and a policy of expansion before other states were strong enough to stop him. From 1938, his drive to war went up a gear and was accelerated by his obsession that he did not have long to accomplish his tasks; that growing international condemnation of Nazism after the Anschluss signalled the start of a grouping of adversaries; that US involvement in the Evian Conference on Jewish refugees in the summer of 1938 (however ineffective) signalled – to Hitler – that the real centre of the 'World Jewish Conspiracy' was in the USA and that this would eventually cause the USA to back Britain and France in a general war. Finally, growing British rearmament from early 1939 suggested that by the early 1940s the odds would be stacked more heavily against Germany's gamble, and this was coupled with Hitler's fear of the eventual power of the USSR. Having started a clock ticking towards war, Hitler was then driven by the inexorable logic of his own extremist position. As Richard Overy has argued, war with Poland was inevitable but Hitler, the gambler, still hoped it would not involve the Western Allies. He hoped he could achieve the destruction of Poland without Britain and France getting involved. But this time Britain and France were determined to stand firm in the hope of deterring further escalation. The two-day delay (1–3 September 1939) was not preparatory to another act of appeasement but was necessary in order to coordinate British and French mobilization.[27]

Consequently, the Second World War broke out because Hitler was prepared to gamble on the possibility of German victory in a swift war, despite the size of the risk. This failed because the British and French finally resisted. Nevertheless, by the summer of 1940 – even with Britain still defiant – it looked as if that massive gamble had actually paid off. However, even then Hitler was preparing for the even bigger future confrontation with the USSR that was more in keeping with the war he had originally envisaged.[28] But these are the subjects of other chapters.

16

NAZI GERMANY, 1933–9: A POPULAR DICTATORSHIP?

How popular was Hitler's dictatorship? While letters to the press do not offer a representative sample of public opinion they do give an insight into the popularity of Hitler.[1] This, at times, included a semi-religious attitude which some Germans developed in their 'relationship' with the Führer.

'Just as in my youth the dear Lord used to appear in my dreams, so now the Führer appears.'

'He is the creator and preserver, the protector of our magnificent, great German Reich.'

'He who serves the Führer serves Germany and he who serves Germany serves God.'[2]

These examples illustrate the semi-religious tone of the Führer-cult that grew up around Hitler. But can the Third Reich, 1933–9, really be described as a 'popular dictatorship'?

How can we measure public opinion in a brutal dictatorship?

Any examination of the measure of support for Hitler's government has to make its assessment without the statistical aids that are used to measure such matters in a modern democracy. The very nature of the Nazi regime meant that, after the general election of March 1933, the manipulation of voting rendered election results meaningless. Similarly, there is no objective mass observation data, or public opinion poll information, that can be consulted. And, with the defeat of Germany in 1945, oral history accounts almost certainly contain an un-measurable element of reconstruction of memories after both the trauma and guilt of the defeat of the Third Reich and global condemnation of Nazi crimes. This particularly applies to accounts concerning support for the Nazi government. Nevertheless, historians do have a number of resources which can be used as barometers of opinion. All were compiled in secret, or only made available to a limited group of interested analysts. As such, they offer a relatively objective set of insights. Consequently, whilst these sources are not without their problems, taken together they can give a general idea of the public mood under Nazism.

Between 1934 and 1936, monthly and bi-monthly reports were compiled for the Ministry of the Interior on public opinion. These were halted by Göring in 1936, partly because the reports revealed negative reactions to Nazi policies and partly to reduce the influence of the Ministry of the Interior in one of the internal rivalries that were so characteristic of the Third Reich.

Late in 1934, Rudolf Hess, acting as Hitler's Deputy, ordered monthly reports to be compiled on the public mood. These were to be collected by Nazi Party functionaries and – again typical of the infighting – were not to be shared with other agencies, specifically the SS Security Service (the SD).

From November 1933, local stations of the secret police, the Gestapo (see below), compiled monthly surveys. These were specifically ordered to be objective and not to doctor the facts. Early Gestapo reports have not survived but their main findings can be learned from the Gestapo's internal news bulletins.

From the end of 1934 until late 1944, the SD also compiled reports focused on the effects of government policy and the identification of actions that caused opposition. By 1939, the SD had somewhere in the region of 3,000 full-time officials and 50,000 part-time agents. As with the Gestapo reports, the SD agents were instructed to be accurate and objective. By early 1945 though, this degree of accuracy was reduced as the SD was threatened with the end of all cooperation from the central government – on the orders of Martin Bormann, who from 1941 was head of the Party Chancellery and Hitler's private secretary. The reason for this threatened severance of communication was the negative nature of the SD reports as the Third Reich disintegrated into defeat. This unwillingness to hear bad news had been a weakness of the upper echelons of the Third Reich since its start. As early as 1936, Hitler had angrily cut short a report of low morale (prompted by rising prices and scarcity of consumer goods) with the words: 'The mood in the people is not bad, but good. I know that better. It's made bad through such reports. I forbid such things in future.'[3]

The final source of information is the Sopade reports. These were gathered by agents on behalf of the Social Democratic Party in exile, first in Prague and then in Paris. They provide particularly useful insights into economic issues, alongside the living conditions of workers. The Sopade reports provide a generally reliable source of information and one whose accuracy was recognized by the Nazi SD and the Gestapo. It is noticeable that the Sopade reports often corroborate the information in Nazi documents. This characteristic enhances both the usefulness and reliability of both sources. It is worth noting that, with the coming of war in 1939, the range of sources greatly reduces; the main source remains the SD reports but there are few other sources for corroboration.

Whilst these sources of information cannot offer us representative samples, they nevertheless do provide us with some insight into the relationship between the Nazi government and the German population.[4]

Terror versus cooperation

The autobiographies of eyewitnesses of the events of the 1930s frequently speak of a sense of being 'watched'. This was true of time spent at work, at leisure and in the home. The sense of threat and of the need to guard one's words shows itself in the underground humour of the period.

> Two men meet. 'Nice to see you're free again. How was the concentration camp?'
>
> 'Great! Breakfast in bed, a choice of coffee or chocolate, and for lunch we got soup, meat and dessert. And we played games in the afternoon before getting coffee and cakes. Then a little snooze and we watched movies after dinner.'
>
> The man was astonished: 'That's great! I recently spoke to Meyer, who was also locked up there. He told me a different story.'
>
> The other man nods gravely and says: 'Yes, well that's why they've picked him up again.'[5]

There certainly was a well-developed machinery of repression, devised to police and punish those who threatened Nazi rule. From the autumn of 1933, Hermann Göring had established a secret state police (the *Geheime Staatspolizei*, abbreviated to *Gestapo*). And, by April 1934, the SS chief Heinrich Himmler had become 'Inspector of the Gestapo', with Reinhard Heydrich running it under him. To start with, Himmler was nominally under the authority of Göring with regard to the Gestapo, since Göring had appointed him to this post as part of a power struggle between himself and the SA under Ernst Röhm. However, after the Night of the Long Knives in June 1934, the SS became fully independent of the SA and soon had absolute control of the Gestapo.[6] This combination of the SS and Gestapo, along with the establishment of concentration camps (now under SS control and replacing the informal detention centres set up by the SA) meant that Himmler was well on the way to creating his police empire: an SS state within the Nazi state. It was a police empire that would last until Himmler's final betrayal of Hitler in April 1945.

Once in operation, the Gestapo set about hunting down enemies. Between October 1935 and May 1936, the Gestapo arrested 7,266 people connected with the banned Communist

Party and the Social Democratic Party. In 1936, the CID (the *Kripo* or criminal police) was also brought under Himmler's authority. Together with the Gestapo it formed the Security Police (the *Sipo*, or *Sicherheitspolizei*). Along with the SS Security Service (the SD) this newly formed Security Police organization was headed by Himmler's deputy, Heydrich. The uniformed regular police (the *Orpo*, or Order Police), in their green uniforms, remained a separate branch of the police structure but were also headed by a senior SS officer. After 1939, a large number of these Orpo were formed into police battalions and were used to maintain control of the occupied territories; these activities included participation in genocide (see Chapter 18).

As well as operating plain-clothes agents, the Gestapo were assisted by Nazi Party informers. Every staircase in a block of flats and every street had its Nazi-appointed Block Warden. Their job was to keep a close eye on their neighbours and to report any dangerous behaviour. As one Sopade report noted, from Berlin in 1937, the Block Warden '. . . is supposed to talk to the housewives about prices and food shortages, he pushes into people's homes, he is supposed to find out what newspapers people read, what their lifestyle is like . . .'[7] Clearly, both surveillance and repression was hard-wired into the system.

However, as the Italian Marxist Antonio Gramsci (died 1937) argued – in an analysis that can usefully be applied to the Third Reich – repressive regimes can hardly expect to use unlimited terror against their subjects. Instead, a technique combining the threat of terror and coercion, alongside building consensus, would be more effective. In this, as we shall see, the Nazis were highly successful. They managed to maintain a sense of surveillance and control whilst actually not having the resources to police the entire nation. There were only around 30,000 members of the Gestapo in the whole of Germany (and by no means were all of these field agents) and, for example, the city of Essen had only 43 Gestapo agents to supervise its population of 650,000.[8] As late as 1940, the Stuttgart branch of the SD instructed agents to be more proactive in their surveillance since, 'These opportunities are all too often neglected.' This should perhaps not be overstated as this detective capability was well in excess of what was available to comparable states. For example, the 12,000 detectives that the Nazis inherited from Weimar in 1933 ensured that Berlin (with about one detective per 1,800 inhabitants) had more than twice as many detectives relative to population as London or Paris. Major non-Prussian German cities averaged one detective per 2,600 inhabitants.[9] But then again, the authorities in London and Paris were not attempting, or claiming, the level of control that the Nazis did.

Consequently, the sense of surveillance was only possible in reality because of the active cooperation of large sections of German society. Clearly, fear was a real feature of life. But it was a fear that was not simply based on the watchfulness of the Gestapo and other branches of the Nazi state; instead it must be recognized that surveillance was actively supported by many ordinary Germans who volunteered information regarding behaviour they thought was out of keeping with the new values of the Third Reich.[10] This cooperation existed on many levels: from established non-Nazi policemen who adapted themselves to the New Order,[11] to neighbours, friends and fellow customers in shops and pubs who informed on those they felt were 'suspicious'.[12] Many of those who were denounced were victims of previous disputes with family members, neighbours or work colleagues, but the data suggests that those most at risk were strangers and the socially marginal (such as vagrants, beggars and alcoholics). Clearly, with regard to these, many denouncers could feel morally justified in upholding the Nazi social order without the embarrassment or guilt that might attend denouncing someone they actually knew.

The evidence for support for the domestic policies of the Third Reich

The Nazis attempted to achieve two apparently contradictory outcomes. On one hand they sought to encourage massive levels of participation in repeated gestures of conformity such as the Hitler salute, contributing to collections and hanging out flags on events such as Hitler's birthday. On the other hand they aimed to depoliticize Germans by turning them into passive consumers. In these two aims they were more successful with the second than the first: while only a minority became committed Nazis, the overwhelming majority learned to live with the regime as it met most of their basic needs and reflected their values in many of its actions.[13] This sense of detachment and passive acceptance is reflected in a Sopade report from Westphalia in 1936: 'Here all public life seems to have died out. We have no idea what is going on in the world . . . the Nazis have succeeded in persuading the masses to leave politics to the men at the top . . . they are ensuring that people are no longer interested in anything.'[14]

A whole set of public rituals were devised in order to create a sense of unity with which people could identify: 30 January celebrated Hitler's coming to power; 24 February commemorated the re-founding of the Nazi Party in 1925; in March, on the Sunday that fell five weeks before Easter, was Heroes' Remembrance Day, which transformed a day of mourning the dead of 1914–18 into a celebration of military heroism; 20 April was Hitler's birthday; 1 May was the National Day of Labour, which replaced the old socialist May Day celebrations; the second Sunday in May was Mother's Day, when mothers of large families received one of the three orders of the Mother's Cross; 21 June was a celebration of the Summer Solstice, an aspect of the pagan pseudo-religion that Nazism encouraged; 12 August was Hitler's mother's birthday and another day on which Mother's Crosses were awarded; late September/early October saw the Harvest Festival celebration at the Bückeberg Mountain, which both sought to unite peasants with the regime and also emphasized the Nazi racial obsession with 'Blood and Soil'; on 9 November, at Munich, the party commemorated those Nazis who had died in the Munich Putsch of 1923 and the 'Blood Banner' (the flag carried in 1923) was paraded.

In addition, between October and March, badges were sold on the streets by Hitler Youth – and also leading Nazis – to raise money for Winter Relief for distressed families. 'One-pot Sundays' were also instituted, on which families were encouraged to eat a simple meal and contribute the money saved to the Winter Relief programme. There was genuine appreciation from poorer members of society for the assistance that this provided. A Block Warden in Upper Bavaria recorded, in 1935, the gratitude of one old man, in whose shabby room 'the picture of the Führer looks down from the smoke-blackened walls'.[15] The whole annual programme of events was designed to foster unity amongst the German racial community of 'National Comrades'. Whilst not all Germans eagerly took part in these events, there is plenty of evidence that many did so with some enthusiasm.

On the other hand there is also plenty of evidence for widespread grumbling at the material shortages and economic problems of the Third Reich. Peasants and owners of small businesses complained at the bureaucratic demands of the government and at the lack of sufficient protection for their sector of society; workers grumbled at lack of bargaining rights, food shortages and forced attendance at Nazi events. But these grumbles scarcely qualify as dissent. And even if they are defined as such, they fall far short of opposition and do not come anywhere near resistance. Furthermore, many of these complaints targeted the system and local Nazis rather than Hitler himself, whom Nazi propaganda successfully presented as a man of the people, with his simple meals and his uniform decorated only with the Iron Cross First Class.[16]

Additionally, the fact that these grumbles were expressed loudly enough to be picked up by Sopade and SD reports indicates that the grumblers never intended their complaints to be seen as truly hostile towards the government. The impact of such grumbles was further reduced by the fact that complaints were usually focused on specific issues and were limited to particular groups, or even sections of groups in society. They were not large-scale confrontations with the overall regime. This was, anyway, highly unlikely as many Nazi policies resonated with many groups in society. Many middle-class people were broadly in favour of many Nazi values, workers were grateful for job security,[17] even churchgoers supported the Nazis' nationalism and their opposition to Bolshevism. Alongside this, the abolition of political parties prevented any organized groups from bringing together aspects of discontent and building an alternative programme with which to challenge the Nazis. In addition, the relentless propaganda, the culture of surveillance and the threat of terror ensured that most people had no access to reliable information. Whilst this fed the rumour-machine, it also meant that it could never really become an alternative to the state's control of information. And anyway, many are recorded as saying, gratefully, that there was now order, stability and work. These things counted for a great deal, as did the tearing up of the hated Treaty of Versailles and the reassertion of Germany's place in the world. As a Sopade report reluctantly admitted in the spring of 1937: 'They [most people] do not want to return to the past and if anyone told them that their complaints about this or that aspect threaten the foundations of the Third Reich they would probably be very astonished and horrified.'[18] This was not an isolated report. Another one, from northern Germany in the summer of 1938, corroborates it with its conclusion that: 'People grumble everywhere about everything but nobody intends this grumbling to represent a hostile attitude to the regime'.[19]

The evidence for support for the foreign policy of the Third Reich

Success in foreign affairs clearly boosted the morale of many Germans and added to the popularity of the Nazi government.[20] There is a great deal of evidence to suggest that this was the case. In the Reichstag election, following the 1936 reoccupation of the Rhineland, it seems clear that: 'Even if the voting was rigged, there was no question that most of the country embraced the beginning of Germany's return to great-power status.'[21] And it was little consolation to attribute this to 'hysterical working-class women' and 'people with limited intelligence', as one Sopade reporter did in 1936.[22] Popular opinion considered that 'Hitler succeeds in simply everything' and 'What a guy, Hitler'.[23] Again, after the Anschluss with Austria, the Sopade reports noted genuinely high levels of support for the action and noted that Hitler was favourably compared with Bismarck.[24] Another Sopade report, from Danzig in early 1939, carried a similar message: 'One may well assert that the whole nation is convinced that Hitler is a great politician. This is solely attributable to his foreign policy successes . . .'[25]

But this did not create what the Nazis intended: a population eager for eventual war. In fact the effect was quite the opposite. It was Hitler's successes *without recourse to war* that so impressed and relieved the average German citizen.[26] When war threatened, anxiety increased. In September 1938, as war with the Czechs and their allies seemed imminent, reports from government agencies in Munich identified a depressed mood amongst ordinary Germans and an unpatriotic listening-in to foreign radio broadcasts, which heightened fears of war. This was despite full theatres, cafés and cinemas, which otherwise indicated a positive feel-good factor at work in society. Similarly, on 27 September, the American correspondent William L. Shirer witnessed the lack of enthusiasm amongst Berliners for a military parade designed to fan their desire for war. In his diary that night he noted how the civilians, pouring out of their workplaces, instead, 'ducked into the subways, refused to look on, and the handful that did stood at the kerb in utter silence . . .'[27] So, if foreign policy increased Hitler's popularity, it was conditional on his keeping Germany out of a war – and this he had no intention of doing.

How strong was opposition before the outbreak of the Second World War?

The regime was active in crushing any opposition. As early as 1933, 'Special Courts', with Nazi judges, were established to deal with political crimes. However, acts of serious political opposition were soon dealt with by a new Nazi court – the People's Court. This left the Special Courts dealing with derogatory remarks about the Nazi Party and its leadership, along with punishing the passing on of rumours deemed unpatriotic. In Munich, the Special Court tried cases ranging from rumours that Göring had transferred his wealth to Switzerland, to reports of brutal treatment in Dachau concentration camp. When, in 1938, a sixty-four–year-old woman in the region of Rhineland-Westphalia was overheard commenting to a companion that 'Mussolini has more political sense in one of his boots than Hitler has in his brains', it became a matter for the Gestapo and the local Special Court.[28] This last case is instructive. The fact that she was arrested five minutes after making the remark was not because of the alertness of an ever-present Gestapo, but rather because another customer had overheard her and gone straight to the telephone in order to report her comment to the authorities.

Such offenders did not pose much of a threat to the regime and this was reflected in their sentences. Most sentences ranged from between one and six months in prison. In Munich, between 1933 and 1939, a total of 4,453 cases were brought to the Special Court in the city. But of these only 1,861 actually came to trial.[29] The others were dismissed by the police and the courts because the accusation did not stand up to scrutiny. This is significant because it indicates that there was nothing remotely approaching a reign of terror in the city.

A comparable statistic is that for the number of prisoners held in concentration camps. In September 1939, there were about 25,000 prisoners held in one of six camps: Dachau, Sachsenhausen, Buchenwald, Flossenbürg, Mauthausen and Ravensbrück. This constituted 0.04 per cent of the total

German adult population aged 15–65 years old, which was 52,581,000.[30] Even allowing for the fact that released prisoners were still subject to police supervision, this was clearly not a nation dominated by the numbers of its concentration camp population.

A Sopade report from Saxony in early 1938 also reveals the lack of real opposition beyond the low-level grumbling at shortages and restrictions that we have already observed: 'Only the continual collections . . . and the periodic shortages of various foodstuffs give these groups cause for slight grumbling. It is extremely rare to hear a critical word from workers who are laid off . . . On the other hand, one cannot speak of popular enthusiasm for National Socialism.'[31]

Nevertheless, even if the majority of Germans' lives were not in danger (unless they directly challenged the government), failure to conform could lead to significant problems. A worker in Karlsruhe was dismissed from his job in 1934 because he refused to sing the Nazi 'Horst Wessel Song' and refused to attend parades.[32] More active opposition was suicidal.

Consequently, evidence for real resistance in the 1930s is limited, sporadic and it was ineffective. Members of the banned Communist Party (the KPD) and Social Democratic Party (the SPD) would rarely work together. The former abused the latter as 'Social Fascists', a bizarre phrase invented in Moscow in the early 1930s in the mistaken belief that the Nazis were less of a threat than their socialist rivals. And the latter distrusted the dictatorial aims of the former and their domination by orders from Moscow. Tellingly, by the mid-1930s, the leadership of both organizations was either in exile, dead or in concentration camps. Of the 300,000 members of the Communist Party in 1933, about 150,000 suffered active persecution, up to and including death. Many others kept their heads down. The main aims of both organizations became to simply keep some kind of connection between members within Germany, gather information and – more dangerously – occasionally distribute illegal pamphlets.

This level of opposition was little threat to the regime, although the Gestapo found itself unable to stamp it out, and a secret report concluded: 'They promote energetically the so-called whispering campaign . . . it has not yet been possible to catch a single one of these persons in the act and bring him to trial.'[33] This offers an apparent contrast to the earlier Sopade report, which suggested that Block Wardens made organization of opposition cells almost impossible. But the contrast is more apparent than real. First, they are focused on different areas of life: the Sopade report looked at the home environment, while the Gestapo report focused on conversations at work. Clearly, the latter was a less easily supervised environment than the former. Second, there is no effective opposition being revealed in either report. Whilst the Gestapo might have been irritated by their inability to track down the 'whisperers', those responsible were not able to mount an opposition that really threatened the regime.

The only real potential for effective opposition lay within the military – and their allies within the civil service – as these alone had the potential to topple the regime.[34] But after the personal oath of military loyalty to Hitler in 1934 and in the context of Hitler's foreign policy triumphs in the 1930s, there was little appetite for opposition beyond a small core. Within the Foreign Office, these included the German ambassador in Rome, Ulrich von Hassell, the ambassador in Moscow, Friedrich Graf von der Schulenburg, and Foreign Office officials in Germany such as Ernst von Weizsäcker and Adam von Trott zu Solz. These were in touch with another centre of opposition, which was – surprisingly – within military intelligence. These included Major General Hans Oster and his boss, Admiral Wilhelm Canaris, the head of the *Abwehr* (counter espionage). These in turn were connected to a small group of senior army officers such as the army's Chief of Staff General Ludwig Beck and (after he was removed from his post for being openly critical of Hitler's warlike moves over Czechoslovakia) his successor, Franz Halder. A number of senior officers were shocked by Hitler's removal of high-ranking officers Blomberg and Fritsch early in 1938 (see Chapter 15),[35] as well as by the likelihood of a disastrous war. However, these groups lacked a coherent political ideology and agenda and were undermined by Hitler's successful gaining of the Sudetenland without a war in the autumn of 1938.[36] Appeasement had left the opposition without a pressing reason for action that would appeal to a wider German audience. It would only be the mounting disaster facing Germany in the Second World War that would prompt these groups to finally act to try to remove Hitler at a time when resistance to the Nazis from other sources was also increasing (see Chapter 21).

Prior to this, the only plot to remove Hitler in the 1930s that came anywhere near succeeding was in November 1939. This was the work of a carpenter named Georg Elser, who acted entirely on his own. The plot – with stolen explosives secreted in a hollowed-out pillar in a Munich beer hall – came astonishingly close to killing Hitler. But Hitler unexpectedly cut short his speech and left thirteen minutes before the time-bomb exploded. Despite torture, Elser always insisted that he had acted alone. However, Hitler was obsessed with the idea that British Intelligence was behind the attempt and, in a bizarre twist, ordered the kidnapping of two British agents in neutral Holland who were in contact with a Nazi agent whom they – mistakenly – thought represented the German resistance to Hitler. In a gun battle with undercover SS Security Service men (led by the same officer who had faked a 'Polish attack' on a German radio station in August), a Dutch intelligence officer died and the two British agents were seized. Although held until their liberation in 1945, the two insisted they knew nothing of the plot.[37] There would be no opposition again that came this close to removing the Führer until July 1944.

How popular was the Nazi government by 1939?
The renowned Canadian historian Robert Gellately has convincingly presented a case that concludes that, during the 1930s, there developed a significant level of support for the

Nazi regime within Germany. Gellately argues that the overall evidence shows that – despite never gaining a majority of votes in free elections – the majority of Germans soon demonstrated a high level of support for the Nazi regime and that, to a significant degree, this support survived until 1945. Gellately makes a thought-provoking claim that the Nazi use of terror against specific categories of 'undesirables' was deliberately kept in the public view because most Germans agreed to some extent with such policies. As a result, the mounting persecution of Jews, communists, socialists and trade unionists, the mentally and physically disabled, then the elimination of Jews and Gypsies met with an alarming level of approval from those – the majority of Germans – who were not in these target groups.[38] Similar arguments have also been made by Adam LeBor and Roger Boyes, who argue that, for a variety of reasons, many ordinary Germans came to terms with the Third Reich and that a surprising degree of consensus existed. They suggest that in such a situation there were choices to be made and that many made the wrong ones.[39] The historian Peter Hoffman has remarked that: 'On the whole, at all times from 1933 to 1945 the majority of German voters, indeed of the entire population, supported the government, albeit with varying degrees of willingness.'[40]

The fragmentary nature of the evidence clearly makes it hard to quantify the extent of this support for the Third Reich.[41] Whilst many historians, as we have seen, stress the extent of collusion others have once more reminded us of the totalitarian aims of the Nazis.[42] Despite this, it seems clear that there was a surprising degree of collusion with the regime. Examples of opposition and nonconformity clearly occurred but these coexisted with the more widespread acceptance of the Third Reich. And it was the latter that stopped the emergence of any really sustained opposition to the regime. Alongside this, the Nazi government, for all its emphasis on 'guns before butter', was very conscious of the role of early consumerism and the working-class desire for holidays, both of which could be – and were – manipulated in order to try to win popular support.[43]

This was buttressed by relentless propaganda, which was accompanied by the ever-present threat of force.

Overall, therefore, one has to conclude that the evidence suggests there was considerable support in Germany for Hitler's dictatorship, even if aspects of it caused resentment. Had Hitler died in August 1939, he would probably have done so as the world leader who had (with all things considered) the greatest extent of popular approval. His regime had – it seemed – brought stability and a sense of national pride. His foreign-policy successes had greatly added to his prestige. Most Germans felt little sympathy for the minorities persecuted by the Nazis, even if they disapproved of the more extreme outworkings of the policies. But, in September 1939, Hitler led Germany into a war that would test that popularity to destruction.

17

THE THIRD REICH AT WAR: THE UNSTOPPABLE BLITZKRIEG, 1939–41

Heinz Guderian was a German army officer who was one of the architects of the new kind of warfare that swept Germany to victory in the first three years of the Second World War. During the 1920s, he realized that tanks could revolutionize future wars. This would be a new type of warfare – *Blitzkrieg* (lightning war). Its impact lay in the grouping of armoured forces in independent units that were not tied to the slower-moving foot soldiers. Coordinated with motorized infantry and airpower, the speed and impact of these armoured thrusts would overwhelm opponents, cut enemy troops off from their command centres, cause confusion and bypass strongpoints. Concentrated power was central to the use of Blitzkrieg. As Guderian once commented: 'You hit somebody with your fist and not with your fingers spread.' Another vital ingredient was the presence of officers who had been trained to understand the potential of this new kind of warfare. This often made up for the fact that, in the advance through France in 1940, many German tanks were inferior in their performance when compared with French tanks. What they lacked in specification was more than made up for by the drive and enthusiasm of the German armoured commanders. As early as 1935, Guderian was put in command of a *Panzer* (tank) Division, although he was not yet a general.

The speed with which the German army overwhelmed Poland's defences in September 1939 proved the accuracy of Guderian's prediction. But it still did not persuade other senior officers that this daring kind of warfare was always worth the risk. In France, in May 1940, Guderian attacked with such speed that he was ordered to halt so that the slower-moving infantry could catch up. Following a furious row with his superior, General von Kliest, Guderian was sacked. At this point, Hitler intervened and Guderian was reinstated. As a result, German troops were at the English Channel only four days after Guderian had initially been sacked. Little wonder then that his troops nicknamed him 'Fast Heinz' and 'Hurricane Heinz'.

Three days later – on 23 May – he was to be frustrated again, when Hitler temporarily halted the advance, afraid his panzers were too exposed by the rapidity of their progress. Guderian was furious, since he felt it was this delay that allowed the retreating British to reach the embarkation port at Dunkirk.

Guderian went on to repeat his rapid panzer advances in the USSR in 1941 but fell out with Hitler over the correct tactics to follow in the face of bitter resistance by the Red Army. Consequently, he was dismissed from his command in December 1941, only to be reinstated in 1943 as commander of Germany's armoured troops in a desperate attempt to halt the relentless advance of the Red Army.

Despite losing one of the largest tank battles in history, at Kursk in 1943, Guderian went on to become Commander of the General Staff in 1944 and presided over the purging of officers whose loyalty to the Nazi regime was open to question. In March 1945, another disagreement with Hitler led to his final dismissal from office. He was captured by US forces in May 1945 and – despite accusations of war crimes by the governments of the USSR and Poland – was released in 1948.

He died in 1954, exactly fourteen years to the day since he had led his panzer units across the river Meuse at Sedan, in the decisive breakthrough that had secured victory in France.[1] But it was in Poland, in September 1939, that he had first unveiled the ferocious power of Blitzkrieg.

September 1939: the settling of unfinished business with Poland

At 0445 hours on the morning of 1 September 1939, Germany invaded Poland. This was the culmination of a complicated relationship with Poland that stretched back to the peace treaties that ended the First World War,[2] and lay under the longer shadow of German ambitions in Eastern Europe that stretched back into the Middle Ages.

When Poland was reconstructed in 1919 (having, since the eighteenth century, been partitioned by Prussia, Russia and Austria), its borders with Germany were a matter of bitter contention. The Treaty of Versailles created a Poland whose western territories were coveted by Germany since it had ruled these areas prior to 1919. A strip of land – the 'Polish Corridor' – provided Poland with access to the sea but left East Prussia separated from the rest of Germany. On the coast, the city of Danzig (modern Gdansk) was loosely overseen by the League of Nations but contained a German population that desired union with Germany. In Silesia, bitter fighting between Poles and Germans only ended when the area was partitioned between the two states. In short, there were plenty of reasons why the relationship with Poland was fraught with difficulty. Yet, in 1934, Germany and Poland signed a non-aggression pact that to optimists might have seemed to have provided the basis for an improvement in relations between the two countries. It was, though, simply a short-term expedient by which Hitler calmed tensions on Germany's eastern border while launching his rearmament programme. And, by 1938, this had become clear. In October of that year, Germany offered the Poles a renewal of the treaty but with such strings attached that the Poles were bound to refuse: Danzig to be annexed by Germany and an extra-territorial motorway and railway to cross the Polish Corridor to link East Prussia with Germany. In April 1939, Hitler unilaterally abrogated the 1934 treaty, and the next five months saw tension rise as Germany made increasing demands on Polish territory. In many ways this was a return to the norm in German–Polish relations, the six years 1934–9 being an exception.

When Germany invaded Poland, it did so secure in the knowledge that this would not provoke war with the USSR. Since August 1939, the Nazi–Soviet Pact had guaranteed non-aggression between these two ideological enemies. Furthermore, only sixteen days after Germany invaded Poland, the destruction of that nation was further underscored by a Soviet attack from the east. Like the Germans, the USSR considered that it too had unfinished business with Poland, having lost land to the new Polish state by the Treaty of Riga (1921), which had ended the Soviet–Polish War of 1919–21. Despite a non-aggression pact with Poland in 1932, relations had remained tense. Stalin had ethnically cleansed Poles from the western borderlands of the USSR and blamed Polish agents for problems in Ukrainian agriculture (which were actually caused by Soviet repression and mismanagement). As a consequence, the invading Red Army seized western Belorussia and western Ukraine from Poland and incorporated these regions into the USSR. At the same time, the Soviet secret police began a reign of terror against the Polish intelligentsia and ruling class. In total, somewhere in the region of 150,000 Poles were killed by Soviet repression. The most infamous atrocity committed by the USSR against the Poles would be the murder of Polish army officers at Katyn Wood in 1940, in which 4,500 officers were executed. It was not until 1990 that the Russians would admit their responsibility for this atrocity.

Poland entered a savage six-year period that would see over 16 per cent of its 1939 population casualties of violence and war-related causes. Of these victims, the largest group would be Polish Jews (numbering about 3 million murdered) but Polish non-Jewish civilian casualties would be in the region of 2.5 million. Given Polish military casualty figures of about 240,000, these enormous civilian figures remind us of the kind of 'New Order' that German conquest was unleashing on Europe.[3] By contrast, the United Kingdom had total casualty figures of about 0.94 per cent of its population; the USA lost 0.32 per cent; Germany (measured as the population within its 1937 boundaries) a figure of just under 10 per cent at highest estimates; the USSR about 14 per cent.

Three days after Germany invaded Poland, the British and French declared war. There is evidence to suggest that, up to the final moment, Hitler had hoped that Britain and France would once more appease him. Paul Schmidt, the German government interpreter, later recalled how the news was received in Berlin. The attention immediately turned to von Ribbentrop. '"What now?" asked Hitler, with a savage look, as though implying that his Foreign Minister had misled him about England's probable reaction.' Göring muttered, 'If we lose this war, then God have mercy on us!' And Goebbels 'stood in a corner, downcast and self-absorbed.'[4] Clearly, the Nazi leadership had deluded itself with regard to the reaction of the Western Allies; the local war in the East was on its way to becoming a World War.

A new kind of warfare . . . racial war

It was clear from the start that the Second World War would be radically different from the experiences of 1914–18. As well as Blitzkrieg, it would be different in the way that large numbers of civilians would be deliberately targeted. For this would be a war that, from the outset, would be marked by brutality towards non-combatants and – especially in Eastern Europe – it would be a race war. In July 1940, senior SS officer Reinhard Heydrich confided to a colleague that, before the invasion of Poland, Hitler had instructed him to liquidate leading Poles, running into the thousands.[5] In 1939, the High Command of the German armed forces issued 'schooling pamphlets' to troops instructing them in the need to destroy all aspects of Jewish influence that 'seeks to set all the people of the world against Germany'.[6]

On 22 August 1939, Hitler met with senior military commanders in preparation for the invasion of Poland. Notes taken by a number of commanders included the following instructions: 'Genghis Khan had sent millions of women and children to their deaths, and did so consciously and with a happy heart. History sees in him only the great founder of states.' Hitler had instructed the SS 'mercilessly and without pity to send every man, woman, and child of Polish ethnicity and language to their deaths . . . Poland will be depopulated and resettled with Germans.'[7] These words reveal a great deal about Hitler but also about his generals – whom he had made partners in this enterprise – for none of them protested in the slightest.[8]

Army units were swiftly involved in war crimes in Poland alongside the SS. On 9 September, the Fifteenth Motorized Infantry Regiment murdered 300 Polish POWs. At least 64 other atrocities against Polish POWs by army units are on record in September 1939. When Admiral Wilhelm Canaris of the Abwehr expressed concern to General Wilhelm Keitel, head of *Wehrmacht* (army) High Command, he was told that the 'matter has already been decided by the Führer'.[9] Keitel went on to say that if the army chose not to play its part within this activity it would go on anyway.[10]

In many ways, the Second World War was two wars. One war was fought in the East against those the Nazis regarded as racial enemies; the other was fought in the West against those who were regarded as generally racially acceptable but politically opposed to the New Order of the Third Reich. On the Eastern Front, atrocity and genocide were woven into the fabric of the war from its start, although it took two years for its terrible characteristics to be fully visible. It was not alone in this character (though the scale was unique to the Eastern

Front) since there were other theatres, such as in the Pacific war, where historians have argued that 'war hates' led to 'war crimes';[11] these comparisons in no way diminish the shocking characteristics and scale of Nazi atrocities. But they remind us that war atrocities were not 'a monopoly of the Nazi regime'.[12] And to this we might add the targeting of civilians in Bosnia and Rwanda in the 1990s as horrific reminders of what human beings are capable of. Nevertheless, two things make Nazi war crimes stand out: firstly their appalling scale and secondly the way in which they were part and parcel of the whole ideological package of the Third Reich. It is these factors that so clearly defined the criminal regime Hitler led and increasingly this criminality involved the German military, not only in the conquests that brought populations under Nazi control, but also in the brutality that accompanied it. But first the war would turn westward.

The 'Phoney War'

On 28 September 1939, less than a month since the invasion, the commander of Polish forces in Warsaw negotiated a ceasefire in the face of unstoppable German attacks. On 5 October, Hitler took the salute at a victory parade through the city and the next day the last organized Polish resistance ended. The British and French, who had declared war on behalf of Poland, were unable to affect the outcome. Neither did they take offensive action against Germany in the west. What followed was a six-month period of limited military activity. In Britain, it became known as the 'Phoney War', or the 'Bore War' (a play on Boer War). In Germany, a popular term was '*der Sitzkrieg*' (the sitting war), which was a play on Blitzkrieg.[13]

The period was not entirely inactive. The RAF dropped propaganda leaflets on Germany and the French began, then reversed, a limited incursion into the Saarland on Germany's western border. Goebbels noted in his diary: 'Absolutely nothing is happening on the West Wall . . . the French have withdrawn to the border. It is impossible to say what they intend to do now. A crazy war.'[14] Over the winter, the USSR invaded tiny Finland (in the 'Winter War') and suffered high casualties, though the outcome of such a one-sided conflict was never in doubt. The Finns were eventually forced, in March 1940, to sign the Treaty of Moscow, by which Finland gave up 11 per cent of its territory and 30 per cent of its economic wealth to the USSR.[15] Later, in 1941, the Finns would join Germany in its attack on the USSR, in what the Finns would call the 'Continuation War'. At the end of the war, Finland would have the curious distinction of being the only ally of Germany that was not occupied by the Allies at the end of the conflict, remained a democracy and in which native Jews suffered no persecution.

In the Atlantic, German U-boats began attacking Allied shipping and, in December 1939, the British scored a high-profile victory when the German pocket battleship *Admiral Graf Spee* was trapped in the neutral port of Montevideo, Uruguay, and was eventually scuttled by her captain. He later committed suicide wrapped not in the Nazi flag but in the Imperial flag of the German navy. The best the propaganda machine of the Third Reich could make of this was that it had been a 'heroic suicide'.[16]

The war in the West

The fighting in the West commenced in Scandinavia. The Allies had plans to send troops to northern Sweden to deny its iron ore to Germany. In addition, the British navy boarded a German vessel, the *Altmark*, to free British POWs whose ships had been sunk by the *Admiral Graf Spee*. It was, incidentally, the last recorded use of a naval cutlass in action. Faced with threats to its iron-ore supplies and British action in Norwegian waters, the Germans invaded Denmark and Norway in April 1940. In Denmark, the occupation was swift due to Denmark's close proximity to Germany, but the fighting in Norway – assisted by French and British forces – continued until June. By that time, the Germans were fighting in France and it was clear that Norway was lost. However, since 1947, a Christmas tree has been given to the people of London each year from the Norwegian people in gratitude for Britain's support for Norway. In Britain, on 10 May 1940, dissatisfaction with the Norwegian campaign led to the replacement of Neville Chamberlain as Prime Minister with Winston Churchill. The era of appeasement was truly over. However, it was to be a significant date for more than this reason – for on that very day, German forces invaded the Netherlands, Belgium and Luxembourg; more significantly, they outflanked the French by advancing through the thickly wooded region of the Ardennes. It was an area that the Allies had considered impassable for tanks; they were wrong.[17]

Whilst Hitler's decisions were to eventually lose Germany the Second World War, in the opening months his gambler's instincts (and undoubtedly a significant degree of tactical insight) came close to winning it for them. It was little wonder that his confidence in his own infallibility – already boosted by the foreign policy successes of the 1930s – soared. The original plan of the German army High Command had been to advance through Belgium and occupy the industrial areas of Northern France. It was Hitler – supported by Generals von Manstein and Guderian – who saw and insisted on the risky opportunity offered by the Ardennes route. It paid off dramatically. From this point, 'France's collapse occurred with the force of an ancient drama . . . For the Greeks, the act of *até* , fateful blindness, always preceded the act of the *catastrophe*.'[18] The French defensive Maginot Line was immediately rendered irrelevant and, by 20 May, Guderian's tanks were at Abbeville, near the Channel, and had cut off the Allied armies in Belgium.

It was then that Hitler made the fateful move to temporarily halt the German advance. The reasons have been much debated and criticized – especially in the light of what was to follow. At the time – although Guderian disagreed – the decision was more understandable. The British seemed broken, the Germans were stretched, tanks needed conserving for what might prove to be a large campaign further south to finish off the French – who it was thought would only admit defeat when Paris was captured – and the Luftwaffe promised to wreak havoc on the British and French forces awaiting evacuation. But German army Chief of Staff, General Halder, disapprovingly noted in his diary: 'Now the political leadership gets the idea of transferring the final decisive battle from Flanders to northern France. In order to disguise this political aim it is explained that the Flanders terrain with its numerous waterways is unsuitable for tanks.'[19]

In the event, the delay allowed the retreating Allies time to strengthen their defences and, eventually, the British succeeded in evacuating about 340,000 troops from Dunkirk and another 220,000 from other French ports (though most of their heavy equipment was left behind). Churchill's 'Miracle of deliverance' had saved the British army (and a great many French soldiers too). The collapse of French resistance followed swiftly. On 22 June, an armistice was signed in the very railway carriage that had witnessed the German humiliation in 1918. At that time, Hitler had lain in a German hospital, temporarily blinded by a gas attack, and had resolved (he later claimed) to reverse the bitter humiliation of 1918. Within twenty-two years, he had done so with a vengeance. The 'Führer Myth' – carefully cultivated through the 1930s – had reached a new level. Hitler did some sightseeing in Paris (the only time he ever visited the city) and the armistice site was destroyed, the railway carriage being removed to Berlin. In 1945, it was moved to Thuringia and was eventually destroyed by the SS. France faced the humiliation of German occupation of the north and west, while the south-east was under the authority of the new French government of Marshal Philippe Pétain, the hero of the 1916 Battle of Verdun. With its capital at Vichy it was accommodating towards the Germans, who now seemed to be the masters of Europe.[20]

On 10 June, the Italians – confident they were joining the winning side – had also declared war on France and Britain.

The entry of Italy into the war on Germany's side was met with cynical humour in some quarters of the Reich. A joke from 1940 quipped: 'The German army HQ receives news that Mussolini's Italy has joined the war. "We'll have to put up 10 divisions to counter him!" says one general. "No, he's on our side," says another. "Oh, in that case we'll need 20 divisions."'[21]

The rapid German successes also prompted the USSR into action. Stalin had assumed that the war in the West would be a long drawn-out affair. Surprised by the speed of German victory, he took the opportunity to seize territory in order to improve the defensive position of the USSR. The Baltic states of Estonia, Latvia and Lithuania were swiftly annexed (in line with the Nazi–Soviet Pact of 1939) and pressure brought to bear on Romania to give up land lost by Russia in 1918. These actions turned German attention eastward. The war diaries of Chief of Staff General Halder reveal how, as soon as late June 1940, discussions were occurring centred on moving German troops eastward. And by July, he was pondering 'how a military blow against Russia can be carried out to force it to recognize Germany's dominant role in Europe'.[22]

The Third Reich triumphant

Britain was now isolated. The failure of the Luftwaffe to gain air supremacy in the Battle of Britain meant that invasion plans were cancelled in September, though fierce debates still rage as to how seriously these were ever entertained by Hitler.[23] In the Atlantic, German U-boats used the newly conquered French ports to launch attacks on British shipping. It was the 'Happy Time' (1940–1), as U-boat commanders termed it, though not for those on the receiving end of torpedoes and gunfire.[24] In September 1940, the Tripartite Pact united Japan, Italy and Germany and stated that any nation (with the exception of the USSR) not currently in the war, which attacked one of the three signatories would be deemed at war with all three. The arrangement formalized earlier agreements between these 'Axis powers'. With Germany triumphant, the other states of Europe began to adjust their stance to accommodate the new realities. In November 1940, Hungary, Romania and Slovakia joined the Tripartite Pact. In March 1941, they were joined by Bulgaria, lured by the promise of regaining land lost to Greece and Yugoslavia following defeat in the First World War. That same month, Prince Paul, the regent of Yugoslavia, signed the pact. After the signing, one Romanian diplomat tried to comfort a counterpart in the Yugoslav delegation with the words: 'A twisted ankle is easier to heal than an amputated foot', a reference to the Yugoslav difficulties in fronting the agreement when they went home compared with Romania's loss of territory in several boundary adjustments that had occurred since 1940.[25] But the situation would prove more serious for the Yugoslav leadership as, later in the month, a military coup – backed by the British – brought to power the 17–year-old King Peter II. Yugoslavia's wavering led to Hitler ordering the invasion of the country in April. In June 1941, Croatia also joined the pact. Curiously, in May 1945, the pro-German Croatian army, retreating into Austria, would be the last Axis army to surrender to the Allies. The British returned them to Yugoslavia and death at the hands of their communist enemies.

Other states too found it advantageous to accommodate the Germans. This included neutrals such as Portugal, Spain, Sweden and Switzerland, who all cooperated to some extent with the Third Reich. Swiss factories made military components, the Swiss National Bank bought gold from the Reichsbank – which itself had been looted from conquered Europe – and the Swiss francs so gained were used by Germany to buy essential materials from other 'neutrals'. Sweden provided iron ore to Germany and allowed German troops to cross its territory. Its stance was complex though, as it also provided shelter for Jews fleeing from Denmark, trained Norwegian and Danish troops who were then able to re-enter these countries in May 1945 and offered humanitarian assistance through the Swedish diplomats Count Folke Bernadotte (who was responsible for arranging safe passage for many concentration-camp inmates) and Raoul Wallenberg (who saved thousands of Jewish lives through issuing people with Swedish passports).

Spain offered economic and military assistance to the Germans but its leader, General Franco, would not risk Spain's future by occupying Gibraltar as the Germans requested. Indeed, after a long and fruitless negotiation with Franco in 1940, Hitler commented that he would rather have teeth extracted than face another such meeting. Clearly, the Führer was not used to being thwarted. From 1943, Spain returned to full neutrality as Germany's defeat loomed and, throughout the war, Jewish refugees were allowed to remain in Spain.

Even the USSR made overtures to Germany regarding joining the Tripartite Pact. These though were not taken up by Germany, already well into its plans to invade the USSR. However, in January 1941, new areas of economic cooperation were agreed between the Third Reich and its intended victim. The Soviets, clearly, were eager to keep Germany friendly for as long as possible. They would be disappointed by the events of 1941. Other states were more cautious. Finland – attacked by the USSR for a second time in June 1941 and soon engaged in war with its old adversary, but alongside the Germans this time – joined the Anti-Comintern Pact in November 1941 but declined to join the Tripartite Pact. The Finns considered their conflict with the USSR to be quite separate from the Second World War. As a result, Helsinki joined London and Moscow as the only capitals of fighting European nations not occupied by an enemy at some time in the Second World War.

Early in 1941, Hitler sent German forces to assist his Italian allies who were struggling in their campaigns in the Mediterranean. Soon, German forces were engaged in Libya and had forced the British back into Egypt. In April, Germany attacked Greece and the wavering Yugoslavia and postponed its planned invasion of the USSR as a result of this action. It would be another fateful decision. In December 1941 – when advanced German patrols saw the sunlight glinting on the golden domes of the

Kremlin and found discarded tickets printed with 'Moscow' in the litter bins of the outlying railway stations of the Soviet capital – they may have reflected on the two-month delay in the attack on the USSR that had been caused by German action in the Balkans. For, at that point, with the Russian winter closing around them, they had not succeeded in capturing the capital of the USSR before the Soviet counter-offensive was launched against them. But all this was unthinkable in the spring and summer of 1941, for then the Blitzkrieg still seemed unstoppable. By the end of May, Germany had defeated Greece and had gone on to invade Crete. The sinking of the German battleship *Bismarck* in May, though, offered a small consolation to the British.

The war turns East
In December 1940, the German military began detailed planning for war in the East. On 22 June 1941, Germany and its allies attacked the USSR in Operation Barbarossa. Named from a crusading German king of the Middle Ages, it was a military operation of epic proportions. Over 3 million troops of Germany and its allies invaded the USSR along a 1,800–mile (2,900–kilometre) front. Alongside the Germans were fighting forces from Croatia, Finland, Hungary, Romania, Italy and Slovakia. Volunteer units from other nations joined them in what many regarded as a crusade against communism. For the Nazis, it was the culmination of their geo-political dreams. Here, at last, was the opportunity to capture vast areas for Lebensraum in the East and to seize the resources of the USSR. More than this, it saw the realization of the Nazi racial and political fantasies that had fused Jews and communists as their ultimate enemies and that regarded the USSR as the home of 'Jewish-Bolshevism'. Whilst frustration with the USA was increasingly leading to Hitler accusing Roosevelt of being in the pay of World Jewry, nothing resonated with Hitler's psyche and Nazi political ideology as much as the war in the East. Soon it would see the greatest casualties in any war. Its

opening weeks would see the start of mass killings of Jewish civilians, which would escalate to the murder of whole communities as the summer progressed and, over the winter, would develop into planning a genocide that sought to encompass all the Jews of Europe.

The attack on the USSR was the largest military operation in human history. And it would destroy the Third Reich.

18

'THE TWISTED ROAD TO AUSCHWITZ': FROM PERSECUTION TO GENOCIDE

In 1941, SS units began the mass murder of Jews in the USSR. Few German soldiers from the regular army objected to these massacres. A rare example was that of two anonymous army field chaplains (one Catholic, one Protestant) who intervened to try to help ninety Jewish children below the age of five, at Bjelaja Zerkow, south of Kiev. They had been abandoned, without food or water, by the SS after the rest of their community had been murdered. A senior army officer – Helmuth Groscurth – then intervened too, in an attempt to delay the killings, but he was overruled by more senior army and SS officers. Eventually, all the little children were killed. One of the SS supervising these murders later stated at his trial how one little fair-haired girl had held his hand while waiting to be shot. An army officer whose organizational input had helped facilitate these final killings was later recommended for promotion. Groscurth's report on the events is shocking because, in this, he concluded not that the killings should not have happened, but, rather, that the horror of the drawn-out affair would have been avoided if the little children had been shot by the SS immediately after the Jewish adults were killed and not left until later.[1]

Brutality and ghettos

Long before 1941, it was clear that Europe's Jews were to be targeted for brutal treatment. SS atrocities against Jews occurred in the first weeks of the Polish campaign in September 1939. However, at first, it was not clear – even to the Nazis – exactly how that brutality would develop. On 21 September 1939, Heydrich, in a speech to SS *Einsatzgruppen* (task groups, special action groups) explained that the *Endziel* (final goal) was a territorial solution whereby all Jews (including Jews from Germany) would be sent to eastern reservations. At this time the destination probably envisaged was the Lublin area, in the eastern part of German-occupied Poland.[2] One of the earliest uses of the term *Endlösung* (Final Solution) appeared in December 1939, in a document produced by the Jewish-affairs specialists of the SS security service (the SD) in Berlin. But at this time it still implied a form of brutal reservation. Whilst it was local initiatives that led to ethnic cleansing in the Warthegau (an area of western Poland annexed by Germany in 1939 and differentiated from occupied Poland, the so-called 'General Government' area), those who administered it did so in the knowledge that their actions were approved of in Berlin.[3]

The confinement of eastern Jews was a clear aim of Nazi policy at this stage. The first ghetto was established at Piotrkow Trybunalski, in October 1939. Larger ones followed. The ghetto at Lodz was set up in April 1940; the Warsaw ghetto was established in October. Soon, 380,000 people were crammed into one quarter of the Polish capital. Many other ghettos were set up in 1940 and 1941. Rapidly sealed off from the outside world, those trapped in them fell victim to hunger, disease and the casual violence of Germans. Jews in Western Europe faced discrimination and restrictions but the full force of Nazi brutality would not target them until later in the war.

In the autumn of 1939, Goebbels visited the Lodz ghetto and

Posen to produce anti-Polish and anti-Jewish films. He commented on the Jews that: 'They are not people but animals. And for that reason, they are not a humanitarian but a surgical task. We have to take steps here, and quite radical ones.' He did not specify what but added that his conclusions had Hitler's full support.[4] In April 1940, Hitler remarked to Kvaternik, deputy head of state of Croatia, that the Jews would be sent somewhere and he did not care where. Clearly, radical solutions were under consideration long before the invasion of the USSR in 1941.

Despite this, as late as 1941, the details of the long-term aims of the Nazis for the Jews of Europe remained unclear. Plans for establishing a reservation around Lublin or transporting Jews to Madagascar were soon seen as being unrealistic. Heydrich's reference to a 'final goal' when he had addressed the leaders of SS Einsatzgruppen in September 1939 remained undefined. With the invasion of the USSR, in June 1941, that objective would be clarified in the most horrific fashion.

The invasion of the USSR: the beginning of genocidal war

In 1941, as the Germans prepared for war against the USSR – and then as they put this plan into operation – there was widespread talk at the highest levels of 'nothing less than serial genocides'.[5] In May 1941, a meeting of state secretaries (gathered to plan the feeding of the invading German army from the produce of the USSR) calculated mass starvation of the civilian population. Later that year (November 1941), Göring told the Italian Foreign Minister, Ciano, that within a year 20–30 million people would starve to death in the USSR. At the same time, SS chief Himmler oversaw the production of a resettlement plan that envisaged the deportation of 31 million people to Siberia, consisting of all Jews, 80–85 per cent of Poles, 75 per cent of Belorussians, and 64 per cent of western Ukrainians.[6]

In addition, Hitler (according to notes made by General Halder from a meeting in March 1941) specifically stated: 'This is a war of extermination.'[7] This specifically related to 'the communist adversary'. But in Nazi terminology so-called 'Jewish-Bolshevism' had already become inextricably mixed and thought processes were incrementally moving towards genocide, even if this policy took some months to be fully articulated and applied. Specific references to exterminating Bolshevik commissars and communist intelligentsia, by special methods outside of normal courts martial, rapidly translated during the summer of 1941 into the physical destruction of anyone regarded as a racial enemy. And this had already been well established in Nazi terms as meaning Jews.

This is clear from a document issued in June 1941 entitled 'Guidelines for the Behaviour of the Troops in Russia'. According to this document: 'This battle demands ruthless and energetic measures against Bolshevik agitators, guerrillas, saboteurs, Jews, and complete elimination of any active or passive resistance.'[8] Three days later – 6 June 1941 – this was published as the infamous 'Commissar Order'. Whilst this specified the shooting of Communist Party officials, the previous instructions (and the way this order would be interpreted) shows that targets had been deliberately vaguely drawn. Any racial enemy was doomed. And all of this involved the regular army. SS preparations were quite separate and more radical still.

It is important to understand the way in which the escalation of the murder and starvation of Jews on a large scale (1939–41), to continent-wide genocide of the Jews (1941–5), took place against the background of the invasion of the USSR in June 1941 and the declaration of war against the USA in December 1941. By that last date, the Third Reich was locked into a titanic struggle that it was by no means certain to win. Nazi racial obsessions held Jews responsible for this expansion of the war. Jews were equated with both communism in the USSR and capitalism in the USA. That two leaders as different as Stalin and Roosevelt were regarded as tools in the hands of an international Jewish conspiracy reveals how wild Nazi fantasies ran. And it shows how these fantasies could be organized so as to blame the Jews for all Germany's misfortunes, whilst the Third Reich, of course, bore no responsibilities whatsoever. It should be noted that it was Hitler who declared war upon both the USSR and the USA – but as far as he was concerned it was the Jews who were to blame. And in this titanic struggle, Nazi hatred of the Jews was now rapidly reaching murderous intensity.

The process leading to the 'Final Solution'

From the early stages of the invasion of the USSR, SS Einsatzgruppen, SD security police units and Order Police battalions (units drawn from the German police force and employed in the occupied territories) began a process of killing people described as 'Jewish-Bolshevik enemies' and encouraging pogroms by the local populations. In Latvia and in the Ukraine, local people took the arrival of German forces as a signal to begin murdering their Jewish neighbours, who in anti-Soviet propaganda were blamed for communist repression.

The operations of the Einsatzgruppen were monitored at the highest levels. On 1 August, Gestapo head Heinrich Müller telegraphed the Einsatzgruppen that Hitler was to be continually informed about their operations. At first, the Jews who were targeted were men. However, during August, the killing expanded to include entire Jewish communities.[9] Many Einsatzgruppen were already improvising and this probably did not result from a specific order, which was once thought to have been issued by Himmler in mid-August 1941.[10] Instead, the shift may, in fact, have been triggered by Hitler's comments at a military conference in July concerning the possibilities offered by anti-partisan drives. This seems to have been reflected in an order by Himmler early in August to the SS second cavalry brigade to target the entire Jewish population of Pinsk in Belorussia, since, he claimed: 'The Jews are the partisans' reserve force.'[11]

Massacres took place in all regions occupied by the Germans. One of the largest was at Babi Yar ravine, in the Ukraine, in September 1941, when 33,700 Jews were shot near Kiev. The

Ukrainian Jewish diarist Iryna Khoroshunova recorded how rumour reached nearby Jewish communities of 'something terrible, horrible going on'.[12] A description of the liquidation of about 8,000 Jews from the ghetto at Borissov in Belorussia, in October 1941, conveys something of the horror of these killings.

> Having been completely undressed they were driven to the graves and were forced to lie face down. The police [mainly Latvians] and Germans shot them with rifles and automatic weapons. In this way more and more groups were driven to the graves and shot . . . At the place of execution there were snacks and schnaps. The police drank schnaps and had a snack in the intervals between shooting the groups of Jews . . .[13]

In a number of cases regular army units assisted the SS and police squads, and many army orders justified these actions as being reprisals against 'Jewish-Bolsheviks'. Years of propaganda had fused these two concepts and this made for a lethal combination in the minds of many soldiers. As early as June 1941, a German army sergeant wrote home and concluded: 'Now Jewry has declared war on us along the whole line, from one extreme to the other, from the London and New York plutocrats to the Bolsheviks'.[14] A little later, a non-commissioned officer wrote home in July 1942: 'The great task given us in the struggle against Bolshevism lies in the destruction of eternal Jewry'; another wrote in June 1942: 'If one sees what the Russian has done here in Russia, only then does one rightly grasp why the Führer began the struggle against the Jews.'[15] Army reprisals against civilians show these views were not isolated. These murders usually involved large numbers of Jews and were coded as anti-partisan drives. The reality is revealed by statistics such as when the army commander in western Belorussia reported killing 10,431 out of 10,940 taken in 'battles with partisans' in October 1941. But since only two Germans died, it is clear these were simply murders of civilians.[16]

Appalling as these killings were, even worse was yet to come. Historians differ in their interpretations as to exactly when the decision was made to escalate mass killings to the total annihilation of all Europe's Jews. A number have argued that mid-September 1941 was the most likely time that Hitler approved the deportation of German Jews and their murder in the East.[17] Mid-October has also been identified as a key date, as, after 15 October, these deportations eastwards extended the scope of Nazi killing. These resulted from Hitler's sudden decision to deport eastward all the Jews in Germany and German-occupied Czech lands. The timing of this decision may have been affected by a wish to make accommodation available for bombed out German civilians, or as a response to a rapidly deteriorating relationship with the USA, exemplified by the US policy of shooting U-boats on sight, issued on 11 September.[18] Other historians have suggested that the move accompanied the Soviet counter-offensive before Moscow and Hitler's declaration of war on the USA in December, which turned the conflict into a world war.[19] This seems more convincing since earlier Himmler had actually suspended the shooting of Berlin Jews sent to Kovno in Lithuania. The order came too late. The 5,000 German Jews had been shot on arrival in the vicinity of the Ninth Fort, a fortification serving as a prison. This seems to suggest that, even as late as the end of November, the final decision to implement genocide had not definitively been made.

Whatever the exact point in late 1941 that the decision was made, there is a great deal of evidence to suggest that the process was accelerating at that time. Himmler, in later conversation with senior SS officers, repeatedly claimed that Hitler had given him the order early that autumn. On 24 September, Goebbels met Hitler and discussed the removal of all Jews from Germany. On 17 October, Hitler referred to the elimination of Jews in Eastern Europe. On 25 October, in a meeting with Himmler and Heydrich, Hitler signalled an end to any Jewish emigration and instead referred to exterminating the

Jews and, that same month, the Gestapo ended all emigration. By November 1941, work had commenced on building an extermination facility at Belzec, and Himmler and Heydrich had discussed gassing facilities at Mogilev, Sobibor and Chelmno, and a large crematorium had been ordered for Auschwitz. In December 1941, at Berlin University, Goebbels referred to Hitler's 'prophecy' (made in January 1939) regarding the destruction of Jewry and added that this was now being realized. The rapid appearance of all these developments clearly indicate that a decision had been made by Hitler in autumn 1941. 'Hitler kept hitting the same notes and sending signals that were impossible to miss.'[20]

On 11 December 1941, Germany declared war on the USA. The next day, Hitler met with Nazi Gauleiters, and Goebbels's diary records the message Hitler gave: 'He prophesied to the Jews that if they once more brought about another world war, they would experience their extermination. That is no mere talk. The World War is here, the extermination of the Jews must be the necessary consequence.'[21] On 18 December, Himmler, after a meeting with Hitler, noted in his desk calendar, 'Jewish question: to be exterminated as partisans'.[22] This was a direct link back to the genocidal character of the instructions for Operation Barbarossa, which had been published earlier in the year. Only now – with the battle stalled before Moscow, the likelihood of a long drawn out struggle with the USSR and the escalation of the scope of the war to include the USA – did the increasing scale and radicalization of the killings culminate in the articulation of the ultimate aim of the Nazi regime. This was the destruction of the entire Jewish population within Nazi-controlled Europe. The Wannsee Conference (which followed in January 1942 and is sometimes presented as the meeting that planned the Final Solution) was, in fact, more a matter of Heydrich imposing his authority on the process[23] and also to make accomplices of the major government ministries involved in the genocide.[24]

Heydrich's role in coordinating this plan can be traced back to Göring's authorization of him to 'submit to my office in the near future an overall plan that shows the preliminary organizational, practical and material measures requisite for the implementation of the projected final solution of the Jewish question (*Endloesung der Judenfrage*).'[25] That this was dated 31 July 1941 reveals how long before the Wannsee Conference this decision had been made. It was a decision closely linked to the invasion of the USSR and one that accelerated lethally in the six months that followed. It came from the very top of the Third Reich, since Göring was Number Two in the Nazi hierarchy and had been granted extensive power over the coordination of Jewish policy by Hitler himself. That no written 'Führer Order' survives, linking Hitler directly to the genocide, is no surprise since one almost certainly never existed. This was simply not the way Hitler operated with regard to government, where he set broad goals and others then engaged in 'working towards the Führer' by competing to put these goals into practice. Furthermore, when it came to the most controversial actions, Hitler was even more adept at avoiding a direct connection between such activities and himself, as we have seen with regard to 'Crystal Night' (Chapter 9). However, all the evidence is clear that the Führer was the driving force behind the genocide that others put into practice. The constant reiteration of his January 1939 Reichstag 'prophecy' is evidence enough of Hitler focusing murderous intent on the Jews of Europe once the Second World War had started. The fact that Hitler consistently mis-dated the original speech to the outbreak of war in September 1939 indicates that, in his own mind, the 'war against the Jews' and the outbreak of the Second World War had become inextricably mixed.[26]

The extermination camps of the 'Final Solution'

In March 1942, 75–80 per cent of the victims of the Final Solution were still alive. By the end of March 1943, only 20–25 per cent of those who were to be murdered were still living. The mass shootings continued after 1941 but the bulk of the killing in 1942 took place at three extermination centres: Belzec, Treblinka, Sobibor. These were the so-called 'Operation Reinhard Camps' and were named after Heydrich, assassinated in June 1942. The killings also took place at centres that functioned as both concentration camps and extermination centres. These were Chelmno, Majdanek and, most infamously, at Auschwitz-Birkenau. In total the Operation Reinhard camps murdered 1.7 million people in their period of operation (March 1942–December 1943). At Auschwitz alone, somewhere in the region of 1 million Jewish people and 250,000 non-Jews were murdered between 1941 and 1945.[27] Here the extermination centre was combined with an industrial complex based on slave labour.[28] Most arrivals were subject to selection at 'the ramp' after their trains arrived. Those fit for work were usually sent to the labour camp. The old, sick, and mothers with children were gassed shortly after arrival. The removal of corpses from the gas chambers and their cremation was carried out by Jewish *Sonderkommando* (special detachment) members, who were periodically also gassed and replaced. A surviving member of the Sonderkommando later described how they opened the gas chamber doors to find the corpses, 'all standing up, some black and blue from the gas. No place where to go. Dead. If I close my eyes, the only thing I see is standing up, women with children in their hands.'[29]

Twins were often selected for medical experiments by SS Dr Mengele, and those with physical abnormalities were singled out since, after execution, they made for interesting dissection. The ghettos were emptied as their inhabitants were transported to these centres of death. Jews from Western Europe were either moved on a temporary basis to these holding-ghettos, or directly to the extermination centres.

Expertise in such killings had been developed since 1940 as the SS gassed Polish inmates of psychiatric hospitals in German-occupied territory, often in mobile gas vans using carbon monoxide from the exhaust. Later models of these mobile gas vans were tested on Soviet POWs at Sachsenhausen concentration camp and then deployed, from November 1941, in southern Ukraine in killing Jewish men, women and children. Soon many of these vans were operating, from the Baltic states to Serbia, as well as in the extermination centre of Chelmno from December 1941. At about the same time the method was applied to fixed gas chambers at Belzec extermination camp.

At Auschwitz, the primary killing agent used was IG Farben's poison gas crystals (Zyklon B), which had originally been invented as a pesticide. About 10,000 kilos were used in the process of mass murder. At Auschwitz, IG Farben also built a complex synthetic fuel and synthetic (buna) rubber plant. The site was out of reach of allied bombing raids, was well connected to the railway system and had a plentiful supply of slave labour. When fully operational, the IG Farben industrial complex at Auschwitz consumed more electricity per day than Berlin. And this was the same industrial company that also researched and developed a wide range of medicines and whose scientists won a number of Nobel Prizes. At the Nuremberg War Crimes Trials, the manufacturers of the poison gas claimed ignorance of its murderous use and were released. The excuses of other managers included claims of having no choice in complying with the dictates of the Nazi regime, but there are allegations that sympathetic US industrial interests colluded in obstructing investigations into the complicity of these managers, in order to shield trans-Atlantic connections, which had existed with this key player in Hitler's rearmament programme, in the period leading up to the Second World War. After the war, the huge cartel was broken up and its constituent companies, including Bayer, Hoechst, BASF and Agfa, resumed business.[30]

At a meeting of senior party and government officials at Posen in October 1943, Himmler spoke about the extermination of the Jews but explained that it could not be publicly discussed: 'This is a glorious page in our history and one that has never been written and can never be written.'[31] Later,

Albert Speer – as he reinvented himself after 1945 – claimed he knew nothing of the genocide; but he was present at Posen to hear Himmler's three-hour-long speech. In the same way, many members of the Order Police would escape justice after 1945 because they were not actually members of the Einsatzgruppen. The same applied to members of the army who had assisted in the genocide, since the responsibility was placed solely on the shoulders of the SS.

From 1941 onwards, Jews across Europe were hunted down. In some countries, such as in Slovakia and Croatia, local authorities generally cooperated willingly; there was also active cooperation offered by the Vichy administration in France. Other states were less cooperative. In Denmark, almost all the country's Jewish population was assisted to escape to Sweden.

In a number of countries, the response to Nazi demands to surrender Jews was complex. The Romanians initially cooperated but then refused in late 1942. By early 1943, the Hungarians too blocked German demands for the deportation of the country's Jews. In Bulgaria, Jews from areas recently annexed from Greece and Yugoslavia were handed over to the Germans but there was greater reluctance to deport Bulgarian Jews in the face of public protests and, in March 1943, planned deportations were stopped. Italy too would not cooperate in deporting its Jews into German hands, despite the anti-Semitism of Mussolini, and there were even examples of Italian officials protecting Jews in Italian-occupied areas of southern France and in Croatia. The Germans reluctantly accepted the refusal of the Romanians but were not willing to relax the pressure on the Hungarians. Here the Jewish population numbered almost 800,000 and its destruction remained a Nazi goal. In 1944, Germany occupied Hungary (which was negotiating changing sides with the Allies). In a concentrated operation, the Hungarian Jewish population was murdered in Auschwitz.

In a continent at war, escape was almost impossible. Until late 1943 (when there was some relaxation), Swiss policy led to most Jews being handed back. Sweden too was similarly closed to refugees until November 1942. After this point the deportation of Norway's Jews prompted a change in policy and, from this moment onwards, Sweden became actively engaged in helping Jews escaping from other Scandinavian countries and in other rescue operations elsewhere. Whether this was prompted by humanitarianism, or by a reassessment of Germany's likelihood of winning the war is hard to decide.

Resistance

That there were relatively few acts of resistance, compared with the numbers murdered, should come as no surprise. First, the logical assumption that to obey would make survival more likely was turned against the victims. They were marked for death whatever they did. Second, the shock and fear of civilians facing brutal, armed men must have had a paralysing effect on many of these terrified people. Third, the very presence of loved ones could make it harder to fight back since there were children to be shielded and comforted. Fourth, for those taken from the ghettos to the killing centres, the effects of malnutrition, disease and exhaustion sapped the will to fight. And for those transported in cattle trucks from Western Europe to an extermination centre such as Auschwitz, the victims were left disorientated and bewildered when they finally arrived. Barking dogs and shouted commands added to this state of shock. Greta Salus remembered her experience and that of others on arrival at Auschwitz in 1943: '*Schneller, schneller, schneller* (faster, faster, faster) – it still rings in my ears . . . utterly addled and half-dazed, as though they had been hit on the head.'[32]

However, there were acts of defiance. In 1943, Jews of the Warsaw ghetto rose in revolt, until crushed by huge numbers of well-armed Nazi forces. Uprisings also took place in Treblinka camp (1943), Sobibor (1943), and in Auschwitz amongst members of the Sonderkommando (1944). Jewish partisan groups also operated in the occupied areas of the USSR.

How was the Final Solution possible?

The appalling crime of the genocide committed against the Jews during the Second World War continues to provoke controversy amongst historians seeking to explain how it was possible. It has been controversially argued that the genocide of the Jews was a peculiarly German phenomenon and arose from a widespread desire across all classes of German society to eliminate the Jews. This desire arose from the very particular nature of German history that produced a unique mindset that gave rise to this process of mass murder.[33] Other historians have offered significantly different interpretations. One contrasting viewpoint uses the records of Order Police Battalion 101 in Poland and the USSR to argue that its members were not racial fanatics, or driven by fear of punishment but, instead, were peculiarly open to indoctrination through a mixture of their age, lack of education, limited skills and marginal employment. Their weakness in the face of peer pressure, careerist ambitions and official racial theory led to them becoming mass murderers. As such, less than 500 men shot 38,000 Jews and dispatched a further 45,000 to the gas chambers of Treblinka in just sixteen months in 1942–3. Less than 20 per cent of the unit refused to obey these murderous orders.[34]

Without in any way minimizing the role of anti-Semitism in Nazi ideology it has also been argued that the Final Solution was part of a wider genocidal policy of ethnic cleansing, in which the Jews were the principle but not the only victims.[35] The complicity of the German nation in the crimes of the Nazis has also been explained by other historians as a state of lethal indifference, by which the steady exclusion of the Jews from German society in the 1930s eventually combined with the crisis of the war to create a situation in which most Germans cared little for what happened to this marginalized section of society. This was especially so when the problems of the war occupied so much of people's lives on the German home front.[36] Others have suggested the phrase 'passive complicity' best describes the acceptance of elimination of the Jews that characterized the outlook of ordinary Germans who were not themselves actively engaged in mass murder.[37]

It is also necessary to remember the active support given to Nazi atrocities by many Latvians[38], Lithuanians[39] and Ukrainians.[40] In Belorussia and Russia, the population was less inclined to actively participate in pogroms but, as the Einsatzgruppen reported in eastern Belorussia, in August 1941, 'The population has developed a hatred and an anger towards the Jew and approves of the Germans' actions . . . but is incapable, of its own accord, of taking the initiative in regard to the treatment of the Jews'.[41] Such examples remind us that the desire to obliterate the Jews was not a uniquely German phenomenon and that, in encouraging pogroms in many Eastern European countries, the Nazis were pushing at an open door and found huge numbers of anti-Semitic collaborators and a great many partners in killing.[42] Neither were such genocidal urges confined to the Second World War. The Rwandan genocide, in 1994, and the mass graves of Srebrenica, Bosnia, in 1995, remind us of the bitter reality that the human capacity for indulging in mass murder was not confined to the years 1939–45.

What is also clear is that the treatment of the Jews was an open secret, for all the Nazi efforts to hide evidence of their crimes.[43] Thousands of German soldiers on the Eastern Front witnessed atrocities, or assisted in carrying them out. Hundreds of railway operatives organized one-way trainloads to eastern destinations. Workers in the Reich Bank processed dental gold from unnamed sources. When Anne Frank – hiding in the Amsterdam attic – could write on 9 October 1942 of having heard news of the gassing of Jews,[44] it is not likely that German civilians knew nothing of the genocide being perpetrated by the government of the Third Reich.

What is also clear is that, while there were many complex factors deciding the course of 'The twisted road to Auschwitz',[45] what drove it was the ideological obsession of the Nazis that the Jews were to blame for all the problems of Germany. And it was that racial scapegoating that finally led to the most monstrous crime in human history.

THE THIRD REICH AT WAR: THE HOME FRONT

By 1943, the following joke was recorded in Germany, reflecting realities of life in the wartime Reich. It purported to be a conversation in a pet shop.

> Customer: 'What kinds of dogs do you have for sale?'
> Salesman: 'Pekinese, dwarf poodles, Yorkshire terriers.'
> Customer: 'Stop, stop – haven't you got a dog big enough for a family of five?'[1]

Clearly, by 1943, with the heady days of victory well behind them, Germans on the home front were beginning to face the realities of a long war.

Food shortages and standards of living

In the early stages of the war, the German conquest of much of Europe cushioned the civilian population within the Reich from many of the harsh realities of war. Germans on the home front benefited from the sausages, furniture, shoes and Christmas geese that the military sent back home from occupied Europe. On a larger scale, looting by government agencies assisted in the financing of the war. It was the economics of plunder, designed to protect the standards of living within the Third Reich itself and enhance the popularity of the Nazi regime.[2]

However, even at the start of the war it was clear that Germany held inadequate food stocks for a drawn-out conflict. From August/September 1939, rationing was introduced for items as varied as bread, cereal products, meat, butter, cheese, sugar and eggs. By mid-1941, fruit was added to the list and potatoes were rationed from April 1942. By the end of that year, non-rationed foodstuffs made up only 0.3 per cent of the food supply of an average German working-class family.[3] The quality of food also declined. For example, bread contained up to 20 per cent barley flour and consequently was bitter tasting. From January 1943, household goods were also rationed, with priority given to victims of bombing raids. Despite the existence of a black market in goods smuggled from neighbouring countries,[4] police enforcement of price controls meant that it was not until the closing months of the war that inflation began to spiral upwards. By that time tobacco had long been established as a substitute currency acceptable for purchasing foodstuff.

Those on the home front were initially classified, for rationing purposes, as being in one of three categories: 'normal consumers' (on 2,400 calories per day), 'heavy workers' (3,600 calories), or 'very heavy workers' (4,200 calories). About 40 per cent of Germans were classified as 'normal consumers'. A fourth category – 'workers on long hours' – was later added with calorific intake between the first two categories.[5]

German women at war

It is surprising that only in the disastrous military situation of 1943 did the Nazi regime finally require women to even register for possible mobilization.[6] In fact, during the first six months of the war (September 1939 to February 1940), the number of women workers had actually declined by 400,000.

This was due to generous allowances given to soldiers' wives in an effort to boost morale. And the number of marriages had gone up dramatically in 1939, as war approached. This trend and the government response did nothing to meet the need for more workers, which by the spring of 1940 was getting desperate. Faced with the requirement to mobilize more workers, the government was torn by a dilemma. With the nightmare of the 1918 collapse of morale always haunting it, the regime was not willing to consider the unpopular option of conscripting women. But, on the other hand, it was reluctant to entice them into work with increased wages since this ran the risk of overly boosting consumer spending with the attendant risk of inflation.[7] Even so, from June 1940, women's wages in the public sector were raised from 75 to 80 per cent of that paid to men. However, despite labour shortages, the regime refused to pay equal wages for equal work. After much pressure to do so from the German Labour Front (DAF) organization, Hitler finally settled the issue in April 1944, saying, 'If one was to equate the wages of women with men then this would be in total contradiction to the national socialist principle of the maintenance of the national community.' Furthermore, he claimed, 'An increase in women's wages would in practice simply mean strengthening the black market.'[8] Nevertheless, by1942, 52 per cent of the German labour force was female (compared with 37.4 per cent in 1939). Even so, fear of antagonizing women – and their soldier-husbands – meant that the Nazis were reluctant to introduce conscription of women. Instead, foreign labour was used, often involving severe coercion.

The reluctance to conscript women was particularly obvious with regard to the armed forces. In 1939, about 16,000 women were employed as secretaries, cooks, telephonists, etc. After September 1939, a little-publicized armed forces recruitment drive took place but – apart from women serving in occupied countries and in the air-attack warning units – none wore military uniform. This was in line with the Nazi social agenda of excluding women from the workplace whenever

possible. But labour demands increased as men were drafted
into the armed services. From 1941, the six months' labour
service expected of young women was extended by another six
months of war service.

In 1942, much to the disapproval of Hitler – but made inevitable by acute labour shortages – women were at last employed
in armaments production. This soon extended into service in
the military. The trend, once started, was unstoppable. In 1943,
women were deployed to service anti-aircraft units. However,
their responsibilities did not include firing the guns. By 1944,
women were operating searchlights. When the war ended in
May 1945, there were a total of 50,000 women working in anti-
aircraft units and 30,000 operating searchlights. In this role
they worked alongside teenagers, Russian POWs, Poles,
Czechs and Hungarians. Göring remarked that his *flak* batter-
ies resembled a meeting of the League of Nations.[9]

In total, somewhere in the region of 570,000 women were
eventually involved in armed services duties of one kind or
another. The extent to which Nazi attitudes had been forced to
change, as a result of the chastening circumstances of the failing
war, is revealed in an order of Hitler's, minuted by Martin
Bormann in February 1945. It involved the raising of a women's
battalion, which the Führer hoped, 'will have a salutary effect
on the attitude of the men'.[10] It was a long way from the early
Nazi slogan of a woman's role being confined to '*Kinder,
Küche, Kirche*' (children, kitchen, church). Even so, many
middle-class women were able to evade war work, a fact that
led to vocal protests from their working-class sisters in the
national community.[11]

Other attempts to control women were seen in varied areas
of life. The Interior Ministry issued a ban on women wearing
trousers other than work and sport clothes. Not surprisingly,
the police found the ban difficult to enforce due to problems in
differentiating work and sport clothes from trousers worn for
reasons of fashion. A police report from Tübingen in April
1942 outlined how hard the job was and explained that in cold

weather it was understandable that some women wore trousers. In the end the matter was resolved by the head of the SS
and chief of all police forces, Heinrich Himmler, in an edict of
December 1944. In it he ordered all police units to stop enforcing the ban. Women trouser-wearers had triumphed over the
fashion enforcers of the Third Reich.

More worrying were the strains that the war brought to
German marriages. A report by the SS Security Service (the
SD) in November 1943 noted that soldiers and their wives
were living such different lives that visits home on leave were
often accompanied by frequent arguments. Another SD report
in April 1944 commented that 'large numbers of women are
tending to be increasingly sexually active. This is particularly
evident in the case of soldiers' wives.'[12] The same report noted
that some women believed their husbands serving abroad had
casual sex and that this made them more inclined to do the
same. More materialistic were the women who – according to
the report – traded sex for silk stockings and other items from
German soldiers who had acquired these in occupied countries. Even more shocking was the evidence for sexual
relationships between German women and prisoners of war
doing labouring jobs in Germany. For this the punishment was
one year in a concentration camp for the German woman
involved. Police were ordered, in January 1940, not to intervene if the local community physically punished such women
by cutting off their hair. Sanctions were particularly severe
when the POW involved was a Pole or Russian. At Königsberg,
'Frau Martha S.' was sentenced to ten years in prison and a
further ten years' loss of civil rights for sexual relations with a
Polish POW.

Despite these negative effects of the war, other women made
a significant unpaid contribution to the war effort. Volunteer
female members of the Nazi welfare organization the NSV
played a valuable role.[13] Mostly funded by voluntary contributions made to the Winter Aid Programme – and numbering
over one million women – the NSV was involved in many

roles, but one of the most high profile was its Railway Station Service. Offering advice and assistance to mothers and children, young people, the old and the infirm, they also dispensed soup and tea. These NSV volunteers were a friendly face to travellers in a nation that was becoming increasingly chaotic. Other NSV volunteers ran crèches in factories. They remind us that Germany had a fairly comprehensive welfare system. But, before their caring role should be overstated, it needs to be remembered that – unsurprisingly in the Third Reich – the official NSV directive, of May 1942, explicitly reminded them that: 'Jews, Poles, Gypsies, asocials etc. should not be looked after.' The care they offered extended only as far as those designated as 'German compatriots'.[14] This brutal racial outlook influenced all the social policies of the Third Reich. A striking example is the response of senior officials to a planned post-war pension scheme; one senior doctor noted disapprovingly that 'from a biological perspective' the scheme would cater for those who had 'become less important for the fate of the nation'.[15]

Living under Allied bombs

Since the German bombing of British cities had failed to break civilian morale, it should come as no surprise to discover that Allied bombing failed to destroy that of German civilians, as some realized at the time.[16] As one Berliner – Ursula von Kardorff – noted in January 1944: 'The catastrophes which are hitting the Nazis and the anti-Nazis equally are binding the nation together.' And she concluded: 'If the British think they are going to undermine our morale they are barking up the wrong tree.'[17] And Ursula was no Nazi; indeed she was unsympathetic to the regime. Nevertheless, as we shall see, whilst the raids did not break the German people they steadily eroded support for the regime. Incidentally, this bombing of German cities was carried out almost entirely by the British and Americans, the Soviets making little contribution to the air bombardment in contrast to their massive ground operations.

Evacuation caused the same distress in Germany as in Britain. A secret report of the SD in November 1943 concluded that the situation of having to be 'guests of strangers and have to ask for every utensil is in the long run intolerable'. Furthermore, 'Reference is frequently also made to the sexual problem and the danger of marriage break-up.' The SD also noted: 'There are already reports to the effect that the morals of evacuated wives are anything but satisfactory.' It is particularly striking how the common stresses of war cross all cultural and national boundaries. The SD noted: 'The longing of the parents and of the children for each other is getting everybody down.' One coalminer sadly commented, 'As long as I'm at work I don't think about it, [the fact his family had been evacuated] but the moment I get home I start worrying. I miss my wife and my children's laughter.' The SD report adds that, as he spoke, the man cried.

Social tensions also understandably increased. In the Dortmund area, in October 1943, some 300 women demonstrated because – having returned home – their ration books had been withdrawn in an attempt to force them to leave the city. The police were called but refused to arrest the women.[18]

However, as the war continued, the horrors of bombing made the need for evacuation obvious. One by one the major cities of Germany were smashed by bombing.[19] An early target was Hamburg.[20] In the firestorms that engulfed Hamburg on the night of 27–8 July 1943, the death toll was 35–40,000 people. A report by the police chief of Hamburg reveals why it was hard to be sure about exact casualty figures. 'On the basis of a layer of ashes in a large air raid shelter, doctors could only provide a rough estimate of the number of people who died there, a figure of 250–300.'[21] Despite official claims that calm was maintained, there is – unsurprisingly – evidence to the contrary. Mathilde Wolff-Mönckeberg, who was there, described how, 'It is hard to imagine the panic and chaos. Each one for himself, only one idea: flight.' But that was not easy with railway stations gutted, trams and underground inoperative; so thousands fled with their belongings loaded onto carts and prams.[22]

Even more infamous was the bombing of Dresden on the nights of 13–15 February 1945, which killed perhaps as many as 25,000 people (although possible figures as high as 40,000 have also been suggested) and destroyed about 39 square kilometres (15 square miles) of the city centre. Kurt Vonnegut's anti-war science-fiction novel *Slaughterhouse-Five* (published in 1969), was based on his own experiences as a prisoner of war at Dresden during the bombing. This attack still attracts major controversies over whether the raid was necessary and whether such high civilian casualties could be justified. It was not until 2005 that the ruined Lutheran *Frauenkirche* (the baroque Church of Our Lady) was finally reconstructed and re-consecrated.[23]

The government authorities made efforts to raise morale with increased rations – including chocolate and real coffee – to those bombed out. In Essen, each adult affected received 50 grams (1.7 ounces) of coffee and half a bottle of brandy. Children received 125 grams (4.4 ounces) of sweets. Mobile canteens also provided free meals for up to three days after a raid. However, by the end of the war, local government was overwhelmed by the scale of the catastrophe. In a survey carried out in Cologne after the war, 90 per cent of those interviewed concluded that bombing was the worst hardship they faced during the war. In contrast, only 10 per cent cited food shortages.[24] There is evidence that this suffering struck at support for the Nazi government. SD reports in June 1943 noted the increase in hostile remarks and the Führer himself was not above criticism. The SD further noted that 'Heil, Hitler' salutes were rare in cities that had experienced heavy bombing. A joke going the rounds had a Berliner and Essener comparing bombing experiences. The Berliner recalled how, five hours after the raid, windows were still falling out of houses. To which the Essener replied that in Essen, fourteen days after the last raid, pictures of the Führer were still flying out of the windows. The fact that this found its way into an official SD report reveals something of the widespread nature of such negative comments.[25]

From 1944, bombing disrupted armaments production, oil supplies, transport systems and the aircraft industry.[26] It also caused German fighters, desperately needed elsewhere, to be deployed defending the home front; German aircraft production became over-focused on building fighters rather than other aircraft.[27] It curtailed industrial expansion (1941–4), then severely damaged it thereafter, additionally forcing dispersal of production.[28]

The economy in wartime

The leaders of the Third Reich were surprisingly reluctant to mobilize the German civilian population for 'total war', a situation not helped by the chaotic nature of Nazi government. In this there was a striking contrast with Britain and even more so with the USSR. There was real tension between Hitler and Goebbels over this issue, with the latter convinced that the resources of the entire German nation needed to be focused on the war. The Propaganda Minister even attempted to mobilize public opinion to put pressure on Hitler to change his mind. On 18 February 1943, Goebbels made a long speech to a carefully selected audience at Berlin's Sports Palace. In it he called for a whole range of radical measures including rallying the whole population to war work, a sixteen-hour working day if it was necessary to achieve victory, women to free men for the front (especially the Eastern Front), harsh measures against draft dodgers and black marketeers, and an equal burden of work across the whole of German society. In this call for 'total war', he ended with the cry that had rallied Germans against Napoleon in 1814: 'Let *volk* (people/nation) rise up and storm break loose'.[29] And yet, even then, Germany never mobilized in a manner comparable with those nations that eventually defeated it.

There were attempts to rationalize war production but, even so, the manufacturing of German military equipment was never standardized in the way it was in the Allied nations, and it failed to replicate the Allied production lines producing huge numbers of fewer types of weapons.[30] Instead, the German system involved too many small industries which made German production far less efficient. This problem was increased by Allied bombing and loss of areas that had supplied Germany with raw materials (such as Romanian oil). However, it was not until 1945 that armaments production collapsed and this was largely caused by the bombing of transport facilities over the winter of 1944–5. Efforts to increase productivity of the German workers included bonuses paid in tobacco and alcohol, preserved vegetables and condensed milk.

From the summer of 1944 onwards, Hitler favoured a policy of destroying industry in areas abandoned by the retreating German army. This was a policy that was ignored by many in these areas. The Armaments Minister, Albert Speer, persuaded Hitler that an alternative policy of crippling factories by removing vital components was better since these factories could then be reactivated if German forces reoccupied these areas. But on 19 March 1945, Hitler ordered that this 'crippling strategy' should finally give way to 'scorched earth'. This same decree stripped Speer of responsibilities in this area of the economy. Speer resisted, persuaded Hitler to revise his destruction order, was eventually reinstated on 30 March and used his influence to exploit ambiguities in the revised decree to block fanatical Nazis in their intentions to destroy industries and infrastructure. Speer consequently has come to be seen as the man who saved western Germany from total self-inflicted destruction. However, he was not alone in this aim since employers and their workers actively resisted attempts to destroy industry. Speer – although genuinely wishing to preserve Germany – was probably also looking to a personal future beyond the Third Reich.

By 1944, German official statistics listed 7.6 million foreign workers and POWs in industry within the territory of the Greater German Reich (the borders of Germany itself, as expanded by Nazi territorial seizures). This made up about 25 per cent of the German labour force by this stage of the war. Most of these were forced labourers, many from Poland and the USSR. There was the usual Nazi racial hierarchy, with workers from Western Europe treated better than Poles and Russians.

More and more of the Gestapo's activities went into policing and punishing these foreign workers within Germany. However, evidence suggests that, from 1941, citizens became less willing to inform, even on 'delinquent' foreign workers – especially after 1944. Though in the case of foreign workers this may in fact indicate that the Gestapo was no longer keeping records of those it shot as 'it began to dispense with even the semblance of regulations'.[31]

Children and young people in the wartime Reich

From January 1943, seventeen-year-olds were called up to assist with air defence. It was this forced mobilization of young people that saw Joseph Ratzinger, later Pope Benedict XVI, conscripted into the auxiliary anti-aircraft corps. In some areas entire classes were conscripted en masse. Some of these boys responded enthusiastically to the opportunity to do their bit. One wrote in his diary, in August 1944, after his unit had shot down two aircraft on the Baltic coast: 'Everyone's very excited; they say it would be great if we got the Flak [anti-aircraft] badge.'[32] Others were less willing. In one town, in March 1945, the Hitler Youth Home Guard unit was locked in a room until they 'volunteered' to join the SS. That same month, sixteen-year-olds were conscripted.

Many of these young soldiers fought in the *Volkssturm* (Home Guard), which was formed in September 1944, as the Reich faced invasion. They dug anti-tank ditches and formed anti-tank units armed with *Panzerfäuste* (bazookas). A famous film clip, from 20 March 1945, shows Hitler talking to and patting the faces of young soldiers in an award ceremony. The youngest recipient was the ironically surnamed Alfred Czech (aged 12 years). He won his Iron Cross for rescuing twelve wounded German soldiers under enemy artillery and machine-gun fire.

Into the abyss

As it became clear that Germany was losing the war and Allied bombing devastated German cities, the country turned to bitter sarcasm:

> 'What will you do after the war?'
> 'I'll finally go on a holiday and will take a trip round Greater
> Germany!'
> 'And what will you do in the afternoon?'[33]

As the Red Army threatened Berlin, the young and old were drafted into the Home Guard. However bravely these fighters were presented in the German propaganda it was obvious to all that they stood no chance against the seasoned Soviet troops. A cynical joke asked: 'Who has gold in his mouth, silver in his hair and lead in his limbs? A Volkssturmmann.'

Another bitter joke detailed the following scenario: 'An officer of the Volkssturm finds only a third of his men on parade: The second third has gone to the post office to collect invalidity pensions and the other third has had to attend confirmation classes.'[34]

Those drafted into this Home Guard were divided into four contingents by a decree of October 1944. The first contingent was made up of those capable of active service (despite their age) and some were sent direct to the front despite the inadequacy of their training. The second contingent was those employed in vital war work and were exempt from immediate deployment. Many men tried to be placed in this contingent. The third contingent included teenagers, while the fourth contingent were those incapable of combat duties but who could be used for guard duties. Whilst many attempted to avoid duties in this ill-prepared and ill-equipped army of doomed men and boys, others threw themselves into the frantic defence of the Fatherland.

This commitment to fight to the end was reinforced by the Nazi regime's refusal to negotiate any form of surrender and the Allies demand, from early 1943, for unconditional surrender. Amongst German civilians, as well as soldiers, there was another major factor that encouraged last-ditch fighting. And this was a sense of complicity in the crimes of the regime. SD reports picked up these sentiments. Amongst victims of bombing were heard comments that this was punishment on Germany for what had been done to the Jews. Most German civilians knew that their nation had not only visited war on Europe but had done so in an appalling fashion. German propaganda in the final months of the war encouraged this sense of being bound together in a 'community of fate'. On the eastern borders of the Reich there was the added terror of the Russians and the revenge they were pursuing against the nation that had caused the deaths of about 26 million citizens of the USSR. Nazi foreign policy – and its failure – had brought the much-feared Red hordes into Germany itself. This fear permeated every level of the home front in the dying days of Hitler's Germany. A new form of greeting became commonplace amongst German civilians: '*Bleib übrig*' (stay alive). The letters 'BU' could be found chalked on walls.

With the arrival of the Red Army in eastern Germany, Soviet actions equalled the worst propaganda fears as huge numbers of German women were brutally raped. Estimates of victims run as high as two million women. The horror of defeat was forced upon the defenceless and helpless. In the aftermath of these atrocities many Germans committed suicide. Others did so as Soviet forces drew closer. Reports of Soviet violence towards civilians preceded the Red Army once it had crossed the eastern borders of the Reich. In the Pomeranian village of Schivelbein, the Protestant pastor wrote of families who 'drowned themselves, hanged themselves, slit their wrists, or allowed themselves to be burned up along with their homes'.

Other eastern German towns saw similar tragedies. In Schönlanke, 500 committed suicide; in Demmin, 700.[35] And everywhere, the Soviet soldiers looted. Watches were particularly highly prized and the famous photograph of Red Army soldiers raising the red flag on the captured Reichstag had to be airbrushed by Soviet censors to remove the multiple watches visible on the wrist of one of the soldiers. Everything moveable was liable to be stolen and shipped eastward. Some Russian soldiers later wrote of their anger at seeing the comfortable state of German farms and homes in East Prussia. Why, they questioned, had those who already possessed so much invaded and devastated the USSR?[36]

In the street-by-street battle for Berlin, in April and May 1945, somewhere in the region of 22,000 German civilians died. As the Red Army advanced, civilians faced terrible dilemmas. To surrender too soon ran the risk of being killed by SS and Nazi paramilitaries if the street was not overrun, or was recaptured. To delay surrender risked being shot by Russian soldiers. Many Berliners – who mistimed their hanging out of white bed-sheets – were hanged on lampposts by fellow Germans as the city disintegrated into chaos. These were the bitter realities of the Third Reich's defeat on the German home front.

20

THE GERMAN RESISTANCE

Coming on top of rearmament and economic revival in the 1930s, Hitler's early victories in the Second World War – once initial fears about the war had been overcome – prompted a wave of national pride. A joke ran: 'What does it mean when the sky is black? There are so many aircraft in the air that the birds have to walk.'[1] But as the war continued and as losses mounted it became increasingly difficult for propaganda to hide the extent of the mounting disaster.[2] As this occurred signs of discontent increased. This was particularly the case if those concerned had been members of now-banned opposition parties. One example was a circus director in the western city of Paderborn, a confirmed Social Democrat opponent of the Nazis who trained his chimpanzees to raise their right arm whenever they saw a uniform, and they even took to saluting the postman. He was denounced and a received an official notice forbidding the chimpanzees from making the salute and threatening 'slaughter'.[3] However, while such forms of opposition could be dangerous to those responsible for them, they scarcely threatened the regime. Despite this, the government became ever more watchful. In September 1939, Roland Freisler, President of the Nazi People's Court, declared the court's vigilance in order to avoid any repetition of 'a stab in the nation's back', which right-wing Germans had alleged had occurred in 1918. But as war defeats mounted, the incidences of opposition that could be termed 'resistance' became more significant. When Freisler made his assertion there were 1,347 people imprisoned as a result of actions by the People's Court; by late 1944, the number had risen to 5,316.

The scale and variety of resistance

Although resistance to the Nazis increased in the war years, it never approached anything like a mass movement. Amongst many Germans such resistance was regarded as highly unpatriotic at a time when Germany was engaged in a fight to the finish with the Allies. This was a problem to those conservative opponents of the Nazis, since they saw themselves as patriotic members of society. Amongst the military this was underscored by the fact that they had sworn an oath of loyalty to Hitler as Führer. It was less of an issue to those left-wing resisters since their primary loyalty was to the international working class. In addition to there being few actual resisters, they also lacked unity of purpose and had no common ideology or goals. Nevertheless, there were Germans who were prepared to risk their lives to oppose the Third Reich.[4]

Communist opponents were badly wrong-footed by the Nazi–Soviet Pact of August 1939, which made the Third Reich and the USSR temporary allies. However, when Germany invaded the USSR in 1941, this freed these opponents from restraints imposed by the pact. Communist cells produced illegal leaflets and newspapers designed to challenge the Nazi control of ideas. Communist guidelines, issued in November 1941, established procedures designed to avoid arrest: 'Meetings in comrades' flats should be avoided if possible since experience has shown that the blocks are often under surveillance . . . One should not go straight from home to the meeting place . . . [cells] should not contain more than three people . . . those partial to alcohol are to be excluded from party work . . .'[5] However, these groups never threatened the regime, since the

Gestapo was successful in infiltrating communist cells and, by early 1943, all the major communist networks had been broken up. Those arrested faced death sentences or a lengthy prison sentence. A group of middle-class left-wing sympathisers made up the group known to the Gestapo as 'the Red Orchestra'.[6] Having better connections than their working-class counterparts, they succeeded in passing secrets to Soviet intelligence, distributed pamphlets and distributed stickers at the Nazi anti-Russian exhibition 'The Soviet Paradise' in May 1942. These stickers read: 'The Nazi Paradise. War, Hunger, Lies, Gestapo. How much longer?' The same exhibition was the target of an arson attack by a group of young Jewish resisters who were also loosely allied to the communists. For this attack more than twenty members were executed and one of the leaders – Herbert Baum – died in prison after terrible torture.

A loose alliance with a very different agenda coalesced around anti-Nazis in the military (such as former Chief of the General Staff, General Ludwig Beck), the Abwehr Military Intelligence (such as Admiral Wilhelm Canaris) and amongst some conservatives (such as the monarchist Carl Goerdeler).[7] During the 1930s, this group opposed the course of Nazi foreign policy, which they feared would lead to a disastrous war. Despite the victories of 1939 against Poland, this group continued to be a source of opposition. As well as fearing defeat they were shocked at the actions of the SS in Poland. A former ambassador to Italy – Ulrich von Hassell – wrote in his diary of 'the shocking bestialities of the SS, especially towards the Jews'.[8] The problem for this group lay in the fact that, as conservative nationalists, many of their foreign-policy goals were unacceptable to Britain and France. An example of this comes from February 1940, when contacts between this group and the British included a requirement that even with Hitler gone, Germany should remain united with Austria, should keep the Sudetenland (taken from the Czechs in 1938) and should have its eastern borders restored to those of 1914 (which would involve the dismemberment of Poland). Not surprisingly, these requirements were unacceptable to the British. As the war progressed, younger rebels became associated with this group. These included Count Peter Yorck von Wartenburg, Count Helmut James von Moltke and the Protestant pastor Dietrich Bonhoeffer. This loose alliance the SS later described as the 'Kreisau Circle' after von Moltke's estate in Lower Silesia.[9] Their aims included a constrained form of democracy, a mixed economy and a European federal structure. In spring 1942, Bonhoeffer met Bishop Bell of Chichester in Stockholm, but when Bell returned to Britain, the Foreign Secretary, Anthony Eden, refused to reply to this overture from the German resistance.

The bomb plot of 20 July 1944: the almost-overthrow of Hitler

By 1943 the Gestapo was closing in on the conservative resistance. In the autumn of that year conspirators within Military Intelligence were seized. In January 1944, von Moltke was arrested. This and the deteriorating war situation spurred the resistance towards more radical action. Chief amongst those arguing for the physical elimination of Hitler was Colonel Count Claus von Stauffenberg.[10] This German officer had suffered massive injuries in North Africa. As a result of an air attack he had lost his left eye, his right forearm and two fingers on his left hand. Whilst he was no liberal democrat he had been horrified by the mass murder of Jews and the mistreatment of Soviet prisoners of war. Like his fellow conspirators, he hoped that by removing Hitler a new German government would be able to negotiate a peace treaty that was both acceptable to the Allies and to Germany. Furthermore, such an achievement would remove from the resisters the stigma of treason in the eyes of the German people. In this their hopes were highly optimistic since, by 1944, the Allies were already committed to the unconditional surrender of Germany.

When the Western Allies launched D-Day on 6 June 1944, the hopes of this group for an acceptable peace suddenly seemed remote. It was now clear that the war was lost. So why would the Allies settle for anything less than total victory? And yet the resisters pressed on. As one of their number – Major General Henning von Tresckow – put it: 'What counts is the fact that in the eyes of the world and of history the German resistance dared to act. Compared with that nothing else is important.'[11] Von Tresckow was a man whose determination to cleanse Germany of Nazism was his overriding aim. Already, in March 1943, he had placed a bomb on a plane carrying Hitler to Smolensk.[12] But the detonator malfunctioned, Hitler survived and the plot remained undetected. It was von Tresckow who had recruited von Stauffenberg and from this action would unfold the plot that came closest to killing Hitler. When it eventually failed, von Tresckow blew off his own head with a grenade on the Eastern Front. By disguising his suicide as an enemy attack he hoped to protect fellow conspirators. However, his role was later uncovered when the Gestapo interrogated other plotters.[13]

On 20 July 1944, von Stauffenberg left a bomb in a briefcase close to Hitler in the Wolf's Lair, the Führer's military headquarters on the Eastern Front.[14] This was located in the Masurian Woods, about 5 miles (8 kilometres) from the East Prussian town of Rastenburg, which is now Kętrzyn in Poland. The unexpected shifting of the briefing to a wooden cabin, as opposed to the usual concrete bunker (which would have concentrated the blast) and an officer moving von Stauffenberg's briefcase so as to put a trestle between it and Hitler, meant that the Führer survived. The plot to mobilize the German Reserve Army – Operation Valkyrie – by pretending that the killing was the work of conspirators within the SS failed once it became known that Hitler was alive and that those ordering the arrests of leading Nazis were themselves the conspirators. Stauffenberg had relied on the German officer corps uniting behind a dramatic attempt to remove the Führer. It did not do so. In reality, many senior officers simply 'adopted a wait-and-see policy and then obeyed the countercommands that arrived soon after from the Führer's headquarters'.[15] As a result, the plot stood on a knife-edge from its start and soon collapsed. Had Hitler really been killed, the outcome might have been very different, but even in that scenario whether the German military leadership would have lined up behind those who had just killed the head of state is open to question. The key issue is that the officer corps lacked the necessary drive to overthrow Hitler.

In the aftermath of the failed assassination, somewhere in the region of 7,000 people were arrested. All those leading the plot paid with their lives, either executed as the plot failed, committed suicide, or hanged after trials by Freisler in the Nazi People's Court. Yet, in one of those strange ironies of history, this notorious Nazi eventually met his death in his own brutal courtroom. On 3 February 1945, the US air force carried out a massive raid on Berlin. A bomb hit the People's Court and Freisler was killed by a falling beam. When his body was recovered he was holding the prosecution file of Fabian von Schlabrendorff, who was on trial that day and faced the death penalty for his role in the 1944 plot. Schlabrendorff survived and, after the war, became a judge in the Constitutional Court of the democratic German Federal Republic from 1967 to 1975.

Others did not escape the vengeance of the regime. Everyone in the Reich named Stauffenberg was arrested and those arrayed before the People's Court were harangued and humiliated. Denied belts for their trousers, they were crudely taunted as they sought to keep them up. The manner of their execution was personally dictated by Hitler. They were to be hanged, with the rope looped around meat-hooks – 'hung up like carcasses of meat' was the Führer's order. As they died their death agonies were filmed and the film shown to Hitler. Von Stauffenberg though had been executed by soldiers loyal to Hitler on the night the plot collapsed. Later, the SS exhumed his body, removed his medals and burned his corpse. Four of his five children were placed in foster homes and were made to use new surnames. Today, in Berlin, his name is remembered in the street name Stauffenbergstrasse (formerly known as Bendlerstrasse), situated south of the Tiergarten, in western Berlin. Nearby is the 'Memorial to the German Resistance', sited near where von Stauffenberg and others were shot in 1944. Field Marshall Erwin Rommel – the hero of the North African campaign – was given the alternative of suicide rather than a trial, so his family would be spared. After his suicide, in October 1944, he was given a state funeral, since Hitler could not bear for the German people to learn that Rommel had betrayed his Führer.

The plotters of 20 July 1944 had come very close to killing Hitler. Another resistance movement centred on Munich never came near removing the Nazi regime, yet in its idealistic courage deserves comparison with the plotters of 1944.

The White Rose Movement: idealistic martyrs

One of the most remarkable examples of political resistance to the Nazis came in the form of the White Rose Movement.[16] It was based mostly in Munich – the home of Nazism – with some members in other parts of Germany, such as Hamburg. Its leadership was provided by students at Munich University, most famously the brother and sister team of Hans and Sophie Scholl. They were assisted by Kurt Huber, who was Professor of Musicology and Philosophy at the university. While their political beliefs were rather undefined, they took inspiration from Christianity and a tradition of German philosophy that emphasized the importance of individual morality and freedom of thought. As such they were on a collision course with Nazism.

In June and July 1942, the group first began distributing anti-Nazi leaflets. At first they targeted educated Munich citizens but later distributed their leaflets in Augsburg, Frankfurt am Main and Stuttgart. They also sent leaflets to addresses in Linz, Salzburg and Vienna. These leaflets were striking in their open attack on Nazi atrocities. Their second leaflet stated, 'Since the conquest of Poland 300,000 Jews have been murdered in that country in the most bestial fashion . . . a crime with which no other in the whole history of mankind can be compared'.[17] This open defence of the Jews and publicizing of Nazi atrocities gives a clear indication of the moral quality of the White Rose Movement. When they distributed this leaflet in mid-1942, Germany still seemed likely to win the war. Clearly, the White Rose was not simply a reaction to a Nazism that seemed set to lose the war – rather they were confronting Nazism for what it was and what it did. The disaster at Stalingrad over the winter of 1942–3 only added impetus to a campaign that was already underway. In February 1943, they asserted: 'Hitler is leading Germany over the precipice. Hitler cannot win the war but only extend it.'[18] This was over a year before the army resisters – coming to the same conclusion – took action. In the same leaflet they argued for an end to Prussian militarism, promotion of European cooperation, a federal German government system in place of centralization, moderate socialism and free trade across the world. Within the new Germany that they looked towards there would be freedom of speech and belief and an end to arbitrary government. So much of what the White Rose stood for presaged the character of post-war Europe; it also inevitably led to their destruction at the hands of the Nazi state.

During February 1943, the White Rose group in Munich increased the tempo of its activities. They painted anti-Nazi slogans on buildings across Munich; these included the words: 'Hitler Mass Murderer' and 'Down with Hitler'. On 18 February, the Scholls scattered leaflets in the corridors and atrium of the university but were caught by the porter. Coincidentally, it was the same day that Goebbels addressed a mass rally in Berlin and called for total war. Although tortured, the Scholls refused to divulge names; nevertheless the Gestapo soon arrested other members of the group. Found guilty of treason by the Nazi Peoples' Court, six of them were guillotined. Other members of the group received sentences ranging from six months to ten years in prison.

Eight days later, the local Nazi boss addressed the Munich student population and the assembled students applauded the porter who had handed over the Scholls to the Gestapo. To what extent these applauding students acted under duress and to what extent they genuinely opposed the actions of the White Rose is difficult to assess. What is clear though is that the majority of students distanced themselves from the dangerous stance of the White Rose and its martyred leaders. It is symptomatic of the general stance of the German population towards the resistance.

The text of their final leaflet was later smuggled out of Germany and published by the Western Allies as 'The Manifesto of the Students of Munich'. Copies of it were dropped over Germany by Allied aircraft.

Today, the square near Munich University is called Geschwister-Scholl-Platz. Two fountains near the university are also monuments to the resisters. One bears the names of Hans and Sophie, the other that of Professor Kurt Huber.

The rise of anti-Nazi youth sub-cultures

The White Rose Movement was ideologically opposed to the Nazis. But this was not the only form resistance took amongst the young.[19] Others were motivated by a resentment of Nazi social control and uniformity. This did not constitute a political opposition but was, instead, a kind of social resistance, which attempted to cast off the constraints of the Third Reich. As we shall see, some of these groups seemed to represent alternative lifestyles; others would have challenged any social order in any community, but opposition could prove fatal in a society as ruthlessly ordered as that of Nazi Germany.

In 1944, the Reich Ministry of Justice reported on the need to combat these youth groups, which were aiming to create a sub-culture at odds with the Nazi view of society. One such group termed itself 'Edelweiss Pirates'. In addition to hostility towards members of the Hitler Youth, their activities suggest that they would have been regarded as anti-social in many societies. The report details how they 'were involved in thefts and robberies . . . have beaten up pedestrians . . . have smeared human excrement on the faces of other national comrades'.[20] Even allowing for the heavily one-sided nature of this source and the possibility that it over-stressed the negative aspects of this group's activities, it does seem fairly clear that this group was as much about rebellion against *any* authority as against specifically Nazi authority. However, while some members focused on anti-social behaviour, others channelled their dislike of social control into more political action. The same report claimed that some – in a Düsseldorf group calling itself the 'Golden Horde' – distributed leaflets declaring 'Down with Hitler – we want freedom'. Other such politically active 'pirates' were reported from Cologne, where some called themselves the 'Navajos'. In Duisburg, they called themselves 'Kittelsbach Pirates' and actively targeted Hitler Youth members. In Essen, the gang called itself the 'Raving Dudes'. Some of these groups may have had communist sympathies.

Official Nazi reports suggest that these groups sought to establish a gang-identity through badges and clothing. Edelweiss or skull badges were displayed; many wore short trousers with white socks and a check-patterned shirt. This was often combined with a white sweater and a jacket. They tended to wear their hair long in an obvious rejection of military-style appearance. As inner-city life became more chaotic as a result of bombing, some of these gangs teamed up with army deserters and foreign workers on the run. In October 1944, a series of police raids led to the hanging of 13 young people in Cologne, including a number of Edelweiss Pirates. However, this failed to destroy the movement.

The complex nature of their resistance to Nazism was revealed after the end of the war, when violent street crimes led to arrests of some members by the Allied occupying powers. Some of the victims of these attacks included displaced persons of Russian or Polish origin. Edelweiss Pirates songs now included the lines:

When the knives flash,
And the Polish coffins whizz past,
And the Edelweiss Pirates attack.[21]

Having rebelled against Hitler, the Pirates were now rebelling against the Allied-dominated post-war German society. As such, they seemed to typify 'a type of youthful protest common to just about any time and any place'.[22] But, since the Pirates had never constituted an organization as such, it is difficult to tell if these acts were perpetrated by the same gangs who had opposed the Nazis or by young people who were appropriating the Pirate 'tag'.

Less complex were those groups termed 'Swing gangs' and the fans of jazz music.[23] These seem to have originated in the Hamburg area and rejected Nazi social norms (as well as social constraints generally). They danced to American and British music, imitated British clothes (wearing tartan designs and carrying umbrellas), drank a lot of alcohol and were – it was claimed - sexually promiscuous. Girls wore short skirts, lipstick and nail-polish. Both boys and girls tended to wear their hair long; in this they were comparable to the Edelweiss Pirates and probably did so for the same reason. In a society as heavily politicized as the Third Reich, these actions were regarded as a threat, but even the Nazis defined them as 'liberal-individualistic gangs' and so differentiated them from the 'politically hostile gangs' such as the Edelweiss Pirates. Official reports suggest that some Swing gangs also indulged in petty crime in order to fund their lifestyle. Some young people described this lifestyle by using the German word '*lottern*' (laziness – probably seen as a rejection of the Nazi work ethic and disciplined behaviour). Some parodied the Nazi salute of '*Sieg Heil*' (Hail Victory) with their own, 'Swing Heil'. From 1941, clampdowns on these groups increased. In that year, over 300 members were arrested. From 1942, Swing gangs were broken up and ringleaders imprisoned. Many ended up being confined in a Youth Detention Camp at Moringen, near Hanover.

The Nazi leadership clearly loathed these young people. SS chief Heinrich Himmler, in a letter written in January 1942, expressed these feelings: 'These young people must remain in the concentration camp for a long time, two–three years.' What was required by the state was the resolution to 'act brutally'.[24] However, the Swing gangs and the Edelweiss Pirates never posed a real threat to the Nazi state. They lacked a clear ideology and organization. Overall, the Pirates offered a more serious challenge than the Swing gangs. The latter were more interested in foreign music, independence and bucking authority than insurrection. As one Swing gang member later put it, 'The main problem was not that we were against the Nazis but that the Nazis were against us'.[25] The Pirates, on the other hand, offered a more violent form of resistance but still lacked a political focus for their energies and 'their non-conformist behaviour tended to be restricted to petty provocation'.[26] Crucially, they failed to attract the support of any but a small minority of German young people.

How significant was the German resistance to Hitler?

The problem with the German resistance was, first, that it involved so few people and, second, it was generally limited to two time periods in the history of the Third Reich. The first characteristic is perhaps the easiest to deal with. Nazi successes in bringing down unemployment, in foreign policy during the 1930s and in the initial stages of the Second World War boosted Hitler's popularity and denied opposition mass support. Once the war was underway, opposition seemed like betrayal of a nation locked in a life-and-death struggle. Combined with a traditional German culture of obedience to the state, this meant that resistance was only ever the stance of a small minority of Germans. This then helps explain the second characteristic. What resistance there was, seems only to have been really noticeable when Hitler was settling into power and opposition groups might still entertain hopes that it was a temporary phenomenon, *and then* in the latter stages of the war when defeat loomed. In short, 'either before Nazism had fully developed its magnetic appeal and integrating potential or after this potential had begun to erode'.[27]

As a consequence, the resisters had little support and therefore little hope of toppling the leadership of the Third Reich. The one attempt that came closest was the army plot of 20 July 1944. But even that plot – for the short time that it seemed likely to affect regime change – could only gather support by claiming that the SS had assassinated Hitler and that the plotters were the true German loyalists acting against an SS coup. This was the only way to convince wavering troops to support them. Clearly, even the plotters recognized the lack of appetite for toppling the government in wartime and in a society so geared to military obedience as Germany. This reveals a great deal about the lack of real desire for resistance in even the final year of the Third Reich. Consequently, it was only ever the Allied victory that was capable of really bringing down the Nazi dictatorship.

As the historian Richard Evans reminds us, until 1943–4, Nazi control of the mass media and the availability of food supplies weakened the urge to resist. And even when the destruction of German cities, from 1943 onwards, turned Germans against their government, Nazi repression and terror – coupled with a renewed emphasis on the belief in self-sacrifice – meant that only small numbers of Germans actively translated complaints into resisting the regime.[28]

Consequently, those brave Germans who resisted the Nazis fully deserve the praise they are now given, not only because they were so courageous, but also because they were so few and yet still they acted, and sacrificed their lives.

21

THE THIRD REICH AT WAR: FROM CONQUEST TO GÖTTERDÄMMERUNG

The Second World War claimed millions of victims; four million of these were Soviet POWs who died in German captivity. Their suffering was terrible, and Göring is said to have commented how in the camps for Russian prisoners of war, 'after having eaten everything possible, including the soles of their boots, they have begun to eat each other'.[1] One of these four million was Stalin's son, Yakov Dzhugashvili. Fighting as a thirty-three–year-old artillery lieutenant in the Red Army, Yakov was taken prisoner near Smolensk in 1941. The Germans later dropped leaflets over Moscow boasting of how they had captured the son of the Soviet leader. In 1943, the Germans offered to exchange him for Field Marshal von Paulus, captured at Stalingrad earlier in the year, but Stalin refused the deal. He and his son had never been close. Stalin had bullied the boy so badly that, in the late 1920s, Yakov had attempted suicide but had instead wounded himself in the head.

The circumstances surrounding Yakov's death in German custody remained clouded at the end of the war but it now seems that he died in April 1943, in Sachsenhausen concentration camp. This was shortly after his father had refused the prisoner exchange. Reports suggest that he deliberately approached the forbidden zone by the camp fence and was shot by one of the guards. In September 2003, the US State Department handed over documents detailing the circumstances of his death, which had been discovered in Berlin in 1945, to Galina Dzhugashvili, Yakov's daughter. Many more millions died as the Second World War slowly turned against Hitler and eventually ended in the total destruction of the Third Reich. It was a destruction rooted in that war against the USSR.

Operation Barbarossa: the war against the USSR

On 21 June, 1941, the day before launching the attack on the USSR, Hitler wrote a revealing letter to Mussolini, the Italian dictator.

'Since I struggled through to this decision, I again feel spiritually free. The partnership with the Soviet Union, in spite of the complete sincerity of the efforts to bring about a final conciliation, was nevertheless often very irksome to me, for in some way or other it seemed to me to be a break with my whole origin, my concepts and my former obligations. I am happy now to be relieved of these mental agonies.'[2]

For the Führer, the strain of working with his ideological enemy had been difficult. But with the attack on the USSR, he had returned to his ideological roots. Even at this point he was incapable of personal honesty. Despite being the one who had launched the attack, he still clearly believed that he could describe himself as having shown 'complete sincerity' in trying to build a lasting relationship with the Soviets. It is a revealing insight into the breathtaking way that Hitler reinvented any 'reality' in order to satisfy his own outlook.

What was beyond dispute was the success that attended the opening weeks of the campaign on the Eastern Front. The three million soldiers of Germany and its allies made astonishing progress. Stalin had ignored intelligence from both his own security agencies and the Allies because he believed the

Germans would not start a war in the East while Britain remained unconquered in the West. As a result, the Soviets were taken by surprise; 50 per cent of the Soviet air force was destroyed on the ground and within three weeks the Germans had advanced 300 miles (500 kilometres) on the northern front, 370 miles (600 kilometres) in the centre and 210 miles (350 kilometres) on the southern front. One senior German officer noted in his diary that it was 'probably no overstatement to say that the Russian campaign has been won in the space of two weeks'.[3]

However, while the Germans deployed a massive 153 divisions, the Soviets had 150 divisions of their own facing this attack. And the German Luftwaffe could only deploy 68 per cent of its strength due to commitments elsewhere. Furthermore, although the forces of the Third Reich were massive, the Red Army had some 2.8 million soldiers in the western districts of the USSR and another million in the southern republics of the USSR and in the Far East. Additionally, those in the Far East were battle tested after having beaten the Japanese in fierce border clashes, including the largest tank battle in history to date, at Khalkhin-Gol, on the Mongolian border, in August 1939. These troops could be deployed westward if the threat from Japan receded, as it did. The statistics were more disturbing yet – from a German perspective. The total population of Germany was 80.6 million. The population under Soviet rule was in the region of 196.7 million. Even allowing for the fact that this included 20.2 million people in territories annexed since 1939, the disparity between the two sides was striking. The USSR would be able to replace dead soldiers faster than the Germans could in a drawn-out war. Hitler's gamble on a short, decisive victory involved playing with very poor odds. And, whilst Russian losses were huge in 1941, so were those of the Germans who, by late September of that year, had sustained 534,000 casualties and were beginning to appreciate something of the enormity of the task they had taken on.

Defeat before Moscow

Hitler's decision to concentrate on the push for Leningrad in the north and into the Ukraine in the south, meant Moscow was not occupied before winter set in. The German troops were not equipped for a Russian winter. It was in this condition that their advance ground to a halt before Moscow. Then, on 5 December, the Soviets launched a massive counterattack.

The Battle for Moscow involved some seven million men and women fighting across a battlefield the size of France. By its end, the victorious Red Army had lost over 900,000 men. The enormity of this casualty figure for one battle is revealed in the fact that it is greater than the combined casualties of the British and Americans for the whole of the Second World War and far higher than the British losses in the entire First World War. It gives an insight into the colossal struggle on the Eastern Front. By the end of the Battle of Moscow, the Third Reich had a bitter taste of exactly what its racist geopolitics had committed it to. In the snows of the winter of 1941–2 lay the beginnings of the catastrophic defeat of the 'Thousand-Year Reich'. To those advocating retreat, Hitler asked: 'Do you want to go back 50 km; do you think it is less cold there?'[4]

Clearly, a major part of the blame for the disaster lay with Hitler.[5] By November, confident of victory, the attention of the Führer had shifted towards the oil fields of the Caucasus and he was content to leave Moscow to be strangled by an encirclement. And, while it was Hitler's determination that had prevented the crisis before Moscow turning into retreat and rout, it was his overconfidence that had launched Germany into that crisis in the first place. But the blame lay wider than this. Errors by senior generals played their part too.[6]

World war

On 11 December 1941, Hitler declared war on the USA. When Japan had bombed Pearl Harbor on 7 December, Hitler had delightedly commented: 'We can't lose the war . . .' And, on 9 December, Goebbels had noted in his diary the vain hope that

'The United States will scarcely now be in a position to transport worthwhile material to England, let alone the Soviet
Union.'[7] Even given the increasing amount of aid the US was
giving to Britain (along with attacking U-boats encountered in
the North Atlantic) it was an astonishing move by Hitler. Now
Germany was at war with the three other superpowers at the
same time. It reveals a great deal about Hitler's outlook on life
as it was a classic example of his policy of '*flucht nach vorn*' (in
essence meaning, 'when in a tight spot, attack'). As always, the
political gambler's instinct was to go for broke. In the past it
had wrong-footed opponents and amazed allies; now it was
escalating crisis into disaster.

The depth of Hitler's denial of his own responsibilities and
his self-delusion can be gauged from a speech he made, on 11
December, to the Reichstag (in one of its rare meetings).
Roosevelt, he claimed, 'bears the main guilt for this war' and,
'From November 1938 onwards, he began systematically to
sabotage any chances of a policy leading to European peace.'
So the Second World War was all Roosevelt's fault. Clearly,
the German invasion of Poland, the attacks on the western
nations and, finally, on the USSR were just the defensive measures of the peace-loving Third Reich, as it faced the heartless
threat of the USA and its allies amongst 'members of the same
nation [the Jews] whom we fought in Germany as a parasitic
human phenomenon'. Roosevelt and the Jews – they were the
ones who had caused it all. It would be almost laughable, were
it not for the layers of slaughtered civilians in the mass graves
at Babi Yar and countless other sites of SS mass shootings, the
bombed cities of Europe, the devastated USSR and the extermination camps being developed in occupied Poland. And, in
case anyone had forgotten Britain's part in apparently causing
the war, von Ribbentrop in his address to the American Chargé
d'Affaires reminded him of the 'outbreak of the European war,
provoked by the British declaration of war against Germany'.[8]
Clearly, the small matter of the German invasion of Poland
had quite slipped the mind of the Nazi Foreign Minister.

With the USA now in the war, the German need to bring the war on the Eastern Front to a satisfactory conclusion was more pressing than ever. In 1942, the aim became to capture the industrial region of the Donets Basin, or Donbas, in eastern Ukraine, and then secure the oil-production areas of the Caucasus. At the same time it was hoped that the siege of Leningrad would be successfully concluded and the Baltic fall completely under German and Finnish control. Despite a failure to destroy Soviet forces along the river Don, Hitler ordered the start of the next phase of planned operations. Furthermore, his overconfidence led him to order the *simultaneous* advance on Stalingrad and into the Caucasus. As a result, neither attack had sufficient strength to accomplish its objectives. As Soviet resistance stiffened at Stalingrad, the German 6th Army was ordered to take the city.[9]

From August 1942 until February 1943, the battle raged street by street. The sacrifice of lives on both sides was enormous and the courage of the Soviet defenders immense. When the Red Army signaller Titayev was sent to re-establish telephone contact between two key positions, his body was later found with the broken wire clenched between his teeth – he had used his own skull as a semiconductor.[10]

As the battle sucked in more German troops, the defence of the flanks was left in the hands of inadequately trained and equipped Romanians. In November, the Soviets struck; a pincer attack shattered the Romanians and trapped the 6th Army in the city. Despite Göring's assurances, the Luftwaffe was incapable of supplying them. A catastrophe was building. On Christmas Day 1942, German radio carried greetings from 'the army on the Volga' to civilians back home. But the transmission was mocked up in a Berlin radio studio, as the troops at Stalingrad were in no position to send Christmas greetings. The fighting in the city was intense and, in the final weeks of the Stalingrad disaster, the German army in the city shot more deserters per day than the British shot in the entire First World War. The 6th Army's commander, General von Paulus, was made a Field Marshal, on the basis that no German Field Marshal had ever surrendered. Von Paulus surrendered the day after his promotion. He is reported to have remarked: 'I have no intention of shooting myself for this Bohemian corporal.' Twenty-four German generals went with him into the prison camps.

In Soviet captivity, von Paulus eventually became a critic of the Nazi regime, made radio appeals to Germany to surrender and, after the war, was eventually released in 1953. This was two years before the German soldiers captured with him at Stalingrad. He settled in Dresden, in communist East Germany, and died in 1957. His body was taken to Baden and buried with his wife, who had died in 1947. Of the 90,000 Germans soldiers captured with him, only about 7,000 survived, to be repatriated by the Soviets in 1955. Another 150,000 German soldiers had been casualties in the city before its surrender; Germany could not survive losses of this magnitude. The Soviets sustained about 1.1 million casualties in the Stalingrad campaign, of which about 480,000 were killed.[11]

The disaster of winter–spring 1942–3 in the USSR was mirrored on other fronts. In North Africa, British and Commonwealth troops inflicted a major defeat on the Germans and Italians at El Alamein in October 1942. Soon the German Afrika Korps were in full retreat, a crisis made worse by an Anglo-American landing in Algeria and Morocco in November (Operation Torch). Vichy French forces in Algeria, Tunisia and Morocco capitulated shortly afterwards. In response, Hitler ordered more German troops to North Africa and the occupation of Vichy France. In May 1943, the last German and Italian troops in North Africa surrendered. A total of 238,000 prisoners were taken by the Allies.

In the Battle of the Atlantic, Germany also faced major problems. It was a clear example of the 'over-stretch' that Hitler had created. In 1939, Admiral Dönitz, chief of U-boat operations, had indicated that 300 U-boats would be necessary to defeat Britain. By 1941, only 22 were operational. Despite a surge in

U-boat successes in the first half of 1942 (due to the slowness of the Americans to learn the lessons of British convoy tactics), by 1943, the tide had turned. Hitler eventually ordered the construction of new U-boats at a time when the Battle of the Atlantic was actually lost. The last significant blow against an Allied convoy occurred in March 1943. As U-boat losses mounted, they were ordered away from the graveyard of the North Atlantic.[12]

The defection of Italy and collapse on the Eastern Front

As the wartime situation worsened for the Third Reich, the weaknesses in Germany's relationships with its allies became more apparent. The Japanese ignored requests from Germany during 1942 and 1943 for an offensive against the USSR. The Japanese had enough on their hands facing the growing Allied threat to their newly won Asian empire. They would not face the USSR on the battlefield until August 1945 when the USSR declared war *on them*.

Regarding Italy, matters were even worse. The loss of North Africa, the realization of the scale of the German defeat at Stalingrad and the ill-concealed contempt of the Germans for their Italian allies undermined their alliance with the Third Reich. When the Allies invaded Sicily in July 1943, the Italian disillusionment with the war boiled over into crisis. A meeting of the Italian Grand Fascist Council voted to transfer command of the Italian armed forces from Mussolini to the King of Italy. The next day, Mussolini was arrested and, by September, the Italians had negotiated a separate armistice with the Allies. The Germans reacted swiftly. They occupied the northern half of Italy and established a strong defensive line south of Rome. Italian soldiers across Europe were disarmed and 615,000 ended up as slave labourers in Germany. It was this tragic German retaliation against the Italians on the Greek islands that features in the novel and film *Captain Corelli's Mandolin*.[13] For the Allies, Italy – under German occupation – was no longer the 'soft underbelly of Europe', as Winston Churchill described it in 1942, but was instead 'the tough old gut' (as the British and American soldiers termed it, borrowing a phrase from the US general Mark Clark). However, the Italian campaign drained German military resources that might otherwise have propped up the Eastern Front for longer.

If 1943 saw the Third Reich shoring up its position in Italy, it also saw mounting catastrophes on the Eastern Front. 'Operation Citadel' was a German plan to destroy the offensive capacity of the Red Army and regain the initiative. It would be centred on Kursk and would entail a colossal clash of armoured forces. However, postponements of the attack date cost the Germans the element of surprise and the eventual battle failed to bring about a German breakthrough. The Red Army had developed to the extent that 'a staged German offensive was defeated in less than two weeks!'[14] It was followed by a series of massive Soviet advances – albeit bitterly contested by the German army, which was tenacious in defence. By November 1943, the Soviets had recaptured Kiev; in January 1944, the German siege of Leningrad was ended; by June 1944, the Red Army had recaptured the Crimea, liberated almost the whole of the Ukraine and had crossed the Romanian border. Then, between June and August, the Soviet offensive – 'Operation Bagration' – destroyed the German Army Group Centre; this victory cleared German forces from Belorussia and eastern Poland, and killed 381,000 Germans, wounded a further 384,000 and captured 158,000. The way was now open for further Soviet advances into East Prussia and the Baltic states. Over the winter of 1943–4, the Third Reich had concentrated over 60 per cent of its military manpower and over 50 per cent of its armoured forces on the Eastern Front, and this had been insufficient to halt the Soviet advances. The casualty figures of Germany and its allies reached almost one million over that winter. The Eastern Front was grinding the Third Reich into the ground.[15] While the British and Commonwealth forces were engaging 12 German and Italian divisions at El Alamein, the Russians were fighting 186 divisions on the

Eastern Front. The scale of the fighting – and German losses – there meant that, from this point onwards, Hitler could only react to the actions of others; the supreme gambler had lost the ability to decide the course of events. He had gambled and failed.

D-Day and the liberation of Western Europe

Then, on 6 June 1944, the much awaited Allied liberation of Western Europe began.[16] With D-Day, Hitler was now facing a ground war in the east, west and south. This was accompanied by increasing ferocity in the aerial bombardment of German cities. Germany failed to repulse the D-Day invasion for a number of reasons. First, there was a strategic error in assuming that the main Allied invasion would target the Pas de Calais. For a month after the landings, the Germans held considerable forces there in anticipation of a second invasion. Second, a compromise between senior German officers meant that tank formations were held back from the coast, despite Field Marshal Rommel's strong belief that proximity to possible landing beaches in Normandy was crucial if a beachhead was to be denied any invading Allied forces. Third, on 6 June, hours were wasted waiting for Hitler to wake up (he always slept late) before German armoured units could be ordered forward to confront the Allies on the beaches.

Additionally, the German troops on the vaunted Atlantic Wall were not the cream of the German army. In fact, the second-rate German units stationed in Normandy also included units of Poles, *Osttruppen* (German military units comprised of Russian volunteers), *Volksdeutsche* (ethnic Germans living outside the Reich) and Russian *Hilfswillige*, or *Hiwi*, paramilitary units (Soviet deserters, prisoners and volunteers). Some of these volunteers became very loyal indeed; 'Panzer Meyer' commander of the 12th SS Panzer Division had a devoted Cossack orderly.[17] But they were no substitute for the battle-hardened troops needed to repulse the Allied invasion.

A major factor in German defeat was the supremacy in the air enjoyed by the Allies. This allowed them to cover their own advances and disrupt German troop movements. Wry German military humour during the battle for Normandy in June 1944 commented on the absence – or ineffectiveness – of the Luftwaffe (and also the inaccuracy of US airstrikes): 'If British planes appear, we duck. If American planes come over, everyone ducks. And if the Luftwaffe appears, nobody ducks.'[18] In fact, it was short-falling American bombs that were responsible for killing Lieutenant-General Lesley McNair, one of the highest-ranking US officers to die in the war (two other US Lieutenant-Generals were also killed in the conflict).

As always, the German army was highly effective when fighting from defensive positions. The battle for Normandy soon turned into a bitterly contested struggle for every high-banked hedgerow, sunken lane and copse of the Norman *bocage* (mixed woodland and pasture). For a while, casualty rates were starting to reach First World War proportions. The fanaticism of SS resistance meant that few SS soldiers appeared in the Allied POW cages as, in a little documented aspect of the war, Allied servicemen frequently gave no quarter to the SS. But in July, the Allies broke out towards Avranches in 'Operation Cobra' and, even though the trap sprung around the Germans at Falaise was not closed as fast as necessary (allowing significant numbers to escape), German losses in both casualties and equipment were still enormous. Eisenhower would later describe how it was 'possible to walk for hundreds of yards, stepping on nothing but dead and decaying flesh'.[19] However, these German losses were still some ten times smaller than those being inflicted by the Russians at the same time in Operation Bagration.

Despite the losses on the Eastern Front, Hitler was certain that the key to victory was in the West. This was a combination of his refusal to admit to the scale of the defeats of the winter of 1943–4, a realization that loss of the Ruhr industrial heartland to the Allies would be a disaster and a delusion that a victory in the West was still possible and this would, in turn, make victory possible on the Eastern Front. As a result, German forces were still tenaciously opposing the advances of the Western Allies in May 1945, as the Red Army was rampaging through eastern Germany.

Attacks by German V1 flying bombs and then V2 rockets on London in 1944 came too late in the war to affect its result. And the Nazi racial obsession that theoretical physics was 'Jewish' (alongside the Allied destruction of the 'heavy water' production plant in Norway in 1943) ensured that Germany was far behind the Western Allies in the research leading to atomic weapons. As a result, no German wonder-weapon could change the course of events, whatever Hitler promised to the contrary.

Paris was liberated on 25 August 1944; US forces had landed in the south of France ten days earlier. But the war was not to be over by Christmas. The airborne landings at Arnhem in September failed in the face of strong German resistance and the Rhine remained a barrier to the Allies until March 1945. Then, in the winter snow of 1944–5, the last German offensive in the West pushed a bulge in the Allied lines (hence its name – the 'Battle of the Bulge') but could not be sustained. Although surprised at first, US army resistance soon slowed the German advance. At Bastogne, in December, the US commander of the 101st Airborne troops defending the town, General Anthony Clement McAuliffe, met the German surrender ultimatum with the one-word reply, 'Nuts!' The squandering of German reserves of men, tanks and fuel in this doomed offensive was down to Hitler's decision. As the historian Max Hastings has commented: 'Only Hitler's personal folly maintained the Ardennes battle.'[20]

Increasingly erratic and flawed in his military decisions since Stalingrad, he unrealistically hoped that a surprise German victory in the West would cause the alliance of the USA and Britain to disintegrate and bring the Western Allies to the negotiating table. And, as his Third Reich imploded, the

Führer reverted more and more to type: wild gambles, refusals to give ground, preposterous versions of reality and a refusal to hear any criticisms of his actions. Field Marshal Paul von Kleist judged Hitler's mentality, by this stage in the war, as being 'more of a problem for a psychiatrist than for a general'.[21] The very personality features and strategies that had once propelled him towards power were now accelerating Germany into the abyss of cataclysmic defeat. There was a savage irony in this.

The disintegration of the Third Reich

The failure of the German Ardennes offensive meant that when, in January 1945, the Soviets launched a new offensive there were no more German reserves to deploy against them. The same was true when the Western Allies resumed their advance in February 1945. In the East, disasters mounted though, even at this late stage, German resistance was tenacious. In February, the German navy succeeded in evacuating four military divisions and 1.5 million civilians from Baltic ports before they fell to the Red Army. It was a feat assisted by the striking inactivity of surface ships of the Soviet's Baltic Fleet.[22] Even so, the evacuation witnessed the worst maritime disaster in history when a Soviet submarine sank the liner *Wilhelm Gustloff*, with the loss of 9,000 civilians. It was German civilians who now suffered the full fury of the Red Army. Black humour in Berlin that winter remarked: 'Enjoy the war while you can, the peace will be terrible.'[23] But the reality was no laughing matter. As Soviet troops crossed the borders of the Reich they murdered and raped in appalling revenge for the Nazi atrocities in the USSR. The German home front disintegrated in unimaginable horrors. (See Chapter 19.)

Finally, in the ruins of Berlin, old men and teenagers fought in the poorly armed ranks of the *Volkssturm* (Home Guard) against Soviet tanks. On 29 April, Hitler married his long-term mistress Eva Braun. In the chaotic last hours of the Third Reich, the only official who could be found to conduct the wedding was Walter Wagner, deputy surveyor of local rubbish collections in a district of Berlin. With the Red Army just a few streets from the Führer Bunker, Hitler dictated his last will and testament. In it he nominated Admiral Karl Dönitz as the new President of Germany and Goebbels as the new Reich Chancellor. At about 3.30 p.m. on Monday 30 April 1945, Hitler (and Eva Hitler) committed suicide in his underground bunker below the Reich Chancellery. Above him, Berlin was in ruins. Hitler's vision of life had finally ended in a destructive defeat reminiscent of Wagner's *Götterdämmerung* (the mythical war of the Norse gods that, in ancient Germanic legend, was thought to bring about the end of the world). Shortly afterwards – on 1 May – Goebbels and his wife Magda also killed themselves; they had earlier poisoned their six children. This left Admiral Dönitz as sole leader of what was left of Germany.

On 2 May, German army units in Berlin surrendered.[24] Over the ruined Reichstag building flew the red and gold hammer and sickle flag of the USSR. It had been improvised from a red tablecloth by a Red Army cameraman, the Ukrainian Jew Yevgenny Khaldei. The famous photograph of its raising on the building had later to be airbrushed to remove the – all too obviously looted – multiple wristwatches visible on the wrist of one of the young Red Army soldiers. The destruction and humiliation of the Third Reich could hardly have been more strikingly staged.[25] At 2.41 a.m. on Monday 7 May, the Chief of Staff of the German Armed Forces High Command, General Alfred Jodl, on behalf of the new German government of Admiral Dönitz, surrendered unconditionally to the Western Allies at Rheims, France. Since no representative of the USSR was at this event, the surrender was repeated two days later in Berlin (backdated to 8 May). The last fighting of the war is usually considered to have ended at about 4 p.m. on Tuesday 15 May when a mixed force of Croatian, Slovenian and Montenegrin allies of the Germans finally surrendered to Yugoslav partisans at Poljana, in Yugoslavia (now in modern Slovenia).

Richard Overy has provided a persuasive analysis of why the Allies won. Amongst his answers a number stand out. Germany was not sufficiently equipped for war in 1939,[26] a situation made worse when it invaded the USSR. Most of its army was unmechanized and heavily dependent on horses; in 1942 alone some 400,000 were sent to the Eastern Front.[27] Furthermore, over 90 per cent of the world's oil resources were controlled by the Allies.[28] Germany was also over-focused on developing new technologies when those it already had required updating.[29] The Western Allies destroyed the Luftwaffe through bombing aircraft factories and the oil industry; alongside deployment of long-range fighters, this meant that, between autumn 1943 and spring 1944, the Luftwaffe was starved of replacement planes and fuel and was shot out of the sky.[30] Crucially, Germany could not compete with the massive Allied commitment, organization and mobilization of resources, both human and technical.

As a result, by May 1945, the Third Reich was utterly ruined. It was to have lasted one thousand years; in the event it had lasted less than thirteen. In that time it had caused the deaths of about 40 million people, had committed genocide against the Jews and had enslaved millions. The Nazi New Order had caused misery beyond imagining but was finally over.

Finally ended was a world in which a German doctor at Auschwitz (in civilian life, Professor of Medicine at the University of Münster) could write the following in his diary: '6–7 September, 1942. Sunday, an excellent lunch: tomato soup, half a chicken with potatoes and red cabbage, petits fours, a marvellous vanilla ice cream. Left at eight in the evening for a special action [the mass killing of Jewish prisoners] . . .'[31]

22

THE LEGACY OF THE
THIRD REICH

Theodor Adorno (1903–69) was a German-born intellectual, sociologist, philosopher, composer and a member of the so-called 'Frankfurt School' (a neo-Marxist group of thinkers who sought to explain the failure of left-wing revolution in Western Europe in the 1930s and the rise of Nazism). Like many, he recognized that the world could not be the same after the horrors of the Third Reich. Whatever one's verdict on his overall political philosophy, he succeeded in summing up something of the profound impact of the Third Reich on the world that came after it: 'After Auschwitz: no poetry.'[1] Nazism had left Europe shattered and traumatized, and its effects are still with us.

In 1945, the Third Reich was brought so low that 'Germany's defeat was unambiguous' and German support for Nazism had collapsed.[2] Hitler's immediate geo-political legacy was the advance of Soviet communism into the heart of Europe and consequently the Cold War that would last until the end of the 1980s. The states that found themselves east of the Iron Curtain did so as a direct consequence of the war that Hitler had launched and lost. But the shockwaves of the end of the Third Reich went further still. An exhausted Britain could no longer sustain its world role. The USA, in its war with Germany, had finally achieved military superpower status, which it still holds, while the cost of achieving its own version of this and maintaining that status would eventually lead to the collapse of the USSR in 1991.[3] Ironically, it was the captured technical expertise of German scientists that made a massive contribution to the development of the post-war age of competing ballistic missiles.[4]

Within Germany itself it was the utter collapse of the Third Reich that saw the nation divided into zones between the victorious Allies, which would, by 1949, begin to harden into two distinct German states – one democratic in the West and the other a one-party-state in the East. In a dramatic reversal of the Nazi drive for Lebensraum in the East, the eastern borders of Germany were redrawn on a massive scale and this process pushed the Polish border far to the west of where it had stood in 1939. The victorious Soviets dismembered East Prussia (dividing it between the USSR and Poland) and the German lands to the east of the rivers Oder and Neisse were incorporated into Poland. This compensated Poland for its land that had been annexed by the USSR further east,[5] and the Oder–Neisse line was recognized by Germany as Poland's western frontier in 1970.[6] As relations between the Western Allies and the USSR rapidly cooled, the planned peace treaty with a reunited Germany did not occur until 1990, after the fall of the Berlin Wall in 1989.

This redrawing of Germany's eastern borders was accompanied by massive population movement as millions of Germans were expelled from the newly liberated states of Eastern Europe. Trekking westward during the winter of 1945–6, hundreds of thousands died. It has been estimated that between 1944 and 1950, somewhere in the region of 12 million Germans were expelled westward.[7] By the latter date only about 12 per cent of the Germans living in Eastern Europe in 1939 were still resident there. It was the largest movement of any ethnic group in modern world history. And it came as a direct consequence of the actions and defeat of the Third Reich. The ethnic map of Europe – already brutally redrawn by the murderous actions of the Nazis – had been redrawn yet again by their defeat. Even in the twenty-first century tensions can still be raised between Germany and its neighbours in Poland and the Czech Republic by debates about compensating Germans expelled from the East and monuments commemorating their expulsion.[8] The ghost of the Third Reich still haunts Central European relations.

More positively, the failure of the League of Nations to prevent the Second World War led to the establishment of the United Nations. In 1945, representatives of fifty countries met in San Francisco to draw up the United Nations Charter. One of its immediate tasks was the care of the vast number of displaced people caused by Nazi policies and by the upheaval of war. The United Nations Relief and Rehabilitation Administration (UNRRA), which eventually was replaced by the International Refugee Organization (IRO), had been created by Allied planners well before the end of the war to deal with the anticipated crisis.[9] The modern Office of the United Nations High Commissioner for Refugees (UNHCR), founded in 1950, continues to develop this legacy of caring for those displaced by war, famine and natural disasters. Today, its staff of about 6,600 work in more than 110 countries and assist about 34 million people.[10]

Paradoxically, the failure of Hitler's bid for European domination and his genocide against the Jews provided a stimulus to the establishment of a Jewish homeland in the Middle East in the state of Israel.[11] Since the late-nineteenth century, Zionist organizations had worked for the creation of a Jewish national state. Anti-Semitism in Europe caused many Jews to embrace this belief and Nazi persecution increased the commitment of many Jews to secure a defensible homeland. By 1945, Jews fleeing Nazi persecution had increased the Jewish population of British-administered Palestine to about 33 per cent of the total population. With the defeat of the Third Reich, many thousands of Jewish survivors sought to escape from Europe to find a new home in the Middle East. Existing trends may well have led to the establishment of Israel, even had Nazism not arisen, but what is clear is that, at the very least, the experiences of the 1930s and 1940s accelerated these trends. This was both from the perspective of Jews wishing to escape a continent that seemed bent on their destruction and from the perspective of an international community more open to Jewish aspirations following the horrors of the Final Solution.[12]

The actions of the Third Reich were also key factors leading to European integration that has transformed Europe since 1945. In 1951, the Treaty of Paris created the European Coal and Steel Community (ECSC). It aimed to strengthen the economies of Europe and make the outbreak of another war between Germany and France unthinkable. Since then, this partnership has been the 'bedrock and motor of European economic integration'.[13] By ensuring the integration of such important industries as coal and steel it turned these two traditional enemies into partners in the future development of Europe. As such it was a direct consequence of the trauma that had torn Europe apart between 1939 and 1945. In the absence of a formal peace treaty ending the Second World War, a revived Germany was peacefully reintegrated into Europe through economic cooperation.[14] This first step in integration was followed by cooperation on a wider front through the European Economic Community (EEC) formed in 1957–8, the forerunner of the modern European Union (EU).[15] The fact that the major states of Europe have been at peace since 1945 and that today Germany and France are allies is due to the transformation of European attitudes following the defeat of the Third Reich. For the same reason, German foreign policy is now committed to non-aggression, in direct contrast with the first forty-five years of the twentieth century, and its energies have been channelled into *economic* expansion.

The appalling atrocities of the Nazi regime led to the prosecution of at least some of those responsible, in the Nuremberg War

Crimes Tribunals of 1945–9. These events played a major part in later developments in international law such as the Genocide Convention of 1948 (defining genocide and declaring it a crime under international law), the Universal Declaration of Human Rights of 1948 and the Geneva Convention on the Laws and Customs of War of 1949 and its 1977 supplementary protocols. The court, established by UN Resolution 827 in 1993, to deal with war crimes committed in the former Yugoslavia, along with the court established by UN Resolution 955 in 1994, to deal with the Rwandan genocide, reveal an international community that now is prepared (if belatedly) to take action against war crimes and genocidal acts. This too can be seen as a long-term legacy of the Third Reich and its final defeat.[16]

Despite the collapse of Soviet communism and the reunification of Germany, which understandably caused historian Allan Bullock to comment that 'The age of Hitler and Stalin is over',[17] the shadow of the Third Reich still lingers, well over half a century after its end. The character of Europe is still defined to a significant extent by the traumas unleashed by Hitler. The ethnic map of Europe in the twenty-first century is hugely different because of the Third Reich. The widespread Jewish culture, which was a characteristic feature of Poland and the western USSR in 1939, no longer exists. The German communities of Eastern Europe are largely gone. Eastern Europe is a different kind of place because of the Third Reich. This is a permanent change.

Positively, there is a clear determination to ensure that the horrors of Nazism are not repeated, by commemorations such as Holocaust Remembrance and educating modern young people about racism and intolerance. Alarming though is the evidence that there are still Holocaust deniers who refuse to acknowledge the enormity of the crimes of the Third Reich, and neo-Nazi groups who look back nostalgically to its ideology and its imagery. These groups are clearly minorities but they remind us that Nazism can still exert an appeal, especially at times of social stress.

That is why it is necessary that the ideology of the Third Reich, its appeal and its terrible effects must be studied and understood. We have to continue to ask ourselves: how was it possible? What were the wide-ranging factors that allowed the Third Reich to prosper and, for over a decade, to expand its influence? In doing this, it is necessary to examine it, not only as a German phenomenon, but also against the backdrop of wider European history and to recognize that its values briefly resonated with many people, principally inside, but also outside Germany. These questions cause us to recognize its unique character and at the same time to identify those features that were related to wider trends, experiences and ideologies. And these did not all vanish with the defeat of Germany in 1945. These are difficult questions and issues because they mean that we cannot label the Third Reich as being so unique that aspects of it could not happen again. Only when we come closer to understanding it can we have the insight necessary to confront its ideology – if it reappears in some new form – with the words of the White Rose movement: 'We will not be silent.'

NOTES

Chapter 1. The Nazi rise to power, 1918–23

1. For an early outline of the career of Anton Drexler, see Heiden, Konrad, *A History of National Socialism*, Alfred A. Knopf, Inc, 1935, reprinted by Octagon Books, 1971, pp. 3–8. See also: Schoenbaum, David, *Hitler's Social Revolution: Class and Status in Nazi Germany, 1933–1939*, W.W. Norton, 1997, pp. 15–16.

2. See Weitz, Eric D., *Weimar Germany: Promise and Tragedy*, Princeton University Press, 2007, and Friedrich, Otto, *Before the Deluge: A Portrait of Berlin in the 1920s*, HarperCollins, 1972.

3. Harman, Chris, *The Lost Revolution: Germany 1918 to 1923*, Haymarket Books, 2003, argues that the failure of revolution in Germany needs to be understood if one is to fully explain the success of the right wing in Germany and the isolation of the USSR.

4. MacMillan, Margaret, *Peacemakers: Six Months That Changed the World: The Paris Peace Conference of 1919 and its Attempt to End War*, John Murray, 2003, explores the complexities of framing the post-war peace treaties and the intractable problems the peacemakers faced.

5. Wheeler-Bennett, John W., *Nemesis of Power: The German Army in Politics 1918–1945* (2nd edn), Palgrave Macmillan, 2005, offers a detailed examination of how the Germany army exercised a

dominating role in the Weimar republic and its part in the rise of the Nazis and its later toleration of Nazi crimes.

6. Carsten, Francis Ludwig, *The Reichswehr and Politics, 1918 to 1933*, University of California, 1974, pp. 78–9.

7. Burleigh, Michael, *The Third Reich, a New History*, Pan Books, 2001, p. 65.

8. Thornhill, Chris, *Political Theory in Modern Germany: An Introduction*, Polity, 2000, p. 101. For an examination of the crisis in the Weimar economy in the 1920s, see Widdig, Bernd, *Culture and Inflation in Weimar Germany*, University of California Press, 2001.

9. Kershaw, Ian, *Hitler, 1889–1936: Hubris*, Penguin Books, 1999, p. 165.

10. Mühlberger, Detlef, *Hitler's voice: the Völkischer Beobachter, 1920–1933*, vol. I, Peter Lang Publishing, 2004, provides a detailed insight into the views of the Nazi party as portrayed in its newspaper.

11. Kershaw, Ian, *The 'Hitler Myth'*, Oxford University Press, 1987, p. 22.

12. Strasser, Otto, *Hitler and I*, Jonathan Cape, 1940, p. 42.

13. Kershaw, Ian, 1999, op. cit., p. 175.

14. Bookbinder, P., *Weimar Germany: The Republic of the Reasonable*, Manchester University Press, 1996, p. 78.

15. Kershaw, Ian, 1999, op. cit., pp. 215–7.

16. Ibid., pp. 244–6.

Chapter 2. The Nazi rise to power, 1924–33

1. Wright, Jonathan, *Gustav Stresemann: Weimar's Greatest Statesman*, Oxford University Press, 2002, pp. 1–2.

2. Mommsen, Hans, *The Rise and Fall of Weimar Democracy*, Forster, Elborg and Jones, Larry Eugene (trans.), University of North Carolina Press, 1998, suggests this interpretation of events.

3. Kershaw, Ian, *Hitler, 1889–1936: Hubris*, Penguin Books, 1999, pp. 224–6.

4. Ibid., pp. 271–7.

5. Goebbels, quoted in Kershaw, Ian, ibid., p. 277.

6. Kershaw, Ian, *The 'Hitler Myth'*, Oxford University Press, 1987, p. 26.

7. For a detailed examination of the history of the SS, see Höhne, Heinz, *The Order of the Death's Head*, translated by Barry, R., Pan Books, 1969.

8. Burleigh, Michael, *The Third Reich, A New History,* Pan Books, 2001, p. 104.

9. Weitz, Eric D., *Weimar Germany: Promise and Tragedy*, Princeton University Press, 2007, emphasizes the confident modernity that seemed to characterize Weimar in the mid-1920s and makes the point it should not just be seen as a mere prelude to the Nazi era. See also: Gay, Peter, *Weimar Culture: The Outsider as Insider*, W.W. Norton, 2001.

10. For insights into the close relationship between von Papen and Hindenburg, see Turner, Henry, A., *Hitler's Thirty Days to Power,* Perseus Books, 1996, pp. 96–7. For an examination of the career of von Papen, see Rolfs, Richard, W., *The Sorcerer's Apprentice: The Life of Franz von Papen,* University Press of America, 1996. And for the relationship between Schleicher and von Papen, see Bendersky, Joseph W., *A History of Nazi Germany: 1919–1945*, Burnham 2nd edition, 2000, pp. 89–90.

11. See Kershaw, Ian, 1999, op. cit., pp. 424–7, for a detailed assessment of the factors that finally led to Hitler's appointment as Chancellor.

Chapter 3. Who voted Nazi? And why?

1. For different interpretations of why so many groups of people voted Nazi, see Brustein, William, *The Logic of Evil: The Social Origins of the Nazi Party, 1925–1933*, Yale University Press, 1998; Fischer, Conan, *The Rise of the Nazis*, Manchester University Press, 2002; Mühlberger, Detlef, *The Social Bases of Nazism, 1919–1933*, Economic History Society and Cambridge University Press, 2003.

2. Kershaw, Ian, *Hitler, 1889–1936: Hubris*, Penguin Books, 1999, pp. 407–8.

3. Burleigh, Michael, *The Third Reich, a New History,* Pan Books, 2001, pp. 68–69.

4. Ibid., p. 105; Noakes, J. and Pridham, G., *Nazism 1919–1945,* vol. I, *The Rise to Power 1919–1934*, University of Exeter Press, 2nd edition, 1998, p. 80.

5. Kagan, Donald, Ozment, Steven E., Turner, Frank, *The Western Heritage: Since 1789*, Pearson Education, 2001, p. 1,037.

6. See Kershaw, Ian, op. cit., pp. 408–9.

7. Burleigh, Michael, op. cit., p. 68.

8. See Kershaw, op. cit., p. 407.

9. A key area explored in Jenkins, Jane and Feuchtwanger, Edgar, *Hitler's Germany*, Hodder Murray, 2000.

10. For an overview of the mixed support provided by German capitalists, see Kershaw, Ian, op. cit., p. 358.

11. Fischer, Conan, *The Rise of the Nazis*, Manchester University Press, 2002, p. 130.

12. Kershaw, Ian, *The 'Hitler Myth'*, Oxford University Press, 1987, p. 30.

13. Quoted in Rothnie, Niall, *National Socialism in Germany*, Palgrave Macmillan, 1987, p. 13.

14. Burleigh, Michael, op. cit., p. 67.

15. Explored in Evans, Richard, *Rereading German History, 1800–1996*, Routledge, 1997.

16. Noakes, J. and Pridham, G., *Nazism 1919–1945*, vol. I, *The Rise to Power 1919–1934*, University of Exeter Press, 2nd edition, 1998, p. 54.

17. Evans, Richard, *The Coming of the Third Reich*, Penguin Books, 2003, p. 264.

Chapter 4. Bringing Germany into line

1. Koshar, Rudy, *Social Life, Local Politics, and Nazism: Marburg, 1880–1935*, University of North Carolina Press, 1986, p. 255. See also the effects on organizations as seemingly apolitical as singing clubs in Allen, William Sheridan, *The Nazi Seizure of Power: The Experience of a Single German Town, 1930–1935*, Franklin Watts, 1965, pp. 220–1.

2. See Rolfs, Richard, W., *The Sorcerer's Apprentice: The Life of Franz von Papen*, University Press of America, 1996.

3. Overy, Richard, *The Dictators: Hitler's Germany and Stalin's Russia*, Allen Lane, 2004, chapter 1, 'Paths to dictatorship', gives an accessible overview of what was hoped for from Hitler's government.

4. Dogan, Mattéi, Higley, John (eds), *Elites, Crises, and the Origins of Regimes*, Rowman & Littlefield, 1998, p. 173.

5. Hayse, Michael R., *Recasting West German Elites: Higher Civil Servants, Business Leaders, and Physicians in Hesse Between Nazism and Democracy, 1945–1955 (Monographs in German History, 11)*, Berghahn Books, 2003, p. 250.

6. An accessible overview of this process can be found in Lee, Stephen J., *European Dictatorships, 1918–1945*, Methuen, 2000. See also Williamson, D. G., *The Age of the Dictators: A Study of the European Dictatorships, 1918–53*, Pearson, 2007.

7. Quoted in Kershaw, Ian, *Hitler, 1889–1936: Hubris*, Penguin Books, 1999, p. 427.

8. Evans, Richard, *The Coming of the Third Reich*, Penguin Books, 2003, p. 315.

9. Krausnick, Helmut, 'Stages of co-ordination', in *The Road to Dictatorship, 1918–1933*, Oswald Wolff, 1964, p. 136.

10. For an excellent overview of the Nazi *Gleichschaltung*, see Kershaw, Ian, op. cit., pp. 435–6.

11. See Levi, Erik, *Music in the Third Reich*, Palgrave Macmillan, 1994.

12. Gallin, Alice, *Midwives to Nazism: University Professors in Weimar Germany, 1925–1933*, Mercer University Press, 1986, p. 87.

13. Burleigh, Michael, *The Third Reich, a New History*, Pan Books, 2001, p. 104.

14. For an examination of the events, see Pritchard, R. John and Mayer, Sydney L., *Reichstag Fire: Ashes of Democracy, Ballantine's Illustrated History of the Violent Century; Politics in Action Number 3*, Ballantine Books, 1972.

15. See his account in Papen, Franz von, *Memoirs*, Andre Deutsch, 1952.

16. Kershaw, Ian, *The 'Hitler Myth'*, Oxford University Press, 1987, p. 54.

17. The newspaper *Miesbacher Anzeiger*, of 22 March 1933, in Kershaw, Ian, 1987, ibid., p. 54.

18. Evans, Richard, op. cit., p. 459.

19. Burleigh, Michael, op. cit., p. 151.

20. Overy, Richard, op. cit., p. 47.

Chapter 5. The revolution eats its own children: the destruction of the SA

1. Shirer, William, L, *The Rise and Fall of the Third Reich*, Simon and Schuster, 1960, p. 220.

2. See Machtan, Lothar (John Brownjohn, trans), *The Hidden Hitler*, Basic Books, 2001.

3. Fischer, Conan, *Stormtroopers: A Social, Economic, and Ideological Analysis, 1929–35*, Allen & Unwin, 1983, provides an overview of the nature of the SA.

4. Campbell, Bruce, *The SA Generals and the Rise of Nazism*, University Press of Kentucky, 2004, pp. 142–3.

5. Hancock, Eleanor, *Ernst Röhm: Hitler's SA chief of staff*, Palgrave Macmillan, 2008, provides a modern biography of the SA leader.

6. Evans, Richard, *The Third Reich in Power*, Allen Lane, 2005, p. 21.

7. Minuth, Karl-Heinz (ed.), *Akten der Reichskanzlei Die Regierung Hitler, 1933–1934*, Boppard, 1983, pp. 630–1. in Evans, Richard, *The Third Reich in Power*, Allen Lane, 2005, p. 20.

8. Sopade report, 26 June 1934, in Kershaw, Ian, *The 'Hitler Myth'*, Oxford University Press, 1987, p. 65.

9 Kershaw, Ian, *Hitler, 1889–1936: Hubris*, Penguin Books, 1999, p. 505.

10. Noakes, J. and Pridham, G., *Nazism 1919–1945*, vol. I, *The Rise to Power 1919–1934*, University of Exeter Press, 2nd edn, 1998, p. 177.

11. Gallo, Max, *The Night Of The Long Knives: June 29–30, 1934*, Da Capo Press, 1997, provides a detailed account of the destruction of the SA. A shorter examination can be found in, amongst other places, Benz, Wolfgang and Dunlap, Thomas (trans.), *A Concise History of the Third Reich*, University of California Press, 2006, pp. 53–57.

12. Noakes, J. and Pridham, G., op. cit., pp. 178–9.

13. Ibid., p. 181.

14. Kershaw, Ian, 1999, op. cit., p. 175.

15. Klemperer, Victor, *The Klemperer Diaries, 1933–1945*, Chalmers, Martin (trans.), Phoenix Press, 2000, pp. 71–2.

16. Noakes, J. and Pridham, G., op. cit., pp. 186–7.

17. Kershaw, Ian, *The 'Hitler Myth'*, Oxford University Press, 1987, p. 86.

18. www.historylearningsite.co.uk/night_of_the_long_knives.htm

19. Von der Goltz, Anna, *Hindenburg: Power, Myth, and the Rise of the Nazis*, Oxford University Press, 2009, provides a detailed examination of the life and significance of Hindenburg.

20. Kershaw, Ian, 1999, op. cit., p. 525.

21. Beaumont, Roger A., *The Nazis' March to Chaos: The Hitler Era Through the Lenses of Chaos-Complexity Theory*, Praeger Publishers, 2000, p. 102.

Chapter 6. Economic transformation, or smoke and mirrors? The Nazi impact on the German economy, 1933–9

1. Pool, James, *Who Financed Hitler?*, Simon & Schuster, revised edition, 1999, focuses on the controversies surrounding the Nazi Party's financial backing.

2. Wiesen, S. Jonathan, *West German Industry and the Challenge of the Nazi Past, 1945–1955*, University of North Carolina Press, 2003, looks at the effects of these relationships for German industry even after the fall of the Third Reich.

3. Overy, R. J., *The Nazi Economic Recovery, 1932–8*, Cambridge University Press, 1996, for example, argues that there was a significant change in Nazi economic policy in 1936–7 with an increase in state power.

4. Evans, Richard, *The Third Reich in Power*, Allen Lane, 2005, p. 325.

5. Freeman, Chris and Louçã, Francisco, *As Time Goes By: From the Industrial Revolutions to the Information Revolution*, Oxford University Press, 2001, p. 270.

6. See Halpern, Paul G., *A Naval History of World War I*, Routledge, 1994.

7. See Brechtefeld, Jörg, *Mitteleuropa and German politics: 1848 to the present*, Palgrave, 1996.

8. Noakes, J. and Pridham, G., *Nazism 1919–1945*, vol. II, *State, Economy and Society, 1933–1939*, University of Exeter Press, 2nd edition, 2000, p. 81.

9. Evans, Richard, op. cit., p. 355.

10. A point made strongly by Weitz, John, *Hitler's Banker*, Little, Brown, 1997.

11. Noakes, J. and Pridham, G., op. cit., pp. 84–5.

12. Ibid., p. 86.

13. Schacht, Hjalmar, *My First Seventy-Six Years*, Wingate, 1955, pp. 362–77.

14. Volkmann, Hans-Erich, 'The National Socialist Economy in preparation for war' in *Germany and the Second World War*, Oxford University Press, 1990, pp. 293–300 and 350–4.

15. See Nicosia, Francis R, and Huener, Jonathan (eds), *Business and Industry in Nazi Germany*, Berghahn Books, 2004.

16. James, Harold, *The Deutsche Bank and the Nazi economic war against the Jews: The Expropriation of Jewish-Owned Property*, Cambridge University Press, 2001, and also see James, Harold, *The Nazi Dictatorship and the Deutsche Bank*, Cambridge University Press, 2004.

17. Noakes, J. and Pridham, G., op. cit., p. 119.

18. Examined in detail in Jeffreys, Diarmuid, *Hell's Cartel: IG Farben and the Making of Hitler's War Machine*, Metropolitan Books, 2008.

19. Evans, Richard, op. cit., p. 349.

20. Noakes, J. and Pridham, G., op. cit., p. 90.

Chapter 7. Reluctant supporters, or sullen opponents? The German workers

1. Baranowski, Shelley, *Strength Through Joy: Consumerism and Mass Tourism in the Third Reich*, Cambridge University Press, 2004, pp. 1–2.

2. Abel, Theodore, *Why Hitler Came to Power*, Harvard University Press, 1986 reprint of the 1938 original, p. 218.

3. Burleigh, Michael, *The Third Reich, a New History*, Pan Books, 2000, p. 133.

4. Schoenbaum, David, *Hitler's Social Revolution: Class and Status in Nazi Germany, 1933–1939*, Doubleday, 1966, W.W. Norton, 1980, p. 4.

5. See references to research, available in English, in Muhlberger, Detlef, *Hitler's Followers: Studies in the Sociology of the Nazi Movement*, Routledge, 1991; Fischer, Conan, 'Workers, the Middle Classes and the Rise of National Socialism', in *German History*, 1991, 9, pp.

357–73; also Fischer, Conan (ed.), *The Rise of National Socialism and the Working Classes in Weimar Germany*, Berghahn Books, 1996.

6. Quoted in Whittock, Martyn, *Hitler and National Socialism*, Heinemann, 1995, p. 21.

7. Herzog, Rudolph, *Heil Hitler, das Schwein ist Tot! (Heil Hitler, The Pig is Dead)* Eichborn-Verlag, 2006, translated and quoted in www.spiegel. de/international/0,1518,434399,00.html

8. Domarus, Max (ed.), *Hitler: Speeches and Proclamations, 1932–1945: the Chronicle of a Dictatorship*, vol. I, Bolchazy-Carducci, 1990, p. 234.

9. Evans, Richard, *The Third Reich in Power*, Allen Lane, 2005, p. 334.

10. Noakes, J and Pridham, G, *Nazism 1919–1945*, vol. II, *State, Economy and Society,1933–1939*, University of Exeter Press, 2nd edn, 2000, p. 177.

11. Safire, William, *Safire's Political Dictionary*, Oxford University Press, 2008, p. 300.

12. Kershaw, Ian, *Hitler, 1936–1945: Nemesis*, Penguin Books, 2001, p. 350.

13. Baranowski, Shelley, op. cit., p.10.

14. Evans, Richard, op. cit., p. 475.

15. Whittock, Martyn, op. cit., p. 21.

16. Burleigh, Michael, op. cit., pp. 672–3.

17. Noakes, J. and Pridham, G., op. cit., p. 177.

18. Housden, Martyn, *Resistance and conformity in the Third Reich*, Routledge, 1997, p. 168.

Chapter 8. The betrayed middle class?

1. Both examples from Eberle, Henrick, and Uhl, Matthias (eds) *The Hitler Book*, John Murray, 2007, quoted in: www.dailymail.co.uk/news/article-487409/Dear-Mr-Hitler--letters-Nazi-leader-reveal-nation-love-monster.html#ixzz0PU3mPYPA

2. Evans, Richard, *The Third Reich in Power, 1933–1939*, Allen Lane, 2005, p. 437.

3. Earlier in the history of the regime, hopes had been high for Nazi regeneration of this craft area, as is explored in Kater, Michael H., *The Twisted Muse: Musicians and their Music in the Third Reich*, Oxford University Press, 1997, p. 132.

4. Schoenbaum, David, *Hitler's Social Revolution: Class and Status in Nazi Germany, 1933–1939*, Doubleday, 1966, W.W. Norton, 1980, p. 4.

5. Evans, Richard, op. cit., p. 435.

6. Burleigh, Michael, *The Third Reich, a New History*, Pan Books, 2001, pp. 80–1.

7. Fischer, Conan, *The Rise of the Nazis*, Manchester University Press, 2002, p. 139.

8. users.stlcc.edu/rkalfus/PDFs/026.pdf

9. Bendersky, Joseph W., *A Concise History of Nazi Germany*, Rowman & Littlefield, 2006, p. 71.

10. Croner, *Soziologie der Angestellten*, Kiepenhauer and Witsch, 1962, p. 196, in Schoenbaum, David, *Hitler's Social Revolution: Class and Status in Nazi Germany, 1933–1939*, Doubleday, 1967, W.W. Norton, 1980, p. 4.

11. Noakes, J. and Pridham, G., *Nazism 1919–1945*, vol. II, *State, Economy and Society, 1933–1939*, University of Exeter Press, 2nd edition, 2000, p. 108.

12. Ibid., p. 109.

13. Ibid., p. 110.

14. Kershaw, Ian, *Hitler, 1936–1945: Nemesis*, Penguin Books, 2001, p. xlvi.

15. Schoenbaum, David, *Hitler's Social Revolution: Class and Status in Nazi Germany, 1933–1939*, Doubleday, 1966, pp. 136–43 and 147–50.

16. Evans, Richard, op. cit., pp. 440–1.

17. Kershaw, Ian, op. cit., p. xxxvi.

18. Noakes, J. and Pridham, G., op. cit., p. 113.

Chapter 9. The persecution of German Jews in the 1930s

1. Tobias, Sigmund, *Strange Haven: A Jewish Childhood in Wartime Shanghai*, University of Illinois Press, 2009. See also, for background, Kranzler, David, *Japanese, Nazis, and Jews: The Jewish Refugee Community of Shanghai, 1938–45*, Yeshiva University Press, 1976.

2. Noakes, J. and Pridham, G., *Nazism 1919–1945*, vol. II, *State, Economy and Society, 1933–1939*, University of Exeter Press, 2nd edn, 2000, p. 327.

3. Barkai, Avraham, 'The German Volksgemeinschaft, from the persecution of the Jews to the "Final Solution"', p. 84, in Burleigh, Michael (ed.), *Confronting the Nazi Past, New Debates on Modern German History*, Collins & Brown, 1996.

4. Ibid., p. 89.

5. Burleigh, Michael, *The Third Reich, a New History*, Pan Books, 2001, p. 72.

6. Dippel, John Van Houten, *Bound Upon a Wheel of Fire: Why So Many German Jews Made the Tragic Decision to Remain in Nazi Germany*, Basic Books, 1996, explores how love for Germany and a sense of identification with it explains why many German Jews chose to stay in Germany.

7. Dawidowicz, L., *The War against the Jews, 1933–45*, Harmondsworth, 1977, pp. 210–11.

8. Merkl, P., *Political Violence under the Swastika, 581 Early Nazis*, Princeton University Press, 1975, pp. 33, 446 ff. See also Niewyk, D. L., *The Jews in Weimar Germany*, Manchester University Press, 1980, pp. 79–81 and Kershaw, Ian, *Hitler, the Germans, and the Final Solution*, Yale University Press, 2008, pp. 155–6.

9. Burleigh, Michael, op. cit., p. 73.

10. Noakes, J. and Pridham, G., op. cit., p. 327.

11. Ibid., p. 329.

12. Kershaw, Ian, *Hitler, 1889–1936: Hubris*, Penguin Books, 1999, pp. 472–3.

13. Quoted in Barkai, Avraham, op. cit., p. 93.

14. Quoted in Noakes, J. and Pridham, G., op. cit., p. 335.

15. Kaplan, Marion, 'The School Lives of Jewish Children and Youth in the Third Reich', *Jewish History*, vol. XI, no.2, Fall 1997, p. 41.

16. See Kershaw, Ian, op. cit., pp. 562–71, for a detailed examination of the origins of these laws and the process of bringing them together.

17. See MacDonogh, Giles, *1938: Hitler's Gamble*, Constable & Robinson, 2009.

18. Gilbert, Martin, *Kristallnacht: Prelude to Destruction*, Harper Perennial, 2007, gives a detailed account of the terrible events.

19. For an insight into how Hitler functioned as the 'activator' who stimulated radical experiments, see Kershaw, Ian, *Hitler, the Germans, and the Final Solution*, Yale University Press, 2008, p. 39.

20. Klemperer, Victor, *The Klemperer Diaries, 1933–1945,* Phoenix Press, 2000, p. 268.

21. Evans, Richard, *The Third Reich in Power*, Allen Lane, 2005, p. 549.

22. Kershaw, Ian, *Popular Opinion and Political Dissent in the Third Reich: Bavaria, 1933–1945*, Oxford University Press, 1983, p. 277.

23. Kershaw, Ian, 2008, op. cit., p. 7.

24. Quoted in Barkai, Avraham, op. cit., p. 96.

Chapter 10. 'Racial hygiene' in the 1930s

1. Bullock, Alan, *Hitler and Stalin: Parallel Lives,* Harper Collins, 1991, p. 1,074. See also Lifton, Robert Jay, *The Nazi Doctors: Medical Killing and the Psychology of Genocide*, Basic Books, 2000; and the study by Weyers, Wolfgang and Ackerman, Bernard, *Death of Medicine in Nazi Germany: Dermatology and Dermatopathology under the Swastika*, Ardor Scribendi, 1998.

2. Weindling, Paul, 'Understanding Nazi racism: precursors and perpetrators', p. 70, in Burleigh, Michael (ed.), *Confronting the Nazi Past, New Debates on Modern German History*, Collins & Brown, 1996.

3. Weindling, Paul, 'Heinrich Zeiss, Hygiene and the Holocaust', pp. 174–87, in Porter, Dorothy and Porter, Roy (eds), *Doctors, Politics and Society: Historical Essays*, Editions Rodopi, 1993, examines the career of Mrugowsky and others working in the field of 'racial hygiene'.

4. Friedlander, Henry, *The Origins of Nazi Genocide: From Euthanasia to the Final Solution*, University of North Carolina Press, 1997, pp. 9–10, provides a comparison of the origins of the eugenics movement in Germany and the USA.

5. For a detailed (and relatively rare) exploration of the impact of Nazism on black people, see Lusane, Clarence, *Hitler's Black Victims: The Historical Experience of Afro-Germans, European Blacks, Africans and African Americans in the Nazi Era*, Routledge, 2002. Also, see Marie, Tina, *Other Germans: Black Germans and the Politics of Race, Gender, and Memory in the Third Reich (Social History, Popular Culture, and Politics in Germany)*, University of Michigan Press, 2003.

6. Weindling, Paul, op. cit., p. 77.

7. Hau, Michael, *The Cult of Health and Beauty in Germany: A Social History, 1890–1930*, University of Chicago Press, 2003, pp. 203–6.

8. Weindling, Paul, op. cit., pp. 77 and 79.

9. Burleigh, Michael, 'Saving money, spending lives: Psychiatry, society and the euthanasia programme', p. 101, in Burleigh, Michael (ed.), *Confronting the Nazi Past, New Debates on Modern German History*, Collins & Brown, 1996.

10. Ibid., p. 108.

11. See Saunders, Will, 'Cross and Swastika: The Nazi Party and the German Churches: To What Extent Did Christians Support Hitler, and for What Reasons?', *History Review*, No. 46, 2003.

12. For an overview of the range of people persecuted as 'social outsiders' in the Third Reich, see Gellately, Robert and Stoltzfus, Nathan (eds), *Social Outsiders in Nazi Germany*, Princeton University Press, 2001.

13. Wippermann, Wolfgang, 'Christine Lehmann and Muzurka Rose: Two "Gypsies" in the grip of German Bureaucracy, 1933–60', p. 113, in Burleigh, Michael (ed.), *Confronting the Nazi Past, New Debates on Modern German History*, Collins & Brown, 1996.

14. Burleigh, Michael and Wipperman, Wolfgang, *The Racial State: Germany 1933–45*, Cambridge University Press, 1991, pp. 120–1.

15. Points brought out clearly in: Lewy, Guenter, *The Nazi Persecution of the Gypsies*, Oxford University Press, 2001.

16. Most controversially argued in Lively, Scott and Abrams, Kevin, *The Pink Swastika*, Veritas Aeterna, 1995.

17. See Steakley, James D., *The Homosexual Emancipation Movement in Germany*, Arno Press, 1975, p. 113 and, Lautman, Ruediger, 'Gay Prisoners in Concentration Camps as Compared with Jehovah's Witnesses and Political Prisoners', p. 204, in Berenbaum, Michael (ed.), *A Mosaic of Victims: Non-Jews Persecuted and Murdered by the Nazis*, New York University Press, 1990.

18. Friedlander, Henry, op. cit., p. 1.

19. Weindling, Paul, op. cit., p. 67.

20. See Burleigh, Michael, *Ethics and Extermination: Reflections on Nazi Genocide*, Cambridge University Press, 1997, which provides a reflection on the linked policies of euthanasia and extermination.

Chapter 11. The Nazi impact on society: young people and education

1. Beevor, Antony, *D-Day*, Viking, 2009, p. 454.
2. Ibid., p. 324. From Colville, Sir John Rupert, *The Fringes of Power*, W.W. Norton, 1985, p. 474.
3. Noakes, J. and Pridham, G., *Nazism 1919–1945*, vol. II, *State, Economy and Society, 1933–1939*, University of Exeter Press, 2nd edn, 2000, pp. 222–3.
4. Ibid., p. 223.
5. Figures based on Evans, Richard, *The Third Reich in Power*, Penguin Books, 2006, p. 272.
6. Noakes, J. and Pridham, G., op. cit., p. 226.
7. Shirer, William L, *The Rise and Fall of the Third Reich*, Pan Books, 1964, p. 319.
8. Rempel, Gerhard, *Hitler's Children: The Hitler Youth and the SS*, University of North Carolina Press, 1990, analyses the way the SS recruited amongst the Hitler Youth. It offers a particularly revealing exploration of the way in which the 'Patrol Service' of the Hitler Youth (designed to pursue ideological and social deviants both within the Hitler Youth and amongst young people generally) became a source of SS recruits to the Gestapo and Concentration Camp guard units (the Death's Head formations). Ralph Lewis, Brenda, *Hitler Youth: The Hitlerjugend in War and Peace, 1933–1945*, Zenith Press, 2000, provides an outline of the history of the Hitler Youth and includes a chapter on the military record of the infamous SS Hitler Youth Division.
9. Noakes, J. and Pridham, G., op. cit., p. 234.
10. Evans, Richard, op. cit., p. 275.
11. Ibid., pp. 278–9.
12. Noakes, J. and Pridham, G., op. cit., p. 233. For more on the conflict between parents and their children in Nazi youth organizations, see Burleigh, Michael, *The Third Reich: A New History*, Pan Books, 2001, p. 236.
13. Kershaw, Ian, *Hitler, 1936–1945: Nemesis*, Penguin, 2001, p. 9.
14. Hermand, Jost, Bettauer Dembo, Margot (trans.), *A Hitler Youth in Poland*, Northwestern University Press, 1993, recounts the brutal regime at Hitler Youth camps, in this case during the Second World War.

15. Noakes, J. and Pridham, G., op. cit., p. 234.

16. Herzog, Rudolph, *Heil Hitler, das Schwein ist Tot!* (*Heil Hitler, The Pig is Dead*) Eichborn-Verlag, 2006, translated and quoted in www.spiegel.de/international/0,1518,434399,00.html. Also quoted in Burleigh, Michael, *The Third Reich: A New History*, Pan Books, 2001, p. 234.

17. Noakes, J. and Pridham, G., op. cit., p. 245.

18. Ibid, p. 237.

19. Figures from Evans, Richard, op. cit, p. 267.

20. Noakes, J. and Pridham, G., op. cit., p. 239.

21. For an overview of Krüger's film career, see Bock, Hans-Michael (General Editor), Bergfelder, Tim (Associate Editor), *The Concise Cinegraph: Encyclopaedia of German Cinema*, Berghahn Books, 2009, pp. 267–8.

22. Evans, Richard, op. cit., p. 269.

23. Utgaard, Peter, *Remembering and Forgetting Nazism: Education, National Identity, and the Victim Myth in Postwar Austria*, Berghahn Books, 2003, pp. 27–8.

24. Severance, John B., *Einstein: Visionary Scientist*, Clarion Books, 1999, pp. 94–5. See also Bendersky, Joseph W., *A History of Nazi Germany: 1919–1945*, Burnham, 2000, p. 138, for how this occurred in the context of the emigration of a number of German intellectuals.

25. Kater, Michael H., *Doctors Under Hitler*, University of North Carolina Press, 1989, pp. 98–9.

26. Panayi, Panikos, *Weimar and Nazi Germany: Continuities and Discontinuities*, Pearson, 2000, p. 87.

27. Noakes, J. and Pridham, G., op. cit., p. 244.

Chapter 12. The Nazi impact on society: women in the Third Reich

1. www.timesonline.co.uk/tol/ news/world/europe/ article626101.ece

2. Pine, Lisa, *Nazi family policy, 1933–1945*, Berg, 1997, p. 40.

3. Clay, C. and Leapman, M., *Master Race: The Lebensborn Experiment in Nazi Germany*, Hodder and Stoughton, 1996, p. 65.

4. Pine, Lisa, op. cit., p. 41.

5. Ericsson, Kjersti and Simonsen, Eva, *Children of World War Two*, Berg, 2005, pp. 16–17.

6. Ibid. p. 18.

7. Sneeringer, Julia, *Winning Women's Votes: Propaganda and Politics in Weimar Germany*, University of North Carolina Press, 2002, p. 19.

8. Ascheid, Antje, *Hitler's Heroines: Stardom and Womanhood in Nazi Cinema*, Temple University Press, 2003, p. 23.

9. Overy, Richard, *War and Economy in the Third Reich*, Oxford University Press, 1995, pp. 48–9. See also Benz, Wolfgang, Dunlap, Thomas (trans.), *A Concise History of the Third Reich*, University of California Press, 2006, p. 100.

10. Bock, Gisela, 'Antinatalism, maternity and paternity in National Socialist racism', p. 120, in Crew, David F. (ed.), *Nazism and German society, 1933–1945*, Routledge, 1994.

11. Ibid., pp. 121–2.

12. Mason, Tim, *Social Policy in the Third Reich: The Working Class and the National Community*, Berg, 1993, p. 235.

13. Kitchen, Martin, *The Third Reich: Charisma and Community*, Pearson, 2008, p. 142.

14. Guenther, Irene, *Nazi chic? Fashioning Women in the Third Reich*, Berg, 2004, p. 5. This study provides an insight into this often neglected area of cultural history.

15. www.marquette.edu/research/documents/discover_2008_ nazi_chic. pdf

16. Quoted in Guenther, Irene, op. cit., p. 6.

17. For an examination of the complex involvement of women in Nazi Germany, the various impacts of the Third Reich on women and an exploration of the controversial question of whether women should be considered as victims of Nazi Germany, see Stephenson, Jill, *Women in Nazi Germany*, Longman, 2001.

18. Kitchen, Martin, op. cit., p. 143.

19. Kompisch, Kathrin, *Taeterinnen: Frauen im Nationalsozialismus (Perpetrators: Women Under National Socialism)*, Boehlau Verlag, 2009. This study provides a detailed analysis of the involvement of women in the Third Reich.

20. For detailed examination of the crimes of Dr Herta Oberheuser, see Spitz, Vivien, *Doctors From Hell: The Horrific Account of Nazi*

Experiments on Humans, First Sentient Publications, 2005; Kater, Michael H., *Doctors Under Hitler*, University of North Carolina Press, 1989; and Nicosia, Francis R., Huener, Jonathan, *Medicine and Medical Ethics in Nazi Germany: Origins, Practices, Legacies*, Berghahn Books, 2002.

Chapter 13. The Nazi impact on society: the Christian Church

1. Steigmann-Gall, Richard, 'Old Wine in New Bottles? Religion and Race in Nazi Antisemitism', p. 287, in Spicer, Kevin P., (ed.), *Antisemitism, Christian Ambivalence, and the Holocaust*, Indiana University Press, 2007, explores the complex issue of how Nazi anti-Semitism was rooted in aspects of Christian history and yet the Nazis were anti-Christian.

2. Old, Hughes Oliphant, *The Reading and Preaching of the Scriptures in the Worship of the Christian Church*, vol. VI, *The Modern Age*, Wm. B. Eerdmans Publishing Company, 2007, pp. 789–90.

3. For an examination of Niemöller's life and influence, see Bentley, James, *Martin Niemöller: 1892–1984*, Free Press, 1984; Niemöller, Martin, *Exile in the Fatherland: Martin Niemöller's Letters from Moabit Prison*, Locke, Hubert G. (ed.), Wm. B. Eerdmans Publishing Company, 1986.

4. Steigmann-Gall, Richard, *The Holy Reich: Nazi Conceptions of Christianity, 1919–1945*, Cambridge University Press, 2003, argues against the view that Nazism was either unrelated to Christianity, or actively opposed to it. In contrast, he argues that many Nazis thought their ideology was based on a Christian understanding of Germany's problems.

5. Dimont, Max I., *Jews, God, and History*, Signet Classic, 2nd edn, 2004, p. 397, outlines the reasons for the Nazi attacks on Christianity.

6. For a thought-provoking examination of Galen's life, including the areas of Nazism he did not confront, see Griech-Polelle, Dr Beth A., *Bishop von Galen: German Catholicism and National Socialism*, Yale University Press, 2002. This is a point also explored in Griech-Polelle, Dr Beth A., 'A Pure Conscience Is Good Enough: Bishop von Galen and Resistance to Nazism', pp. 106–122, in Bartov, Omer, Mack, Phyllis (eds), *In God's Name: Genocide and Religion in the Twentieth Century*, Berghahn Books, 2001.

7. Kershaw, Ian, *Hitler, 1936–1945: Nemesis*, Penguin, 2001, p. xxxvi.

8. Ibid., pp. 40–1.

9. Hesse, Hans (ed.), *Persecution and Resistance of Jehovah's Witnesses During the Nazi Regime, 1933–1945*, Berghahn, 2001, and Penton, M. James, *Jehovah's Witnesses and the Third Reich: Sectarian Politics Under Persecution*, University of Toronto Press, 2004, provide analysis of the impact of the Third Reich on the Jehovah's Witnesses.

10. Conway, John S., *The Nazi Persecution of the Churches, 1933–1945*, Ryerson Press, 1968, p. 59.

11. Steigmann-Gall, Richard, op. cit., pp. 6–7, has an examination of this analysis of Nazism.

12. Stein, George H., *The Waffen SS: Hitler's Elite Guard at War, 1939–1945*, Cornell University Press, 1966, pp. 122–3, examines the 'holy war' outlook of the SS.

13. Morris, Brian, *Religion and Anthropology: A Critical Introduction*, Cambridge University Press, 2006, p. 293.

14. Stackelberg, Roderick, *The Routledge Companion to Nazi Germany*, Routledge, 2007, p. 137.

Chapter 14. The Nazi impact on society: the control of ideas

1. Weinberg, Gerhard L., *Germany, Hitler, and World War II: Essays in Modern German and World History*, Cambridge University Press, 1995, p. 65.

2. Brode, Douglas, *Multiculturalism and the Mouse: Race and Sex in Disney Entertainment*, University of Texas Press, 2005, pp. 105–6.

3. Parker, P.M. (ed.), *Adolf: Webster's Quotations, Facts and Phrases*, ICON Group International, 2008, p. 228, adapted from an article in Wikipedia.

4. Anger, Kenneth, in MacDonald, Scott, *A Critical Cinema: Interviews with Independent Filmmakers*, University of California Press, 2006, p. 51.

5. Witek, Joseph, *Art Spiegelman: Conversations*, University Press of Mississippi, 2007, p. 91.

6. Laqua, Carten, *Mickey Mouse, Hitler, and Nazi Germany: How Disney's Characters Conquered the Third Reich*, Hermes Press, 2009.

7. Welch, David, *Hitler: Profile of a Dictator*, University College London Press, 1998, p. 6.

8. Kershaw, Ian, *Hitler, 1936–1945: Nemesis*, Penguin, 2001, p. 33.

9. Evans, Richard, *The Third Reich in Power, Penguin Books*, 2006, p. 130.

10. Ibid., pp. 130–1.

11. Beevor, Anthony, *D-Day*, Viking, 2009, p. 122. Using material from the National World War II Museum, Eisenhower Center archive, New Orleans, USA.

12. Welch, David, *The Third Reich: Politics and Propaganda*, Routledge, 1993, provides a detailed examination of Nazi use of propaganda throughout the period of the Third Reich.

13. Klemperer, Victor, *The Klemperer Diaries, 1933–1945*, Phoenix Press, 2000, p. 82.

14. Evans, Richard, op. cit., p. 212.

15. Ibid., p. 132.

16. Friedländer, Saul, *The Years of Extermination: Nazi Germany and the Jews, 1939–1945*, Phoenix, 2008, examines the origins of the latter two films, pp. 19–22.

17. For an overview of Goebbels's impact on film, see Moeller, Felix, *The Film Minister: Goebbels and the Cinema in the Third Reich*, Axel Menges, 2001, and Welch, David, *Propaganda and the German cinema, 1933–1945*, I.B. Tauris, 2001.

18. Craig, Steve, 'How America adopted radio: Demographic differences in set ownership reported in the 1930–1950 U.S. censuses', *Journal of Broadcasting and Electronic Media*, June 2004, p. 15, www.allbusiness.com/information/internet-publishing-broadcasting/172664-1.html

19. Huener, Jonathan, Nicosia, Francis R., *The Arts in Nazi Germany: Continuity, Conformity, Change*, Berghahn Books, 2006, p. 95, remind us that during the war even the ban on jazz was reversed in order to stop Germans tuning into foreign radio stations.

20. Vondung, Klaus and Ricks, Stephen D. (trans.), *The Apocalypse in Germany*, University of Missouri Press, 2000, p. 172.

21. McElligott, Anthony and Kirk, Tim (eds), *Working towards the Führer: Essays in Honour of Sir Ian Kershaw*, Manchester University Press, 2003, p. 100.

22. Wistrich, Robert S., *Who's Who in Nazi Germany*, Routledge, 2nd edn, 1995, pp. 24–5, provides an overview of Breker's career.

23. Koepnick, Lutz Peter, *Walter Benjamin and the Aesthetics of Power*, University of Nebraska Press, 2nd revised edn, 1999, p. 99.

Chapter 15. Germany and the world, 1933–9

1. Noakes, J. and Pridham, G., *Nazism 1919–1945*, vol. III, *Foreign Policy, War and Racial Extermination*, University of Exeter Press, 1988, pp. 727–8.

2. Ingrao, Charles W. and Szabo, Franz A. J. (eds), *The Germans and the East*, Purdue University Press, 2008, gives an overview of the relationship between Germany, German speakers and German colonists in Eastern Europe from the medieval period to the modern day.

3. See Young, William, *German Diplomatic Relations 1871–1945*, iUniverse, 2006, for a detailed examination of the extent to which continuity can be demonstrated in German foreign policy and the extent to which the Nazi leadership dominated the German foreign office.

4. For an analysis of the way in which German foreign policy after 1933 was dominated by the Nazi plans for ruthless German exploitation of Eastern Europe, see Carr, William, *Arms, Autarky and Aggression: Study in German Foreign Policy, 1933–1939*, Hodder Arnold, 1972.

5. Bendersky, Joseph W., *A History of Nazi Germany: 1919–1945*, Burnham Inc., 2000, p. 177.

6. Quoted in Jäckel, Eberhard, *Hitler's World View: A Blueprint for Power*, the President and Fellows of Harvard College, 1981, pp. 34–5.

7. Noakes, J. and Pridham, G., op. cit., pp. 609–16, explains how Hitler's foreign-policy aims changed between 1919 and 1924. An earlier focus on opposition to Britain and France, in order to revise the Treaty of Versailles, gave way to one that stressed conquering Lebensraum at the expense of the USSR – which he had come to think of as a Jewish-dominated state. And this might be accompanied by an alliance with Britain, which would isolate France.

8. Quoted in McDonough, Frank, *Hitler and Nazi Germany*, Cambridge University Press, 1999, p. 70.

9. Aron, Raymond and Mahoney, Daniel, *Peace and War: A Theory of International Relations*, Transaction Publishers, 2003, p. 42.

10. Patterson, Ian, *Guernica and Total War*, Profile Books, 2007, p. 68. See also Russell, Frank, D., *Picasso's Guernica: The Labyrinth of Narrative and Vision*, Allanheld & Schram, 1980.

11. Thomas, Hugh, *The Spanish Civil War*, Modern Library, 2001, provides a detailed examination of the conflict. See also Esenwein, George Richard, *The Spanish Civil War: A Modern Tragedy*, Routledge, 2005.

12. Noakes, J. and Pridham, G., op. cit., pp. 667–75, outlines the process by which the creation of the Rome–Berlin axis accompanied a growing disillusionment with the possibility of working with Britain.

13. Weitz, John, *Hitler's Diplomat: The Life and Times of Joachim von Ribbentrop*, Houghton Mifflin, 1992, provides a detailed biography of von Ribbentrop.

14. Noakes, J. and Pridham, G., op. cit., p. 680, while recognizing the omission of the east from Hitler's conversation, concludes that the Memorandum did constitute something of a programme by which Germany would 'pursue a more aggressive policy abroad'. The details of the Memorandum are provided on pp. 680–7.

15. Source: *Documents on Germany Foreign Policy 1918–1945*, Series D, vol. I, *From Neurath to Ribbentrop (September 1937 – September 1938)*, Washington, United States Government Printing Office, 1949.

16. MacDonogh, Giles, *1938: Hitler's Gamble*, Constable, 2009, p. xiii.

17. Hillenbrand, Fritz Karl Michael, *Underground humour in Nazi Germany, 1933–1945*, Routledge, 1995, p. 133.

18. Ibid., p. 133.

19. Utgaard, Peter, *Remembering & Forgetting Nazism: Education, National Identity, and the Victim Myth in Postwar Austria*, Berghahn Books, 2003, pp. 28–9.

20. Cited in Williams, Warren W., 'The Road to the Austrian State Treaty', in *Journal of Cold War Studies*, vol. II, no. 2, Spring 2000, pp. 97–107. See also Steininger, Rolf, Bischof and Günter, Gehler, Michael (eds), *Austria in the Twentieth Century*, Transaction Publishers, 2008.

21. Shen, Peijian, *The Age of Appeasement, The Evolution of British Foreign Policy in the 1930s*, Sutton, 1999, explores the origin, evolution and nature of appeasement.

22. Gray, Colin S., *War, Peace and International Relations: An Introduction to Strategic History*, Routledge, 2007, p. 110.

23. Taylor, A. J. P., *The Course of German History*, Hamish Hamilton, 1945.

24. Taylor, A. J. P., *The Origins of the Second World War*, Hamish Hamilton, 1961.

25. For this insightful set of conversations, see *BBC History Magazine*, vol. X, no. 9, September 2009, pp. 70–2.

26. For an accessible and succinct overview of the interpretation that Hitler bears primary responsibility for the outbreak of war in 1939, see Henig, Ruth, 'The Origins of the Second World War', *New Perspective*, vol. 3, no. 1, September 1997.

27. Overy, Richard, *1939: Countdown to War*, Allen Lane, 2009.

28. Henig, Ruth, op. cit.

Chapter 16. Nazi Germany, 1933–9: a popular dictatorship?

1. For letters showing Hitler's popularity, see Eberle, Henrick and Uhl, Matthias (eds) *The Hitler Book*, John Murray, 2007.

2. Noakes, J. and Pridham, G., *Nazism 1919–1945*, vol. II, *State, Economy and Society, 1933–1939*, University of Exeter Press, 2nd edn, 2000, p. 378.

3. Kershaw, Ian, *The 'Hitler Myth': Image and Reality in the Third Reich*, Oxford University Press, 1989, p. 76.

4. For an overview of the source-base, see Bankier, David, *The Germans and the Final Solution: Public Opinion under Nazism*, Blackwell, 1996 (paperback edn), pp. 4–10.

5. Herzog, Rudolph, *Heil Hitler, das Schwein ist Tot!* (*Heil Hitler, The Pig is Dead*), Eichborn-Verlag, 2006, translated and quoted in www.spiegel.de/international/0,1518,434399,00.html

6. For a detailed history of the Gestapo, 1933–7, see Browder, George C., *Hitler's Enforcers: The Gestapo and the SS Security Service in the Nazi Revolution*, Oxford University Press, 1996.

7. Noakes, J. and Pridham, G., op. cit., p. 324.

8. Gellately, Robert, *The Gestapo and German Society, Enforcing Racial Policy, 1933–1945*, Oxford University Press, 1990, examines the issue in detail.

9. Browder, George C., op. cit., p. 85.

10. Gellately, Robert, op. cit., pp. 129–30.

11. Ibid., p. 253.

12. Ibid., p. 258. Whilst not all historians accept Gellately's view, even a critic of his arguments, such as Eric Johnson, does not deny either the importance of popular denunciation in maintaining the Third Reich, or the targeted nature of repression. See Johnson, Eric, *Nazi Terror: The Gestapo, Jews, and Ordinary Germans*, Basic Books, 1999.

13. Noakes, J. and Pridham, G., op. cit., p. 185.

14. Ibid., p. 382.

15. Kershaw, Ian, op. cit., p. 66.

16. Ibid., p. 72 and p. 104.

17. Ibid., p. 66.

18. Noakes, J. and Pridham, G., op. cit., p. 386.

19. Ibid., p. 387.

20. Kershaw, Ian, op. cit., p. 71, quotes Sopade reports that noted how opposition to Hitler was made harder by the popularity of the return of the Saar to Germany and the reintroduction of conscription, both in 1935.

21. Gellately, Robert, *Lenin, Stalin and Hitler: The Age of Social Catastrophe*, Jonathan Cape, 2007, p. 312. Kershaw, Ian, op. cit., goes as far as suggesting that Hitler himself was converted to his own 'Führer Myth' after his success over the reoccupation of the Rhineland.

22. Kershaw, Ian, op. cit., p. 127.

23. Ibid., pp. 127 and 129.

24. Gellately, Robert, 2007, op. cit., p. 313.

25. Noakes, J. and Pridham, G., op. cit., p. 378.

26. See evidence quoted in Kershaw, Ian, op. cit., pp. 134–7.

27. Shirer, W. L., *The Rise and Fall of the Third Reich*, Pan Books, 1964, p. 488.

28. Noakes, J. and Pridham, G., op. cit., pp. 285–6.

29. Ibid., pp. 286–7.

30. www.feldgrau.com/stats.html

31. Noakes, J. and Pridham, G., op. cit., p. 384.

32. Ibid., p. 293.

33. Ibid., pp. 396–7.

34. Thomsett, Michael C., *The German Opposition to Hitler: The Resistance, the Underground, and Assassination Plots, 1938–1945*, McFarland & Company, 1997, pp. 39–49, provides a detailed examination of the growth of resistance within sections of the military in the 1930s and its connections to other centres of opposition within the establishment.

35. Ibid., p. 46.

36. See Shirer, W.L., op. cit., p. 505.

37. Moorhouse, Roger, *Killing Hitler: The Plots, the Assassins, and the Dictator who Cheated Death*, Bantam, 2006, brings together the numerous plots to kill Hitler, with chapter 2 explaining the role of Elser. Duffy, James P. and Ricci, Vincent L., *Target Hitler: The Plots to Kill Adolf Hitler*, Greenwood Publishing Group, 1992, pp. 25–34, provides a detailed account of the plot, along with the controversial conclusion that Himmler was possibly implicated in this attempt to kill Hitler.

38. See Gellately, Robert, *Backing Hitler: Consent and Coercion in Nazi Germany*, Oxford University Press, 2001, especially pp. 35–69, for the links between the Nazi press and popular prejudices within German society.

39. LeBor, Adam and Boyes, Roger, *Seduced by Hitler: The Choices of a Nation and the Ethics of Survival*, Sourcebooks, 2001.

40. Hoffman, Peter, *German Resistance to Hitler*, the President and Fellows of Harvard College, 1988, p. 51.

41. For analysis of the academic scholarship on popular opinion, see Kershaw, Ian, *The Nazi Dictatorship: Problems and Perspectives of Interpretation*, Edward Arnold, 2000, pp. 183–217.

42. See Burleigh, Michael, *The Third Reich: A New History*, Pan Books, 2001, for an example of the attempt to reintroduce the concept of totalitarianism to the study of the Third Reich. For comparison, see also Jarausch, Konrad H. and Geyer, Michael, *Shattered Past: Reconstructing German Histories*, Princeton University Press, 2003, pp. 149–62.

43. For further exploration of this issue, see Baranowski, Shelley, *Strength Through Joy: Consumerism and Mass Tourism in the Third Reich*, Cambridge University Press, 2004.

Chapter 17. The Third Reich at war: the unstoppable Blitzkrieg, 1939–41

1. Guderian later wrote a biography entitled *Panzer Leader*, Michael Joseph, 1952. For a modern assessment of Guderian's career see Macksey, Kenneth, *Guderian: Panzer General*, Greenhill Books, new edn, 2003. Also, Hart, Russell A., *Guderian: Panzer Pioneer or Myth Maker?*, Potomac Books, 2006, provides a study that claims that substantial parts of the Guderian-myth were created by Guderian himself in his post-war memoirs.

2. Zaborowski, Marcin, *Germany, Poland, and Europe: Conflict, Co-operation, and Europeanization*, Manchester University Press, 2004, provides a detailed analysis of German–Polish relations in the twentieth century.

3. The Polish Institute of National Remembrance (IPN) puts the total figure of Polish war dead at between 5,620,000 and 5,820,000. The IPN's figures include Polish Jews, ethnic Poles and other ethnic groups living within Poland's 1939 borders. Materski, Wojciech and Szarota, Tomasz, *Polska 1939–1945. Straty osobowe i ofiary represji pod dwiema okupacjami*, Institute of National Remembrance (IPN) Warsaw, 2009.

4. Noakes, J. and Pridham, G., *Nazism 1919–1945*, vol. III, *Foreign Policy, War and Racial Extermination*, University of Exeter Press, 1988, p. 757.

5. Gellately, Robert, *Lenin, Stalin and Hitler: The Age of Social Catastrophe*, Jonathan Cape, 2007, p. 353.

6. Ibid., pp. 353–4.

7. Ibid., p. 355.

8. Bloxham, Donald, *Genocide on Trial: War Crimes Trials and the Formation of Holocaust History and Memory*, Oxford University Press, 2001, p. 130, identifies a large number of ways in which the German army contributed to war atrocities.

9. Gellately, Robert, op. cit., pp. 362–3.

10. On Keitel's contribution to genocide, see Bloxham, Donald, *The Final Solution: A Genocide*, Oxford University Press, 2009, p. 264; and Grant, R. Gordon, *Genocide: The Final Solution to the Jewish Question*, Trafford 2002, pp. 18–19.

11. Dower, John, *War without Mercy: Race and Power in the Pacific War*, Pantheon Books, 1986, pp. 3–15 and 33–73.

12. Browning, Christopher, *Ordinary Men: Reserve Police Battalion 101 and the Final Solution in Poland*, Penguin Books, 2001, p. 160.

13. For a study of British activity during the 'Phoney War', see Smart, Nick, *British Strategy and Politics During the Phony War: Before the Balloon Went Up*, Praeger, 2003.

14. Quoted in Lightbody, Bradley, *The Second World War: Ambitions to Nemesis*, Routledge, 2004, p. 46.

15. For an overview of the Winter War, see Kulkov, Evgeni Nikolaevich, Rzheshevski, Oleg Aleksandrovich, Shukman and Harold, *Stalin and the Soviet–Finnish War, 1939–1940*, Frank Cass Publishers, 2002; and Engle, Eloise, Paananen, Eloise and Paananen, Lauri, *The Winter War: the Soviet Attack on Finland, 1939–1940*, Stackpole Books, 1973.

16. Schumann, Willy, *Being Present: Growing up in Hitler's Germany*, Kent State University Press, 1991, p. 54.

17. Frieser, Karl-Heinz and Greenwood, John T, *The Blitzkrieg legend: the 1940 Campaign in the West*, US Naval Institute Press, chapter 4, 'The 1940 Ardennes Offensive', pp. 100–14, provides a detailed analysis of this successful application of Blitzkrieg.

18. Ibid., p. 144.

19. Noakes, J. and Pridham, G., op. cit., p. 776.

20. Paxton, Robert O., *Vichy France: Old Guard and New Order, 1940–1944*, Columbia University Press, revised edn, 2001, analyses how Vichy pursued a double agenda of an authoritarian and racist 'national revolution' at home whilst also attempting to persuade the Germans to accept the 'new France' as a partner in Hitler's 'new Europe'.

21. Herzog, Rudolph, *Heil Hitler, das Schwein ist Tot! (Heil Hitler, The Pig is Dead)*, Eichborn-Verlag, 2006, translated and quoted in www.spiegel.de/international/0,1518,434399,00.html

22. Noakes, J. and Pridham, G., op. cit., pp. 782–3.

23. Evans, Martin Marix, *Invasion!: Operation Sealion, 1940*, Pearson Education, 2004, argues the case for the intention being a serious one. Robinson, Derek, *Invasion, 1940*, Robinson Publishing, 2006, argues that it was the threat posed by the Royal Navy, rather than the RAF, which was the real factor that stopped a German invasion alongside the inadequate German preparations.

24. A 'Second Happy Time' occurred January–August, 1942 when a lack of organized defensive measures allowed U-boats to sink large numbers of Allied merchant ships along the eastern coast of the USA.

25. Bossy, Raoul V., Bossy, George H., (ed. & trans.) and Bossy, Michel-André, *Recollections of a Romanian Diplomat, 1918–1969: Diaries and Memoirs of Raoul V. Bossy* , vol. II, Hoover Institution Press, 2003, p. 401.

Chapter 18. 'The twisted road to Auschwitz': from persecution to genocide

1. Friedländer, Saul, *The Years of Extermination: Nazi Germany and the Jews, 1939–1945*, Phoenix, 2008, pp. 215–9.
2. Ibid., pp. 30 and 187, and Gellately, Robert, *Lenin, Stalin and Hitler: The Age of Social Catastrophe*, Jonathan Cape, 2007, p. 370.
3. Kershaw, Ian, *Hitler, the Germans, and the Final Solution*, Yale University Press, 2008, p. 19.
4. Gellately, Robert, op. cit., p. 372.
5. Ibid., p. 425.
6. Ibid., pp. 423–5.
7. Ibid., p. 422.
8. Ibid., p. 426.
9. Burrin, Philippe, *Hitler and the Jews: The Genesis of the Holocaust*, Edward Arnold, 1994, pp. 94 ff.
10. Gellately, Robert, op. cit., p. 451.
11. Friedländer, Saul, op. cit., p. 207–8.
12. Ibid., p. 198.
13. Noakes, J. and Pridham, G., *Nazism 1919–1945*, vol. III, *Foreign Policy, War and Racial Extermination*, University of Exeter Press, 1988, p. 1,099.

14. Friedländer, Saul, op. cit., p. 211.
15. Gellately, Robert, op. cit., p. 447.
16. Ibid., p. 448.
17. Browning, Christopher, R, *The Origins of the Final Solution: The Evolution of Nazi Jewish Policy, September 1939–March 1942*, Lincoln Neb, 2004, p. 371.
18. Friedländer, Saul, op. cit., pp. 263–7, identifies the significance of the mid-October deportations and traces its roots back into events occurring during September.
19. Gerlach, Christian, 'The Wannsee Conference, the fate of German Jews, and Hitler's decision in principle to exterminate all European Jews', p. 106–61, in Bartov, Omer (ed.), *The Holocaust: Origins, Implementation, Aftermath*, Routledge, 2000.
20. Gellately, Robert, op. cit., p. 456.
21. Ibid., p. 458.
22. Ibid., p. 458.
23. Cesarani, David, *Eichmann: His Life and Crimes*, Vintage 2005, p. 111.
24. Longerich, Peter ,'The Wannsee Conference in the Development of the "Final Solution"', available online at the House of the Wannsee Conference: Memorial and Educational Site website.
25. House of the Wannsee Conference online documents, found at: www.ghwk.de/engl/authorization.htm
26. Kershaw, Ian, op. cit., pp. 89–116, convincingly identifies Hitler's central role in the genocide of the Jews. This includes analysis (p. 104) of the frequent references – over a dozen – Hitler made, between 1941 and 1945, to his 30 January 1939 Reichstag 'prophecy' and his consistent misdating of this to 1 September 1939. This repetition was clearly designed to discourage humanitarian feelings towards Jews by ordinary Germans, spurred followers to more radical anti-Semitic actions and 'indicated to "insiders" Hitler's knowledge and approval of the genocide' (p. 104).
27. Hilberg, Raul, *The Destruction of the European Jews*, vol. III, rev. ed., Holmes and Meier Publishers, 1985, p. 894.
28. For a detailed and very accessible examination of the origins, administration and murderous impact of Auschwitz, see Rees, L., *Auschwitz: the Nazis and the Final Solution*, BBC Books, 2005.

29. Ibid., p. 234.

30. Jeffreys, Diarmuid, *Hell's Cartel: IG Farben and the Making of Hitler's War Machine*, Metropolitan Books, 2008, provides a thought-provoking analysis of the role of the company.

31. Gellately, Robert, op. cit., p. 541.

32. Friedländer, Saul, op. cit., p. 505.

33. Goldhagen, Daniel, *Hitler's Willing Executioners, Ordinary Germans and the Holocaust*, Abacus, 1996.

34. Browning, Christopher, *Ordinary Men: Reserve Police Battalion 101 and the Final Solution in Poland*, Penguin Books, 2001, especially pp. 159–89.

35. Gellately, Robert, reviewing Daniel Goldhagen's book in *The Journal of Modern History*, vol. 69, no. 1, (March 1997), p. 190.

36. See Kershaw, Ian, *Popular Opinion and Political Dissent in the Third Reich: Bavaria, 1933–1945*, Oxford University Press, 1983, p. 277. Also, Kershaw, Ian, 2008, op. cit., p. 7.

37. Kulka, Otto Dov and Rodrigue, Aaron, 'The German Population and the Jews in the Third Reich: Recent Publications and Trends in Research on German Society and the "Jewish Question"', *Yad Vashem Studies 16* (1984), pp. 430–5.

38. See Lumans, Valdis O., *Latvia in World War II*, Fordham University Press, 2006, pp. 210–62. See also, Press, Bernhard, *The Murder of the Jews in Latvia: 1941–1945*, Northwestern University Press, 2000.

39. Arad, Yitzhak, 'According to Jewish Sources', in Bankier, David and Gutman, Israel (eds), *Nazi Europe and the Final Solution*, Yad Vashem, Jerusalem, in association with Berghahn Books, 2009, p. 238.

40. Ibid., p. 241.

41. Ibid., p. 236. Also p. 240.

42. Gitelman, Zvi Y., *Bitter legacy: Confronting the Holocaust in the USSR*, Indiana University Press, 1997, explores both the collaboration of local people with the Nazi genocide and the reluctance to confront this past in many areas of the former Soviet Union.

43. Bankier, David, *The Germans and the Final Solution: Public Opinion under Nazism*, Blackwell, 1996, p. 156, concludes that the German public clearly knew about the crimes but shirked responsibility by

deflecting it onto others. Disapproval, when expressed, was usually linked to fear of retribution for the crimes as wartime defeat loomed, not moral opposition to the genocide.

44. Friedländer, Saul, op. cit., pp. 438–9.

45. To quote the title of the book by Karl A. Schleunes: *The Twisted Road to Auschwitz, Nazi Policy toward German Jews, 1933–39*, University of Illinois Press, 1970. His interpretation of the Final Solution as a product of unplanned evolution rather than pre-meditated design is not one followed in this chapter, but the phrase is used in this chapter's title to remind readers of the complex and varied circumstances that finally coalesced and led to the mass murder of the Jews.

Chapter 19. The Third Reich at war: the home front

1. Hillenbrand, F.K.M., *Underground Humour in Nazi Germany, 1933–1945*, Routledge, 1995, p. 184.

2. Aly, Götz, *Hitler's Beneficiaries: Plunder, Racial War, and the Nazi Welfare State*, Metropolitan Books, 2007.

3. Noakes, Jeremy (ed.), *Nazism 1919–1945*, vol. IV, *The German Home Front in World War II, A Documentary Reader*, University of Exeter Press, 1998, p. 511.

4. Whiting, Charles, *The Home Front – Germany*, Time-Life Books, 1982, p. 63.

5. Noakes, Jeremy, op. cit., p. 512.

6. Bendersky, Joseph W., *A History of Nazi Germany: 1919–1945*, 2nd edn, Rowman & Littlefield, 2000, p. 213.

7. Mason, Tim, *Social Policy in the Third Reich: The Working Class and the 'National Community'*, Berg, 1993, p. 236.

8. Noakes, Jeremy, op. cit., p. 354.

9. Boog, Horst, Krebs, Gerhard and Vogel, Detlef, Cook-Radmore, Derry (trans.), *Germany and the Second World War*, vol. VII, *The Strategic Air War in Europe and the War in the West and East Asia, 1943–1944/5*, 2006, Clarendon Press, p. 225.

10. Noakes, Jeremy, op. cit., p. 342.

11. Stephenson, Jill, *The Nazi Organisation of Women*, Croom Helm, 1981, p. 216.

12. Noakes, Jeremy, op. cit., p. 386.

13. Stephenson, Jill, op. cit., pp. 178–213, analyses the role of the NSV during the war years.

14. Noakes, Jeremy, op. cit., p. 276.

15. Ibid., p. 294.

16. Nalty, Bernard C., (ed.) *Winged Shield, Winged Sword 1907–1950: A History of the United States Air Force*, University Press of the Pacific, 1997, p. 189.

17. Noakes, Jeremy, op. cit., p. 565.

18. Ibid., pp. 362–5.

19. See Friedrich, J., *The Fire: The Bombing of Germany, 1940–1945*, Columbia University Press, 2008.

20. See Lowe, Keith, *Inferno: The Devastation of Hamburg, 1943*, Viking, 2007.

21. Noakes, Jeremy, op. cit., p. 556.

22. Ibid., p. 557.

23. Recent works examining the bombing of Dresden include: Taylor, Frederick, *Dresden: Tuesday, 13 February, 1945*, Bloomsbury Publishing, 2005; Addison, Paul, Crang, Jeremy A. (eds), *Firestorm: The Bombing of Dresden 1945*, Pimlico, 2006.

24. Overy, Richard, *The Penguin Historical Atlas of the Third Reich*, Penguin, 1996, p. 103.

25. Noakes, Jeremy, op. cit., p. 568.

26. Overy, Richard, *Why the Allies Won*, revised edition, Pimlico, 2006, pp. 152–3.

27. Ibid., pp. 395–6.

28. Ibid., pp. 156–163.

29. For analysis of the significance of this speech, see Bytwerk, Randall L. (ed. and trans.), *Landmark speeches of National Socialism*, Texas A & M University Press, 2008, pp. 112–39.

30. Overy, Richard, 2006, op. cit., pp. 247–9, pp. 266–7.

31. Gellately, Robert, *The Gestapo and German Society: Enforcing Racial Policy 1933–1945*, Oxford University Press, 1990, p. 261.

32. Noakes, Jeremy, op. cit., p. 411.

33. Herzog, Rudolph, *Heil Hitler, das Schwein ist Tot!* (*Heil Hitler, The Pig is Dead*), Eichborn-Verlag, 2006, translated and quoted in www.spiegel.de/international/0,1518,434399,00.html

34. Hillenbrand, F.K.M., op. cit., p. 190.
35. Evans, Richard, *The Third Reich at War*, Penguin, 2008, pp. 732–3.
36. Ibid., p. 708.

Chapter 20. The German resistance

1. Herzog, Rudolph, *Heil Hitler, das Schwein ist Tot!* (*Heil Hitler, The Pig is Dead*), Eichborn-Verlag, 2006, translated and quoted in www.spiegel.de/international/0,1518,434399,00.html

2. Hoffmann, Hilmar, Broadwin, John (trans.), Volker R. Berghahn (trans.), *The Triumph of Propaganda: Film and National Socialism, 1933–1945*, Berghahn Books, 1997, explores the diminishing influence of propaganda films during the Second World War. See also, Welch, David, *The Third Reich: Politics and Propaganda*, Routledge, 1993, which provides a detailed examination of Nazi use of propaganda throughout the period of the Third Reich.

3. Herzog, Rudolph, op. cit.

4. For an overview of those opposing Hitler, see Mommsen, Hans, McGeoch, Angus (trans.), *Alternatives to Hitler: German Resistance Under the Third Reich*, I.B. Tauris & Co Ltd, 2003.

5. Noakes, Jeremy (ed.), *Nazism 1919–1945*, vol. IV, *The German Home Front in World War II, A Documentary Reader*, University of Exeter Press, 1998, p. 586.

6. See Brysac, Shareen Blair, *Resisting Hitler: Mildred Harnack and the Red Orchestra*, Oxford University Press, 2000.

7. For the Abwehr's role, see von Klemperer, Klemens, *German Resistance Against Hitler: The Search for Allies Abroad, 1938–1945*, Oxford University Press, 1992, pp. 23–5.

8. Noakes, Jeremy, op. cit., p. 597.

9. See Hoffmann, Peter, *The History of the German Resistance, 1933–1945*, McGill-Queen's University Press, 3rd edn, 1996, chapter 17, 'The Kreisau Circle', pp. 192–7.

10. Hoffmann, Peter, *Stauffenberg: A Family History, 1905–1944*, Cambridge University Press, 1997, explores the life of this famous German resister.

11. Noakes, Jeremy, op. cit., p. 618.

12. Wistrich, Robert S., *Who's Who in Nazi Germany?*, Routledge, 2nd edn, 1995, p. 260.

13. Stackelberg, Roderick, *The Routledge Companion to Nazi Germany*, Routledge, 2007, p. 250.

14. For details of the plot, see Galante, Pierre, Howson, Mark, Silianoff, Eugène, Ryan, Cary, *Operation Valkyrie: The German Generals' Plot Against Hitler*, Harper & Row, 1981. Also, Jones, Nigel, *Countdown to Valkyrie: The July Plot to Assassinate Hitler*, Frontline Books, 2009.

15. Mommsen, Hans, 'German Society and the Resistance against Hitler', p. 257–8, in Leitz, Christian (ed.), *The Third Reich: The Essential Readings*, Wiley-Blackwell, 1999, p. 271–2.

16. Dumbach, Annette and Newborn, Jud, *Sophie Scholl and the White Rose*, Oneworld Publications, 2007, offers a recent account of the movement. An older study can be found in: Scholl, Inge, Schultz, Arthur R. (trans.), *The White Rose: Munich, 1942–1943*, Wesleyan University Press, 1983.

17. Noakes, Jeremy, op. cit., p. 458.

18. Ibid., p. 457.

19. See Peukert, D., 'Youth in the Third Reich', pp. 30–7, in Bessel, R. (ed.) *Life in the Third Reich*, Oxford University Press, 1987.

20. Noakes, Jeremy, op. cit., p. 450.

21. Kenkmann, A., 'Navajos, Kittelsbach und Edelweisspiraten', p. 157, in Breyvogel, W. (ed.), *Piraten, Swings und Junge Garde*, Dietz, 1991. Quoted in Housden, Martyn, *Resistance and Conformity in the Third Reich*, Routledge, 1996, p. 89.

22. Housden, Martyn, *Resistance and Conformity in the Third Reich*, Routledge, 1996, p. 89.

23. See Peukert, D., *Inside Nazi Germany: Conformity, Opposition and Racism in Everyday Life*, Yale University Press, 1987.

24. Noakes, Jeremy, op. cit., p. 460.

25. Quoted in Welch, David, *The Third Reich: Politics and Propaganda*, Routledge, 1993, p. 78.

26. Welch David, ibid., p. 78.

27. Broszat, Martin, 'A Social and Historical Typology of the German Opposition to Hitler', pp. 25–34, in Large, David Clay, *Contending*

with Hitler: Varieties of German Resistance in the Third Reich, Cambridge University Press, 1991, p. 26.

28. Evans, Richard, *The Third Reich at War*, Penguin, 2009, p. 761.

Chapter 21. The Third Reich at war: from conquest to Götterdämmerung

1. Manvell, Roger, Fraenkel, Heinrich, *Goering,* Simon & Schuster, 1962, p. 262.

2. Noakes, J. and Pridham, G., *Nazism 1919–1945*, vol. III, *Foreign Policy, War and Racial Extermination*, University of Exeter Press, 1988, p. 817.

3. General Halder, recorded in ibid., p. 818.

4. Ibid., p. 829.

5. See Jones, Michael, *The Retreat: Hitler's First Defeat*, John Murray, 2009.

6. For an exploration of the conflict in the wider context of the war, see Mawdsley, Evan, *World War II*, Cambridge University Press, 2009, chapter 6, 'The Red Army versus the Wehrmacht, 1941–1944', pp. 164–87; also, Braithwaite, Rodric, *Moscow 1941*, Profile Books, 2006, for an exploration of the impact of the struggle on the city of Moscow and its population; and also, Nagorski, Andrew, *The Greatest Battle: Stalin, Hitler, and the Desperate Struggle for Moscow That Changed the Course of World War II*, Simon & Schuster, 2007, for another examination of this titanic struggle.

7. Henig, Ruth, *The Origins of the Second World War, 1933–41*, Methuen and Co. Ltd, 2nd edn, 2005, p. 63.

8. Noakes, J. and Pridham, G., op. cit., p. 831–2.

9. For a detailed examination of the battle, see Beevor, Antony, *Stalingrad*, Viking, 1998.

10. Roberts, Andrew, *The Storm of War*, Allen Lane, 2009, p. 333.

11. See Erickson, John, *Barbarossa: The Axis and the Allies*, Edinburgh University Press, 1995, Table 12.4; Overy, Richard, *Russia's War: A History of the Soviet Effort 1941–1945*, Penguin, 1998; Beevor, Antony, *Stalingrad: The Fateful Siege: 1942–1943*, Penguin, 1999.

12. An in-depth study of the U-boat war can be found in Westwood, David, *The U-boat War: The German Submarine Service and the Battle of the Atlantic, 1935–45*, Conway Maritime Press, 2005.

13. Bernières, Louis De, *Captain Corelli's Mandolin*, Vintage, 1993.

14. Dunn, Walter S, *Kursk: Hitler's gamble, 1943*, Praeger Publishers, 1997, p. 185.

15. A detailed examination of the war from the Russian perspective can be found in Merridale, Catherine, *Ivan's War: Life and Death in the Red Army, 1939–1945*, Picador, 2007.

16. Examined in detail in Beevor, Antony, *D-Day*, Viking, 2009.

17. Ibid., p. 340.

18. Ibid., p. 291.

19. Roberts, Andrew, op. cit., p. 487.

20. Hastings, Max, *Armageddon: The Battle for Germany, 1944–45*, Macmillan, 2004, p. 263.

21. Roberts, Andrew, op. cit., p. 531.

22. Grier, Howard D, *Hitler, Dönitz, and the Baltic Sea: The Third Reich's Last Hope, 1944–1945*, Naval Institute Press, 2007, pp. 102–3.

23. Carruthers, Bob and Trew, Simon, *Servants of Evil: New First-hand Accounts of the Second World War from Survivors of Hitler's Armed Forces*, Zenith Press, 2005, p. 208.

24. The battle for Berlin is examined in detail in: Beevor, Antony, *Berlin: the Downfall*, Viking, 2002. See also, Evans, Richard, *The Third Reich at War*, Penguin, 2009, pp. 707–26, for an overview of the last weeks of the war.

25. For details of this example of airbrushing – and many others – see King, David, *The Commissar Vanishes: The Falsification of Photographs and Art in Stalin's Russia*, Metropolitan Books, 1997.

26. Overy, Richard, *Why the Allies Won*, revised edition, Pimlico, 2006, p. 245.

27. Ibid., pp. 264–5 and p. 265.

28. Ibid., p. 279.

29. Ibid., pp. 297–9.

30. Overy, Richard, ibid., pp. 150–2.

31. Noakes, J. and Pridham, G., op. cit., p. 1,204.

Chapter 22. The legacy of the Third Reich

1. Often quoted in this form, or in the forms 'Writing poetry after Auschwitz is barbaric', 'No poetry after Auschwitz' or 'There can be no poetry after Auschwitz'.

2. Evans, Richard, *The Third Reich at War*, Penguin, 2009, pp. 738–9.

3. Overy, Richard, *Why the Allies Won*, revised edition, Pimlico, 2006, p. xiv.

4. Ibid., p. 298.

5. Hoffmeister, Gerhart and Tubach, Frederic C, *Germany: From the Nazi Era to German Unification*, Continuum, 1992, p. 56.

6. For an overview of the so-called '*ostpolitik*', see Buchanan, Tom, *Europe's Troubled Peace, 1945–2000*, Blackwell, 2006, pp. 171–3. Also, von Dannenberg, Julia, *The Foundations of Ostpolitik: The Making of the Moscow Treaty between West Germany and the USSR*, Oxford University Press, 2008.

7. Ther, Philipp and Siljak, Ana, *Redrawing Nations: Ethnic Cleansing in East-Central Europe, 1944–1948*, Rowman & Littlefield Publishers, 2001, p. 62.

8. Ingrao, Charles W, Szabo, Franz A. J., *The Germans and the East*, Purdue University Press, 2008, pp. 423–5.

9. Shephard, Ben, *The Long Road Home: The Aftermath of the Second World War*, Bodley Head, 2010, explores the refugee crisis following the war and the attempts to respond to it.

10. For an overview of the history of the UN, see Krasno, Jean E., *The United Nations: Confronting the Challenges of a Global Society*, Lynne Rienner Publishers, 2004. Also, Luard, Evan, Heater, Derek Benjamin, *The United Nations: How it Works and What it Does*, 2nd edn, Macmillan, 1994.

11. For an overview of the history of Israel, including its origins, see Gilbert, Martin, *Israel: A History*, Doubleday, 1998.

12. For an analysis concluding that Nazi genocide was the most important impetus for the formation of the state of Israel and a key feature in defining the identity, ideology, and politics of Israel, see Segev, Tom and Watzman, Haim (trans.), *The Seventh Million: The Israelis and the Holocaust*, Domino Press, 1991.

13. Dedman, Martin, *The Origins and Development of the European Union 1945–1995: A History of European Integration*, Routledge, 2002, p. 2.

14. Ibid., p. 2.

15. For a detailed examination of its history, see Kaiser, Wolfram, Leucht, Brigitte and Rasmussen, Morten (eds), *The History of the*

European Union: Origins of a Trans- and Supranational Polity 1950–72, Routledge, 2008.

16. Recent examples of genocide and the role of the international community in response to genocide and potential genocidal situations have been surveyed in Totten, Samuel (ed.), *Genocide at the Millennium*, Transaction Books, 2005. This is the fifth volume in the series *Genocide: A Critical Bibliographical Review*.

17. Bullock, Allan, *Hitler and Stalin: Parallel Lives*, Harper Collins, 1991, p. 1,079.

BIBLIOGRAPHY

Abel, Theodore, *Why Hitler Came to Power*, Harvard University Press, 1986 reprint of the 1938 original.

Bankier, David, *The Germans and the Final Solution: Public Opinion under Nazism*, Blackwell, 1996.

Bankier, David and Gutman, Israel (eds), *Nazi Europe and the Final Solution*, Yad Vashem, Jerusalem, in association with Berghahn Books, 2009.

Baranowski, Shelley, *Strength Through Joy: Consumerism and Mass Tourism in the Third Reich*, Cambridge University Press, 2004.

Bartov, Omer (ed.), *The Holocaust: Origins, Implementation, Aftermath*, Routledge, 2000.

Bendersky, Joseph W., *A Concise History of Nazi Germany*, Rowman & Littlefield, 2006.

Bloxham, Donald, *The Final Solution: A Genocide*, Oxford University Press, 2009.

Brechtefeld, Jörg, *Mitteleuropa and German politics: 1848 to the Present*, Palgrave, 1996.

Browder, George C., *Hitler's Enforcers: The Gestapo and the SS Security Service in the Nazi Revolution*, Oxford University Press, 1996.

Browning, Christopher, *The Origins of the Final Solution, The Evolution of Nazi Jewish Policy, September 1939–March 1942*, University of Nebraska Press and Yad Vashem, 2004.

Bullock, Allan, *Hitler and Stalin: Parallel Lives*, Harper Collins, 1991.

Burleigh, Michael, *The Third Reich, a New History*, Pan Books, 2001.

Burrin, Philippe, *Hitler and the Jews: The Genesis of the Holocaust*, Edward Arnold, 1994.

Campbell, Bruce, *The SA Generals and the Rise of Nazism*, University of Kentucky Press, 2004.

Carr, William, *Arms, Autarky and Aggression: Study in German Foreign Policy, 1933–1939*, Hodder Arnold, 1972.

Cesarani, David (ed.) *The Final Solution: Origins and Implementation*, Routledge, 1994.

Childers, Thomas, *The Nazi Voter, The Social Foundations of Fascism in Germany, 1919–1933*, University of North Carolina Press, 1983.

Childers, Thomas (ed.), *The Formation of the Nazi Constituency*, 1919–33, Stanley Paul, 1987.

Childers, Thomas and Caplan, Jane (eds), *Reevaluating the Third Reich: New Controversies, New Interpretations*, Holmes and Meier, 1993

Collier, Martin and Pedley, Philip, *Germany 1919–45*, Heinemann, 2000.

Crew, David F. (ed.), *Nazism and German society, 1933–1945*, Routledge, 1994.

Domarus, Max (ed.), *Hitler: Speeches and Proclamations, 1932–1945: The Chronicle of a Dictatorship*, 4 volumes, Bolchazy-Carducci, 1990.

Eberle, Henrick, and Uhl, Matthias (eds), *The Hitler Book*, John Murray, 2007.

Evans, Richard, *The Coming of the Third Reich*, Allen Lane, 2003.

Evans, Richard, *The Third Reich in Power*, Allen Lane, 2005.

Evans, Richard, *The Third Reich at War*, Penguin, 2009

Fischer, Conan (ed.), *The Rise of National Socialism and the Working Classes in Weimar Germany*, Berghahn Books, 1996.

Fischer, Conan, *The Rise of the Nazis*, Manchester University Press, 2002.

Friedlander, Henry, *The Origins of Nazi Genocide: From Euthanasia to the Final Solution*, University of North Carolina Press, 1997.

Friedländer, Saul, *The Years of Persecution: Nazi Germany and the Jews, 1933–39*, Phoenix, 1998.

Friedländer, Saul, *The Years of Extermination: Nazi Germany and the Jews, 1939–1945*, Phoenix, 2008.

Friedman, Saul, S., *A History of the Holocaust*, Mitchell Vallentine, 2004.

Friedrich, Otto, *Before the Deluge: A Portrait of Berlin in the 1920s*, Harper Collins, 1972.

Gellately, Robert, *The Gestapo and German Society, Enforcing Racial Policy, 1933–1945*, Oxford University Press, 1990.

Gellately, Robert, *Backing Hitler: Consent and Coercion in Nazi Germany*, Oxford University Press, 2001.

Gellately, Robert, *Lenin, Stalin and Hitler: The Age of Social Catastrophe*, Jonathan Cape, 2007.

Gilbert, Martin, *The Holocaust: A History of the Jews of Europe During the Second World War*, Holt Paperbacks, 1987.

Gitelman, Zvi Y., *Bitter legacy: Confronting the Holocaust in the USSR*, Indiana University Press, 1997.

Goldhagen, Daniel, *Hitler's Willing Executioners, Ordinary Germans and the Holocaust*, Abacus, 1996.

Grant, R. Gordon, *Genocide: The Final Solution to the Jewish Question*, Trafford, 2002.

Guenther, Irene, *Nazi chic? Fashioning Women in the Third Reich*, Berg, 2004.

Hancock, Eleanor, *Ernst Röhm: Hitler's SA chief of staff*, Palgrave Macmillan, 2008.

Heiden, Konrad, *The Führer*, Houghton-Mifflin, 1944.

Hillenbrand, F. K. M, *Underground Humour in Nazi Germany, 1933–1945*, Routledge, 1995.

Hoffmann, Peter, *The History of the German Resistance, 1933–1945*, McGill-Queen's University Press, 3rd edn, 1996.

Hoffmann, Peter, *Stauffenberg: A Family History, 1905–1944*, Cambridge University Press, 1997.

Hoffmeister, Gerhart and Tubach, Frederic C, *Germany: From the Nazi Era to German Unification*, Continuum, 1992.

Höhne, Heinz, Barry, R. (trans.), *The Order of the Death's Head*, Pan Books, 1969.

Huener, Jonathan and Nicosia, Francis R., *The Arts in Nazi Germany: Continuity, Conformity, Change*, Berghahn Books, 2006.

Ingrao, Charles W. and Szabo, Franz A.J., *The Germans and the East*, Purdue University Press, 2008.

James, Harold, *The Deutsche Bank and the Nazi Economic War Against the Jews: The Expropriation of Jewish-Owned Property*, Cambridge University Press, 2001.

James, Harold, *The Nazi Dictatorship and the Deutsche Bank*, Cambridge University Press, 2004.

Jarausch, Konrad H. and Geyer, Michael, *Shattered Past: Reconstructing German Histories*, Princeton University Press, 2003.

Jeffreys, Diarmuid, *Hell's Cartel: IG Farben and the Making of Hitler's War Machine*, Metropolitan Books, 2008.

Johnson, Eric, *Nazi Terror: The Gestapo, Jews, and Ordinary Germans*, Basic Books, 1999.

Jones, Larry Eugene, *German Liberalism and the Dissolution of the Weimar Party System, 1918–1933*, University of North Carolina Press, 1988.

Kater, Michael H., *Doctors Under Hitler*, University of North Carolina Press, 1989.

Kershaw, Ian, *The 'Hitler Myth'*, Oxford University Press, 1987.

Kershaw, Ian, *Hitler, 1889–1936: Hubris*, Penguin Books, 1999.

Kershaw, Ian, *The Nazi Dictatorship: Problems and Perspectives of Interpretation*, Edward Arnold, 2000.

Kershaw, Ian, *Hitler, 1936–1945: Nemesis*, Penguin Books, 2001.

Kershaw, Ian, *Hitler, the Germans, and the Final Solution*, Yale University Press, 2008.

Klemperer, Victor, Chalmers, Martin (trans.), *The Klemperer Diaries, 1933–1945*, Phoenix Press, 2000.

Large, David Clay, *Contending with Hitler: Varieties of German Resistance in the Third Reich*, Cambridge University Press, 1991.

Lee, Stephen J., *European Dictatorships, 1918–1945*, Methuen, 2000.

Leitz, Christian (ed.), *The Third Reich: The Essential Readings*, Wiley-Blackwell, 1999.

Levi, Erik, *Music in the Third Reich*, Palgrave Macmillan, 1994.

Lusane, Clarence, *Hitler's Black Victims: The Historical Experience of Afro-Germans, European Blacks, Africans and African Americans in the Nazi Era*, Routledge, 2002.

MacDonogh, Giles, *1938: Hitler's Gamble*, Constable, 2009.

McDonough, Frank, *Hitler and Nazi Germany*, Cambridge University Press, 1999.

McElligott, Anthony and Kirk, Tim (eds), *Working towards the Führer: Essays in Honour of Sir Ian Kershaw*, Manchester University Press, 2004.

Machtan, Lothar, Brownjohn, John, (trans.), *The Hidden Hitler*, Basic Books, 2001.

Marie, Tina, *Other Germans: Black Germans and the Politics of Race, Gender, and Memory in the Third Reich (Social History, Popular Culture, and Politics in Germany)*, University of Michigan Press, 2003.

Mason, Tim, *Social Policy in the Third Reich: The Working Class and the 'National Community'*, Berg, 1993.

Moeller, Felix, *The Film Minister: Goebbels and the Cinema in the Third Reich*, Axel Menges, 2001.

Muhlberger, Detlef, *Hitler's Followers: Studies in the Sociology of the Nazi Movement*, Routledge, 1991.

Nicosia, Francis R. and Huener, Jonathan, *Medicine and Medical Ethics in Nazi Germany: Origins, Practices, Legacies*, Berghahn Books, 2002.

Nicosia, Francis R., and Huener, Jonathan (eds), *Business and Industry in Nazi Germany*, Berghahn Books, 2004.

Noakes, J. and Pridham, G., *Nazism 1919–1945*, vol. I, *The Rise to Power 1919–1934*, University of Exeter Press, 2nd edition, 1998.

Noakes, J. and Pridham, G., *Nazism 1919–1945*, vol. II, *State, Economy and Society, 1933–1939*, University of Exeter Press, 2nd edition, 2000.

Noakes, J. and Pridham, G., *Nazism 1919–1945*, vol. III, *Foreign Policy, War and Racial Extermination*, University of Exeter Press, 1988.

Noakes, Jeremy, *Nazism 1919–1945*, vol. IV, *The German Home Front in World War II, A Documentary Reader*, University of Exeter Press, 1998.

Overy, Richard, *War and Economy in the Third Reich*, Oxford University Press, 1995.

Overy, Richard, *The Nazi Economic Recovery, 1932–1938*, Cambridge University Press, 1996.

Overy, Richard, *The Dictators: Hitler's Germany and Stalin's Russia*, Allen Lane, 2004.

Overy, Richard, *Why the Allies Won*, revised edition, Pimlico, 2006.

Overy, Richard, *1939: Countdown to War*, Allen Lane, 2009.

Panayi, Panikos, *Weimar and Nazi Germany: Continuities and Discontinuities*, Pearson, 2000.

Pine, Lisa, *Nazi family policy, 1933–1945*, Berg, 1997.

Rees, L., *Auschwitz: The Nazis and the Final Solution*, BBC Books, 2005.

Rempel, Gerhard, *Hitler's Children: The Hitler Youth and the SS*, University of North Carolina Press, 1990.

Schacht, Hjalmar, *My First Seventy-Six Years*, Wingate, 1955.

Schoenbaum, David, *Hitler's Social Revolution: Class and Status in Nazi Germany, 1933–1939*, W.W. Norton, 1980.

Shirer, William, L., *The Rise and Fall of the Third Reich*, Simon and Schuster, 1960.

Smith, Lyn, *Forgotten Voices of the Holocaust: A New History in the Words of the Men and Women Who Survived*, Ebury Press, 2006.

Stackelberg, Roderick, *The Routledge Companion to Nazi Germany*, Routledge, 2007.

Steigmann-Gall, Richard, *The Holy Reich: Nazi Conceptions of Christianity, 1919–1945*, Cambridge University Press, 2003.

Stephenson, Jill, *Women in Nazi Germany*, Longman, 2001.

Stibbe, Matthew, *Women in the Third Reich*, Arnold, 2003.

Strasser, Otto, *Hitler and I*, Jonathan Cape, 1940.

Ther, Philipp and Siljak, Ana, *Redrawing Nations: Ethnic Cleansing in East-Central Europe, 1944–1948*, Rowman & Littlefield Publishers, 2001.

Thomsett, Michael C., *The German Opposition to Hitler: the Resistance, the Underground, and Assassination Plots, 1938–1945*, McFarland & Company, 1997.

Tobias, Sigmund, *Strange Haven: A Jewish Childhood in Wartime Shanghai*, University of Illinois Press, 2009.

Turner, Henry, A., *Hitler's Thirty Days to Power*, Perseus Books, 1996.

Von der Goltz, Anna, *Hindenburg: Power, Myth, and the Rise of the Nazis*, Oxford University Press, 2009.

Walters, Guy, *Hunting Evil*, Bantam Press, 2009.

Weinberg, Gerhard L., *Germany, Hitler, and World War II: Essays in Modern German and World History*, Cambridge University Press, 1995.

Weitz, Eric D., *Weimar Germany: Promise and Tragedy*, Princeton University Press, 2007.

Weitz, John, *Hitler's Diplomat: The Life and Times of Joachim von Ribbentrop*, Houghton Mifflin, 1992.

Weitz, John, *Hitler's Banker*, Little, Brown, 1997.

Welch, David, *The Third Reich: Politics and Propaganda*, Routledge, 1993.

Welch, David, *Hitler: Profile of a Dictator*, University College London Press, 1998.

Welch, David, *Propaganda and the German cinema, 1933–1945*, I. B. Tauris, 2001.

Wheeler-Bennett, John W., *Nemesis of Power: The German Army in Politics 1918–1945* (2nd edn), Palgrave Macmillan, 2005.

Widdig, Bernd, *Culture and Inflation in Weimar Germany*, University of California Press, 2001.

Williamson, D.G., *The Age of the Dictators: A Study of the European Dictatorships, 1918–53*, Pearson, 2007.

Winkler, Heinrich August, *Germany: The Long Road West*, vol. I, *1789–1933*, Oxford University Press, 2006.

Wistrich, Robert S., *Who's Who in Nazi Germany*, Routledge, 2nd edn, 1995.

Wright, Jonathan, *Gustav Stresemann: Weimar's Greatest Statesman*, Oxford University Press, 2002.

Zeman, Z, *Nazi Propaganda,* Oxford University Press, 1964.

GLOSSARY OF SOME KEY GERMAN WORDS AND TERMS

Anschluss: union, with Austria.

Der Stürmer: The Stormer, Nazi paper.

Drang nach Osten: drive to the east.

Einsatzgruppen: task groups, or special action groups; *Einsatzgruppe*: task group.

Freikorps: Free Corps, nationalist ex-soldiers, post WW1.

Kristallnacht: Crystal Night, the Night of Broken Glass, 1938.

Führer: Leader.

Gauleiter: regional Nazi Party boss.

Gestapo: Secret State Police.

Gleichschaltung: coordinating, bringing into line.

Lebensraum: Living Space.

Mitteleuropa: middle Europe, Central Europe.

Mittelstand: middle class.

Schutzstaffel: Protection Formation, the SS.

Sturmabteilung: Storm Division, the SA, brownshirts, stormtroopers.

Völkisch: ethnic/racist; *volk*: race, the German ethnic group.

Völksgemeinschaft: racial/national community.

INDEX